# Naval Occasions 1939 Through 1956

Michael H. Coles

Copyright © 2015 Michael H. Coles

All rights reserved.

ISBN: 15119398832
ISBN-13: 9781519398833

# DEDICATION

For those in peril on the sea.

# ACKNOWLEDGMENTS

Many thanks are due to the generous people who helped or encouraged my research. Especial thanks to Sir Michael Howard, H. P. Willmott, Kenneth Jackson, Peter Nash, and the late Edgar Lee. Their assistance was invaluable, but the views incorporated are, unless otherwise indicated, entirely my own. Marilyn Shames also played a vital role as editor.

# CONTENTS

|   | Acknowledgments | i |
|---|---|---|
|   | Introduction | ii |
| 1 | The Loss of HMS *Royal Oak* | 1 |
| 2 | *Decima Flottiglia Mas* | 17 |
| 3 | The Channel Dash | 37 |
| 4 | Sicily, 1943 | 61 |
| 5 | Destruction of the *Scharnhorst* | 97 |
| 6 | Hitler's Fleet in Being | 123 |
| 7 | Ernest King and The British Pacific Fleet | 153 |
| 8 | Failed Deterrence, Korea 1950-53 | 183 |
| 9 | Bedcheck Charlie | 209 |
| 10 | Suez, 1956 | 221 |
|   | Notes | 243 |
|   | About the Author | 273 |

# INTRODUCTION

Atomic bombs dropped on Hiroshima and Nagasaki brought the war against Japan (the last of the Axis powers still fighting) to a close in 1945. However, although the global conflagration was officially over, there were major issues still unsettled, one of them being the division of the Korean peninsular into two belligerent halves. It seemed only a moment passed between the end of the Pacific War and June, 1950 when North Korea invaded South Korea, beginning what has become known as the "Forgotten War".

Events moved fast that June. The United Nations intervened in support of the South, with America, the least exhausted of the western powers, firmly in the lead. Britain and its Commonwealth supplied a carrier task group to provide close air support to their troops fighting under the United Nations command. There were many who thought World War III was beginning, with several players from the preceding event involved, except that the Germans and Japanese, having had enough war over the previous decade, wisely decided to sit this one out, gathering instead enormous economic benefits from the rest of the free world's rearmament. By 1951 I had joined the Royal Navy as a carrier pilot, and thus found myself in the middle of this unexpected conflict.

It was many years later, having left the Navy and moved to the United States, that I enrolled as a graduate student at Columbia University. To start studying history seriously at that time in my life, and to write about naval matters, seemed to represent a logical step on the academic ladder.

I was a schoolboy during World War II and, as most schoolboys did, watched the main events with close and often personal interest. For various reasons - mainly I think because I spent my wartime summers in the Isle of Wight, close to Portsmouth, Britain's main naval base - much of my attention focused on the Royal Navy, and contemporary naval battles. Our concern was mainly the European and Atlantic theaters; once the *Repulse* and *Prince of Wales* had been sunk by Japanese airpower, there seemed little the Royal Navy could do in the Pacific until the island-hopping Americans got closer to South East Asia.

It was George Orwell, I believe, who first pointed out that history is written by the winners, although, like many useful aphorisms with doubtful antecedents, authorship is also frequently attributed to Winston Churchill. Regardless of its true origins, the phrase does have merit, and reminds us that each side in a military conflict produces its own legends and heroes, much as the victors would like to claim them exclusively as their own.

Most of the articles contained in this book were written towards the end of the last century and relate to naval matters. Many of them also involve the Royal Navy, which happens to be the service I know most about. The stories told in this book are included mainly because the events and the principal characters (friend or enemy), appealed to me. There is no brilliant historic rationale to the selections, just the fact that they led to narratives I appreciated. However, I do think they demonstrate that the enemy side contained some genuine heroes, and that fate scatters courage throughout the battlefield without showing much in the way of favoritism.

The book opens with an account of how Gunther Prien, commanding German submarine *U-47*, penetrated Britain's supposedly secure fleet anchorage at Scapa Flow, in the North of Scotland, sinking the battleship *Royal Oak*. Winston Churchill, then First Lord of Britain's Admiralty, described this exploit as "a remarkable feat of professional skill and daring" - a rare admission of enemy competence from such a high level (see Chapter One). It was not long, however before the Italians demonstrated similar skills and enterprise when they introduced midget submarines inside the seemingly well protected harbor of Alexandria. It was later in the war, and maybe both sides were less courteous, but the Italians failed to attract similar praise from the British Prime Minister (Chapter Two).

German Vice Admiral Otto Ciliax showed a commensurate level of audacity when in early 1942 he brought two German battle cruisers in broad daylight the length of the English Channel to the safety of their home port, an event the London *Times* described as mortifying to the pride of British sea power (Chapter Three).

The book is Eurocentric, focusing on Italy and Germany, rather than the Japanese, as the enemies and trying to ensure that the courage and skill of those two fleets get their fair share of recognition (at least at the tactical level). It is also designed to trace the trajectory of relative naval power over the war years 1939 through 1945 and thereafter. In 1939 most would have agreed that the Royal Navy represented the world's most powerful aggregation of naval power, although still possessing insufficient assets to adequately protect Britain's overseas possessions. Moreover, a significant German battleship building program had begun shortly after Hitler's rise to power in 1933, which, together with the creation of a massive U-boat fleet, represented a growing threat to other European naval powers

All of this ambitious construction became embodied in the German Navy's 1937 "Z" Plan which envisaged a strong well-balanced blue water fleet that, when completed, would be capable of challenging the Royal Navy in a global conflict. "When completed" was the crucial condition: Hitler had promised his naval staff that war with Britain would not occur before 1946, and construction proceeded along that time line. Thus the navy that Germany went to war with in 1939, though a powerful and dogged adversary, was doomed to be outnumbered by its principal enemy. Outnumbered though it was, while still in being it did represent an existential threat to British trade, particularly when Hitler invaded Russia and Britain assumed the brunt of escorting the convoys that brought crucial American supplies to that beleaguered country.

Thus, starting with the well-known *Bismarck* in 1941, the Royal Navy embarked on a campaign to exterminate the remaining German battle fleet: hapless *Gneisenau* (badly wounded by the RAF, then scuttled in 1945 to block Gdynia harbor in Poland); *Scharnhorst* (sunk in 1943 - see Chapter Five); and *Tirpitz* (eventually sunk in 1944 - see Chapter Six). Each of these vessels appeared almost unsinkable, and was manned by crews determined not to surrender, despite the punishment they took.

Bearing in mind the theme of this book, we must not forget that it was the British who, having battered the battleship *Scharnhorst* into wreckage off North Cape, honored the few survivors by saluting them before they were led away to captivity, and later dropped a wreath over the spot where their ship went down.

The mathematics of relative naval power never ceased to plague the German naval staff: The loss of HMS *Hood* during the *Bismarck* action, though devastating to British naval morale, meant far less in terms of British strategic battleship dispositions than the contemporaneous loss in that encounter of one of Germany's only remaining two heavy battleships, mattered to her enemy.

Even so, it was not until the final destruction of battleship *Tirpitz* that Britain could rest assured that her vital trade routes, though still subject to the U-boat threat, would no longer be at risk from attack by big-gunned surface warships.

World War II was three years old before Germany's occupation of Europe appeared less than permanent, when the Allies' invasion of Sicily demonstrated that the war could be won by irresistible economic power, translated into material battlefield superiority. The Axis conducted a brilliant fighting retreat across the island, but 50,000 German troops appeared doomed to be penned into the eastern end, unless they could escape across the narrow Straits of Messina in the face of what appeared to be overwhelming Allied sea and air power. Chapter Four tells how legendary German general Hans-Valentin Hube, assisted by an energetic young naval captain, was given full command over the means of escape, enabling what historian Samuel Eliot Morison calls an "outstanding maritime retreat of the war." It is in this chapter that the United States Navy, largely committed to the Pacific theater, makes its first significant presence in the Atlantic and Mediterranean.

As the German Navy became less of a threat in European waters, the British began to be concerned about their standing vis-à-vis the United States in the Pacific. Once the incredible American military/industrial complex got to work in 1941, it achieved miracles of design and construction, so that by mid-1943 the largest naval armada the world had ever seen was assembling in the Pacific. There was no way that British industry, already stretched to its limits to replace three years of battle and U-boat losses, could hope to be anything but a junior player in this game. But Winston Churchill was eager for the Royal Navy to play a leading role in the defeat of Japan, and insisted that the British White Ensign fly alongside the Stars and Stripes as a co-equal. It is clear from the historical record that American naval leaders feared that the British might not be much help, and indeed might even be a hindrance.

A number of historians covering this last period of the naval war started from the position that American Chief of Naval Operations Ernest King didn't like the British, and determined to keep them out of "his" war. The more I read about this, the more I concluded that King wasn't the petty man his British critics made him out to be: he was actually being pretty sensible. The resulting analysis (Chapter 7) appeared in the *Journal of Military History* in its January 2001 issue.

The Korean War, which started in 1950 with what seemed a rather futile invasion of the South by the North, surprised the American forces occupying the area south of the 38th Parallel, who found themselves and their local allies rapidly driven back to the Pusan perimeter at the southern end of the peninsula. A brilliant amphibious operation planned and commanded by U.S. General Douglas MacArthur landed United Nations ground forces well behind the North Korean lines in September 1950, following which the North Koreans remaining in the South were rapidly killed, captured or driven north. The war seemed just about over, except for the nagging question: what action would the Chinese take as United Nations armies drew closer to their border on the Yalu River?

Washington's assumption that Beijing would not be troubled as the American-dominated United Nations Armies came closer, may go down as one of the greater strategic errors of history. Blame is now liberally heaped on Douglas Macarthur, who sadly has few defenders. However, when I was a "mature" student at Columbia the Korean War was still very much on my mind and a significant factor in my studies (Chapter Eight), and I still believe that equal or more responsibility lies with the General's political superiors, and particularly Secretary of State Dean Acheson. At the time in question however, Acheson was busy creating the grand alliance that kept the Russian armies out of Europe for the rest of the twentieth century, and was thus hard to fault.

Should the Korean War be included as part of what is essentially a naval history? The answer becomes simple as soon as one contemplates the impossibility of fighting a war on a distant shore, with no landward communication routes, and without the advantage of uncontested sea power. Added to the communications benefits provided by the United Nations' navies, was the tremendous firepower available to its armies when supported by naval air and by ship borne gunnery.

## NAVAL OCCASIONS - 1939 THROUGH 1956

I wrote Chapter Eight in 1990, and we have learned a lot more about Beijing's diplomacy since then, but I have yet to come across evidence disproving my thesis that, if Washington had taken Chinese concerns seriously in 1950, a lot of lives might have been saved, and diplomatic damage avoided, over the ensuing decades.

Chapter Nine is a small addendum to the Korean War narrative, a piece of the conflict I was personally involved in, and which, I think, played a positive role without too much damage or loss of life.

Unpopular wars that create internal conflict and remain unsupported by political consensus or traditional allies tend not to produce national heroes, and such was certainly true of British Prime Minister Anthony Eden's short lived 1956 attempt to remove Gamil Abder-Nasser as Egypt's head of State. No heroes came out of the resulting small war, nor was much given out by way of awards. But looked at objectively, it was a classic example of how navies and armies can cooperate: the French and British navies escorted troops and supplies securely into the Egyptian theater, brought them safely to the beaches, and provided copy-book close air support after landing. The matter became an ignominious mess when Washington - acting brutally but sensibly - demonstrated that Britain couldn't mount a major military campaign far from home without the benefit of American approval, or at least tacit acquiescence. Noteworthy too is the fact that the United States has never been so popular in the Middle East, before or since. Suez is frequently cited as a key way station in Britain's imperial decline; indeed I look at it as the end of the Empire that I knew, and admired without reservation, throughout my youth. My account of the event (Chapter Ten) was first published in the *Naval War College Review*, Autumn 2006.

Michael H. Coles
Shelter Island, NY
September 14, 2015

# 1 THE LOSS OF HMS *ROYAL OAK*

*(First published in World War II. January/February 2005)*

World War II was only ten weeks old on October 18, 1939. All Germany was elated that day, and no one more than submarine captain Gunther Prien. Proudly wearing his recently awarded Knight's Order of the Iron Cross (Germany's highest war decoration), he picked up the phone and called his mother: "I just sank a battleship," he told her. Hitler, who was described as "beside himself with joy," later entertained Prien and his crew in his private apartment to the sounds of crowds cheering in the streets. Well-wishers from all over the country sent gifts and messages of congratulation to the handsome young captain and his crew.[1]

Germany's jubilation that day was not just the outcome of Prien's feat in sinking the British battleship *Royal Oak*, notable as that was. Possibly more significant was the fact that he had managed to penetrate Scapa Flow, considered one of the world's most defensible naval bases. Located at the western end of the narrow waters between Britain and Norway, this well sheltered 120 square mile deep water anchorage controlled the German Navy's access from the North Sea into the Atlantic, and was thus of vital strategic importance to the British. Moreover, having torpedoed and sunk the aircraft carrier *Courageous* a month earlier, the German Navy appeared to have developed the means to deal with its principal naval adversary.² Scapa Flow represented additional bitter memories to the German Navy. It was there, in July 1919 that Germany's World War I battle fleet, interned by the victorious allies, had responded to a prearranged signal and scuttled itself. Seventy-three warships were settled on the bottom of the anchorage, a humiliation providing further justification for Nazi Germany's revisionist foreign policy.

HMS *Royal Oak*

Winston Churchill, then Britain's First Lord of the Admiralty, announcing the loss of *Royal Oak* to Parliament, congratulated Prien: "When we consider that during the whole course of the last war this anchorage was found to be immune from such attacks on account of the obstacles imposed by the currents and net barrages, this entry of a U-boat must be considered as a remarkable exploit of professional skill and daring."

Prien's exploit was, in fact, more of a moral than a strategic victory. *Royal Oak* was a rather slow old battleship, left behind in an otherwise nearly empty anchorage because she could not keep up with the rest of the fleet. Thus, although important, the material loss was of less significance than the death of over 800 well-trained seamen. Moreover, now made aware of the vulnerability of Scapa Flow to submarine attack, the British took precautions to ensure that the feat would not be repeated.[3]

The Orkneys, a circle of low-lying islands enclosing Scapa Flow, stretch some seventy miles from north to south. The Pentland Firth, one of the world's most turbulent stretches of water, separates the Orkneys from the northerly point of Scotland. Currents there can flow as fast as 14 knots and there can be as much as 6-foot difference between the water level inside and outside the channels leading into the anchorage. A submerged submarine, with a maximum underwater speed of about 7 knots would be virtually helpless in such waters.[4]

Despite its strategic importance, Scapa Flow was poorly defended when war broke out. There was disagreement between the Admiralty and the Commander in Chief of the Home Fleet, Admiral Sir Charles Forbes, as to whether the fleet should be based there or further south in the Firth of Forth. Forbes believed the Orkneys represented a more efficient base for his heavy units but questioned their safety. Although the main entrances were reasonably well protected, he urged the Admiralty to place more block ships in the lesser entrances to the east. His Chief of Staff is said to have described Scapa Flow "as devoid of protection as a man caught in a storm without an umbrella."[5] Winston Churchill, who had assumed control of the Admiralty just before the outbreak of war, recalled being surprised by the unreadiness of the defenses, noting that the anti-submarine booms at each of the main entrances to the south of the anchorage had only single lines of netting, while the principal protection for Kirk Sound, one of the narrow approaches from the east, was the remnants of block ships placed there during the previous war. He further observed that the increased size and speed of modern submarines had reduced the defensive significance of the extraordinarily strong local tides.[6]

When *Royal Oak* first arrived at Scapa Flow shortly before the outbreak of war one of her officers, a submariner by training, wrote a formal report indicating that he felt he could bring a small submarine into the harbor through Kirk Sound. A survey of the entrances made in May of 1939 noted that, despite the navigational difficulties involved " . . . it is safe to assume that an intrepid submariner, in war time, would take risks no discreet mariner would think of taking in peace time . . . the possibility of a hostile submarine entering Scapa Flow cannot therefore be excluded . . ." Nevertheless the Admiralty, determining that there was little likelihood of an enemy submarine penetrating the anchorage, denied any further expenditure on obstructions. The local naval commander boldly disagreed with this conclusion and successfully requested four additional block ships. The first was in place on September 8. *Royal Oak* was already resting on the bottom when the fourth, destined for Kirk Sound, arrived at Scapa Flow.[7]

Admiral Doenitz, commander of Hitler's submarine fleet, had long been convinced that an operation against Scapa Flow was possible. Recent aerial reconnaissance photographs showed that the main entrances to the south and west were well defended and thus probably impassable. The four eastern entrances, on the other hand, still provided possibilities although they were narrow, plagued with fierce tides, and partially obstructed. Of these Doenitz felt that Holm Sound, leading into Kirk Sound, represented the most vulnerable passage. His confidence in the vulnerability of Scapa Flow was reinforced by reports from submarine *U-14*, captained by Lieutenant Horst Wellner, which had made a comprehensive reconnaissance of the area during a prior patrol.[8]

Doenitz decided that an attempt should be made, and that the man to do it was Gunther Prien, commander of *U-47*. "If it were possible to create the perfect U-boat commander out of the best personality traits available, Doenitz would probably have created Prien," wrote Robert Stern in his history of the U-boat war. Although only 31 years old, he had fifteen years of sea-going experience, starting as a boy seaman on a sailing ship and including four years as an officer in the newly re-created U-boat service. Prien, recalled Doenitz later, had all the personal and professional ability required for the task, a great personality, plenty of zest and energy, single minded dedication to his service; a simple, frank and courageous fighting man intent only on doing his job.[9]

*Royal Oak* was one of five ships of the "R" Class (others were *Royal Sovereign, Ramillies, Revenge,* and *Resolution*). She was commissioned in 1916, just in time to take part in the Battle of Jutland although she made little contribution to the fighting. The "R's" each mounted eight fifteen-inch guns in four turrets: two forward and two aft. Heavy layers of armor plate, up to thirteen inches thick, were designed to protect their decks, sides and turrets, although none was provided below the waterline. In 1922, recognizing *Royal Oak*'s vulnerability to underwater attack, "blisters" had been added along her lower sides in the expectation that a torpedo would explode against this extra surface, leaving the main hull intact. The bottom of the ship, still unshielded, remained her most vulnerable part. Effective damage control required that the ship be divided into numerous separate compartments accessible only by watertight doors and hatches, many of them armored and thus requiring powerful machinery to open them.[10]

*U-47*, Prien's command, was one of Doenitz' newest U-boats. A Type VIIB, it was an improved version of the German navy's original "wolf pack" design, which was in turn based on one of the more successful World War I U-boats. Extremely maneuverable and an excellent sea boat, the Type VIIs were first launched in 1938 and continued in production throughout the war. Displacing some 750 tons when surfaced, they carried a crew of between 45 and 55, depending on task, within a hull 215 feet long and 20 feet wide. Two diesel engines gave the boats a maximum speed of 17 knots on the surface while electric motors provided up to 8 knots when submerged. Maximum diving depth was 650 feet. The boats had four torpedo tubes in the bow and one in the stern. Carrying only 14 torpedoes, the Type VIIs frequently found their patrols limited by lack of these weapons rather than food or fuel.[11]

*U-47* left Kiel on October 8, 1939 and proceeded carefully north, running on the surface at night and lying on the bottom during the day. Her aim was to arrive at Scapa Flow on Friday, October 13; there would be a new moon providing scant illumination, and the tides, among the highest of the year, would be best suited for the difficult passage in and out. Only Prien, his first lieutenant (Ober Leutenant Englebert Endrass) and the helmsman knew the destination, although the fact that *U-47* was very lightly loaded must have aroused suspicions among the rest of the crew.[12]

Unknown to Prien, and possibly also to Doenitz, German naval Commander-in-Chief Admiral Raeder had chosen the same time to mount a surface operation whose effect would largely undermine all the U-boat admiral's careful planning. The affair was typical of the poor communication between Germany's surface and under-sea navies. On October 7 a force consisting of a battle cruiser, a cruiser and nine destroyers was ordered to patrol the southwest coast of Norway in the hope that it would lure the Home Fleet out of Scapa Flow and into a trap consisting of over a hundred bombers and dive bombers and four U-boats. The plan worked as intended: on October 8, as *U-47* headed for the open sea, the Admiralty ordered the Home Fleet to sweep the Norwegian waters. Too slow for the main fleet, *Royal Oak* followed out with two escorting destroyers to patrol northeast of the Orkneys. Appalling weather probably hindered both sides impartially: the British failed to find the German task force, and none of the German bombers could locate the Home Fleet. The German ships returned to their base at Kiel, but Admiral Forbes, still concerned about the safety of Scapa Flow, decided to disperse most of his fleet to other ports. The only heavy units remaining there on October 12 when a Luftwaffe reconnaissance plane flew over were *Royal Oak*, the aircraft carrier *Furious* and the battle cruiser *Repulse*. Later the same day, however, *Repulse* and *Furious* sailed for mainland ports, leaving *Royal Oak* the only operational capital ship in the anchorage. Nevertheless, although Prien would not find the opportunities promised by the earlier reconnaissance flights, a number of valuable smaller targets remained, including six cruisers (one heavy, five light) and eight destroyers. Thus, at least in the eyes of Prien's contemporaries, *U-47's* exploit represented an embarrassing failure on the part of the naval staff, despite being a brilliant public relations coup.[13]

*U-47* spent the daylight hours of October 13 submerged off the Orkneys while her crew rested. It was not until 5 P.M. that her skipper told his crew of its mission. Although he noted in his log that their morale was splendid, he remained under no illusions regarding the difficulties to be faced, assuming that the British would provide Scapa Flow with the same level of protection they had given it in the 1914-1918 war.[14]

Prien surfaced at 7:15 P.M. and set course for Scapa Flow. Forced to submerge briefly to avoid detection by a passing merchant ship, he resurfaced and entered Holm Sound at 11:30 P.M. now some half hour after the desirable time of high water. Caught in a strong following current, he was taken through the channel at a breathtaking speed; an ebbing tide flows from the North Sea into the Atlantic and thus into the eastern entrances of Scapa Flow. Before he expected it he was in Kirk Sound, two block ships just visible to port. The boat swung wildly, first grounding, then hitting an anchor cable off one of the block ships, but by skillful use of helm and engines Prien was able to free her and bring her into the anchorage.

To Prien's surprise the night was extraordinarily bright, the Aurora Borealis (Northern Lights) illuminating what appeared to be empty waters to his south. Turning to the north he spied what he thought were two battleships lying anchored close into the mainland; he could see no other warships. The southernmost and closest target he identified correctly as an "R" Class battleship; the farther one, which was largely blanketed by *Royal Oak*'s hull, he mistook for the battle cruiser *Repulse*. (It was in fact the old seaplane tender *Pegasus*.) Arguably, given the fact that it was night, he was deep within a vital enemy naval base, and understandably nervous, Prien can be forgiven for thinking he saw what he had been told would be there.[15]

Remaining on the surface he fired one torpedo at the northernmost ship, two at the one to the south. After a long three and a half minutes an explosion was heard; Prien thought it came from the ship he still assumed to be *Repulse*. He heard nothing from the other vessel. Swinging his boat around, he fired his stern torpedo while reloading his bow tubes; this shot apparently missed. Turning again he fired three of his forward tubes. Three minutes later there were sounds of violent explosions, followed by loud rumbling noises. Prien reported seeing columns of water and fire leaping from the stricken ship, while large pieces of debris flew through the air. Still confused as to which ship he had hit with his first salvo, and uncertain of the northernmost vessel's identity, Prien made for the entrance convinced that he had sunk *Royal Oak* and damaged *Repulse*.[16]

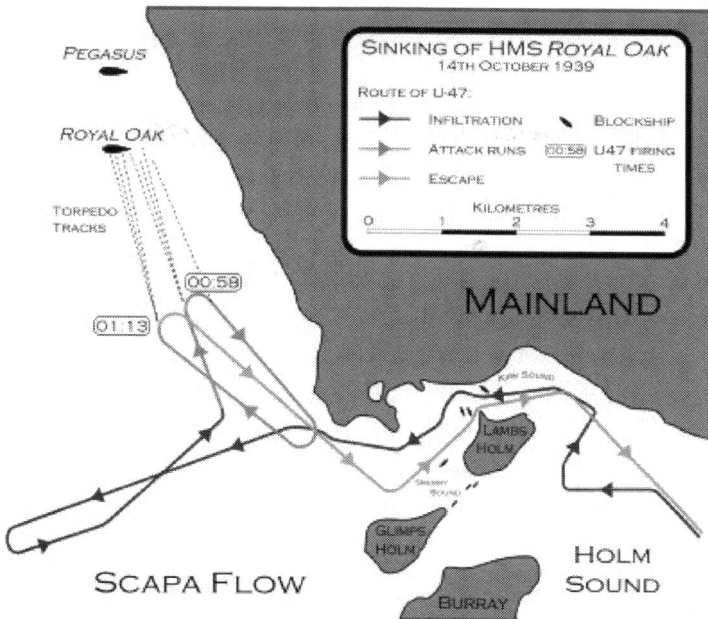

Route of *U-47* into Scapa Flow to sink the HMS *Royal Oak*

Shortly after 1 A.M. on October 14 those on board *Royal Oak* felt the shock of an explosion near the bow, waking most of the men not already on watch. The ship's commanding officer, Captain W. G. Benn, RN went forward to investigate, assuming that the ship had suffered an internal explosion, probably in the paint store. There was evidence that water was entering that compartment, but there seemed to be no fire; all damage appeared localized at the bow. No one suggested that the ship might have been torpedoed. Although pumps were started to drain the flooded compartment, no orders were given to close watertight doors or portholes. As her captain later recalled "I had no thought other than that a local explosion had taken place . . . I had not even thought of the ship being torpedoed. I felt no uneasiness about the safety of the ship." Captain Benn's comfort was institutional: the Royal Navy's instructions regarding the state of readiness to be assumed by ships in harbor included the clear statement "In a defended port, the only form of surprise attack that need be anticipated is from the air."[17]

Twelve minutes after the first detonation there was another shattering explosion, followed shortly by two more. All were on the starboard side of the ship, and had an immediate and catastrophic effect. The great vessel slowly heeled over to starboard and then, accelerating as she went, continued to roll until she capsized and sank at just before 1:30 A.M., only twenty-five minutes after Prien's first torpedo hit. Subsequent inspection by divers indicated that the third and fourth torpedoes tore a 30-foot hole in the starboard bulge causing massive flooding of after engine spaces. The last torpedo, hitting an unprotected area just aft of the bow, blew out a large area of the double bottoms, causing generator room flooding and loss of power.[18]

Although *Royal Oak* remained calm after the first explosion, conditions on board following the second salvo rapidly became chaotic. It was soon apparent that little could be done to save the ship. Moreover as power failed and all the lights went out, it became impossible to give a general order to abandon ship, the command being passed by word of mouth. Australian D. T. W. Harris recalled: "The first of the many heroes I was to meet that night. Torch in hand, he calmly guided sailors to the upper deck gently urging them on in a cool reassuring voice: 'Steady boys, keep moving boys, keep calm.'[19]"

The shell supply for *Royal Oak*'s 15-inch main armament was located in four magazines below the waterline; adjacent storages contained the cordite propellant charges. The turrets revolved on armored barbettes, which protected the ammunition on its dangerous passage up to the guns. Cordite was very temperature sensitive; if it became overheated it could explode and blow up the ship. To avoid such a disaster a series of vents were installed that permitted the gas from burning cordite to escape before it reached an explosive pressure. While the human impact could be horrifying, the material effect on the ship's fighting ability was manageable: she would still remain afloat and able to fire her remaining heavy weapons.[20]

What now happened in *Royal Oak* is consistent with this scenario: orange colored flames spread rapidly inside the living and machinery spaces, burning gasses appearing around the funnel casing. The after end of the ship was engulfed in black smoke, living spaces filled with fumes, while burning hammocks added to the confusion; holes appeared in some decks and others caved in. Several men were blown through doors and hatches or clear out of portholes.[21]

The Court of Enquiry, questioning why the loss of life was so heavy, concluded that since the main threat to *Royal Oak* was believed to be from the air, a large proportion of the crew was stationed below what they thought was the safety of the armored decks, behind securely closed watertight hatches. Very few men escaped from these spaces: many of the through-deck access routes were closed by sliding doors made of heavy steel and as the heel of the ship increased the doors slammed shut, held closed by their own substantial weight. Other access doors opened vertically and, in the absence of power, men below were trapped, struggling to get out. A heroic Marine corporal supported such a hatch on his shoulders to allow others to get by. It appears too that many of the men who did manage to escape lacked their own life belts. *Royal Oak*'s complement included some 175 boy-seamen (under 16) on board for training. Only 32 survived.[22]

One of the ship's launches was made fast to a boom on the starboard side. As the crew attempted to cast off they saw the ship turning over on top of them. A piece of steel from the mast fell into the launch and sank it while the funnel, detached from the upper works, fell between the launch and the side of the ship. Men in the sea watched in horror as the two forward 15-inch turrets, each weighing over 700 tons, swung slowly round and then slid into the water.[23]

Available to *Royal Oak* whenever she was at Scapa Flow was a fishing trawler, *Daisy II* that fortunately had been lying along the battleship's port side. Her skipper, Richard Gatt, who was sleeping on board, rushed to cast off his lines and then began to rescue those fortunate enough to have gotten clear of the ship. He brought about thirty survivors on board before further rescue became difficult due to the heavy coating of oil on the water and the greasiness of the ropes, but he continued to circle, blowing his horn, flashing his navigation lights and throwing lifebuoys in the water. As the alarm spread, boats from *Pegasus* and from the shore reinforced *Daisy II*'s rescue efforts.[24]

Seaman Stan Cole recalled the nightmare of struggling in pitch darkness to make his way out of his mess deck, trying to find one of the few available ladders, then repeating the process through several more decks until he reached the outside. Someone shouted for him to jump before the ship went down. He attempted a dive, but found himself face downwards sliding over the torpedo bulge. In the water he joined with others, swimming as best they could, some with injuries, others terribly burned. He was picked up by a passing boat and transferred to *Daisy II*, still searching the wreckage-strewn waters. Skipper Gatt then transferred his load of shocked survivors to the nearby *Pegasus*.[25]

While frantic rescue work went on, naval vessels urgently searched Scapa Flow, but to no avail: illusory contacts were reported and depth charges were dropped, but there was no immediate evidence of an enemy submarine. It was only when Prien returned to Germany and announced his success that the British were able to establish just how *Royal Oak* had been sunk.[26]

Immediately after firing his last salvo, Prien withdrew at high speed, remaining on the surface. All went well until *U-47* reached the narrow passage she had entered only two hours earlier. Here she encountered the tide, now running against her at its maximum flow of 10 knots, with the water in the channel very nearly at its lowest depth. Running his diesel engines at maximum power Prien managed to clear the southernmost boom then, making an emergency turn, he was just able to scrape past the mole jutting out from Lamb Holm towards the block ships. Threading his way through the narrow gap, he found himself once more in open water. Behind him he could see bright lights over Scapa Flow, and hear what appeared to him to be heavy depth charging. At daylight he dived and lay on the bottom, waiting for nightfall safe in forty fathoms of water.[27]

Prien's decision to withdraw might appear questionable in the light of other targets still available in Scapa Flow. Although he had correctly established that most of the British capital ships had moved elsewhere, there were still valuable cruisers and destroyers lying to the south of the harbor. On the other hand, he knew he had sunk one battleship and thought he had at least damaged a battle cruiser. His torpedo tubes were empty and valuable time would be needed to reload. The light was sufficient for him to be seen on the surface now that his presence was known, and he was unable to attack at night submerged using only his periscope. He also thought that a stationary motorist had seen him on the way in. All these seem reason enough for him to withdraw, save his boat and crew, and survive to fight another day.[28]

*U-47* returned to Kiel the way she had come; submerged during the day and running on the surface at night. During one night at sea she stopped while Prien's First Watch Officer, Ober Leutnant S.G. von Varendorff, led a party of sailors who climbed out onto her hull casing and painted on the conning tower a picture of a charging bull-- the "Bull of Scapa Flow," as the boat would be known for the rest of her short life.[29]

"Bull of Scapa Flow" on conning tower of *U-47*

Prien continued in command of *U-47* becoming by the time of his last voyage, Germany's second ranking U-boat ace. On March 7, 1941 he attempted a wolf-pack attack on a homeward bound British convoy some 200 miles south of Iceland, meeting well-organized resistance by the convoy escort. Only two ships in the convoy were damaged, and one of the attacking U-boats surrendered with most of its crew. Undaunted, Prien came back to the attack the next day. Early the following morning *U-47* was detected by HMS *Wolverine*, which was officially credited with her destruction after a five-hour running battle.[30]

In hindsight, therefore, Gunther Prien's famous exploit would seem to be fairly straightforward; clearly courageous, well planned and executed at the tactical level, probably lucky, but otherwise not the stuff that mysteries are made of. Yet, for several decades after the event, even after release of the Admiralty papers covering the episode, the matter generated considerable controversy.

Prien congratulated by Hitler
(Photo courtesy of http://ww2gravestone.com)

Prien's own description of *Royal Oak*'s sinking appeared in a book published in Germany in 1940 and is generally consistent with subsequent accounts and the conclusions of the Admiralty Court of Enquiry. However, a later English version created considerable resentment among British survivors, who insisted that *Royal Oak* could not have succumbed to a torpedo, there must be some other explanation for her loss, and *U-47*'s log must thus be a forgery. The main focus of their concerns was discrepancies between Prien's account of the event and their own recollections; some even suggested that Prien never actually make his way into Scapa Flow, sabotage again being one likely explanation of the loss.[31] From the German side, on the other hand, Naval historian and former U-boat commander Bodo Herzog asserts categorically that the account of *Royal Oak*'s sinking in Prien's log is an accurate reflection of what happened.[32]

Shortly after the end of the war too, there began a series of unsubstantiated rumors concerning Prien's death. The most consistent claimed that *U-47* had not been sunk, as the British authoritatively claimed, but that Prien and his crew had met some other fate. Moreover, unlike *Royal Oak*'s sinking, Admiralty accounts of *U-47*'s destruction do not entirely dispel doubt; there remains some question as to whether any wreckage was actually sighted. Naval historian Paul Kemp (*U-Boats Destroyed: German Submarine Losses in the World Wars*) was also equivocal: "In the absence of any firm evidence," Kemp wrote, "the cause of the loss of this submarine and her famous commanding officer remains a mystery."[33]

Although all the acceptable evidence indicates that it was indeed *U-47* that sank *Royal Oak*, the question of *U-47*'s destruction and thus Prien's death is more complex. However, it does seem safe to assume (as does Paul Kemp) that Lieutenant Commander Gunther Prien and his crew died in action, as so many of their fellows were destined to do. In Scapa Flow, hard to see against the dark heather of the surrounding moors, is a green buoy marking the spot where *Royal Oak* lies, designated an official war grave and thus undisturbed to this day.[34]

# 2 DECIMA FLOTTIGLIA MAS

And the sinking of the Royal Navy battleships
*Queen Elizabeth* and *Valiant*
By Italian Navy frogmen
In Alexandria Harbor, December 1941

The Italian Navy entered World War II very ill-prepared for the kind of warfare their British opponents were ready for, and their German allies expected them to fight. It only takes a cursory look at a map of the Mediterranean Sea, and the disposition of British and Italian imperial possessions, to realize why, as historian James Sadkovich wrote, a war of convoys was the only sort of naval war that made sense in the Mediterranean context, and the British fleet gave the protection and interdiction of convoys top priority.[1] But the Italian fleet was starved in several important areas: radar, aircraft carriers, antisubmarine weaponry, anti-aircraft cruisers, submarines and night fighting.[2] Thus handicapped, Italy hoped to neutralize the threat from greater powers, and particularly the Royal Navy, its principal opponent in the Mediterranean, by developing cheap and "insidious" assault weapons that would allow them to cripple the British fleet in the early stages of a conflict.[3] In terms of fleet actions, Italian building strategy emphasized speed over armor, but lacking the resources to provide either in sufficient quantity, their post-1940 construction was always too little and too late. But as we shall see, the near destruction of two British battleships deemed safely at anchor in Alexandria harbor, did illustrate the wisdom of squeezing insidious assault weapons out of limited budgets. My main motivation for writing this piece was a belief that the Italians have received insufficient credit for such singular World War II exploits.

One of the first things to be seen by a visitor to the Italian Naval Museum in Venice is a large torpedo with two seats mounted on top. This is the weapon with which the Italians were able to affect one of the most daring and cost-effective naval victories of World War II. Next to the torpedo is a plaque in English written by the captain of one of the two British battleships sunk by this exploit, describing the event. Astonishingly, the account finishes with the story of how the captain subsequently presented Italy's highest military decoration to one of the participants.

A Human Torpedo SLC or "Maiale" similar to the one that can be seen today outside the Naval Museum

In March 1945 Charles Morgan was the British Admiral Commanding the Taranto and Adriatic theater. An armistice between

Italy and the Allies had been in effect since September 1943. The Crown Prince of Italy, visiting Taranto on an inspection tour, was making a presentation of medals.

> *"The first officer to be decorated with the Italian Gold Medal for Valor (equivalent to our Victoria Cross) was Lieutenant de la Penne for his attack on HMS Valiant on December 19th 1941.*
>
> *After the citation had been read out to the parade, Lieutenant de la Penne came forward onto the platform.*
>
> *As he did so the Crown Prince turned around and said 'Come on Morgan, this is your show!'*
>
> *I stepped forward, took the medal from the crown Prince's hand and pinned it on Lieutenant de la Penne's breast.*
>
> *I thus had the pleasure of decorating Lieutenant de la Penne with the highest award granted by the Italian Navy for the very courageous and gallant attack he made on my ship three years and three months before!*
>
> C. E. Morgan
> 18th October 1946"

The Italian Navy in World War I pioneered the use of small special attack units whose objectives were enemy harbors, mostly Austrian. A particularly successful operation was the sinking of the Austrian battleship *Viribus Unitis*, sunk by a hand-steered torpedo piloted by two intrepid Italian seamen. The Italian naval authorities had this legacy very much in mind in 1935 when war with Britain seemed imminent over the Abyssinian question. Attention was given to the procurement of equipment capable of challenging the superior naval power. It is not surprising that the main focus was development of weapons capable of penetrating the Royal Navy's heavily defended Mediterranean bases and sinking major fleet units there.[4]

Four principal weapons resulted from these inter-war studies: "pocket submarines," designed to carry two to four men each, equipped with two torpedo tubes; explosive motor boats whose mission would be high speed penetration of enemy harbors, guided by a driver who would leap over the side a few seconds before impact; limpet mines that would be carried by frogmen for attachment to the bottom of ships' hulls; and two-man guided torpedoes with detachable warheads.[5]

It was using the last of these that the Italians scored their greatest success. Two junior officers, Sub-Lieutenants Teseo Tesei and Elios Toschi, both experienced deep sea divers, were responsible for the initial development, producing by the end of 1935 a vessel that looked like a torpedo but was in reality a miniature submarine 22-foot long, 21 inches in diameter, with a detachable 500 lb. warhead. It was powered by electric motors driving two axial propellers. The crew of two sat astride it in tandem. The pilot, who was always an officer, sat in front facing the instrument panel and shielded by a windscreen. He maneuvered by using compressed air buoyancy tanks and airplane style steering controls. Behind the pilot sat his assistant, an enlisted man whose backrest was a chest containing working tools, net cutters, clamps, and plenty of rope. The crew wore specially designed rubber suits that covered the entire body with the exception of face and hands. Self contained underwater breathing apparatus (SCUBA), using oxygen fed into a mouth piece, allowed up to six hours of submerged travel and provided the capacity to go down as far as 100 feet. The intended method of attack involved night penetration of an enemy harbor. The approach would be made under the target vessel, the warhead detached and then slung between the bilge keels by a line clamped at each end. Fuses could be set for up to two and a half hours, giving the crew time to escape. The official name for the weapon was SLC (Siluro a Lenta Corsa, or slow running torpedoes). But, finding the weapon awkward and hard to control, the Italians christened them *Maiales*, or "Pigs[6]." Given their very limited range, they had to be brought close to their target by some independent means, submarines proving the most effective transporters. Initially they were carried strapped to the submarine's foredeck, resulting in considerable reduction in the boat's maneuverability.

*Maiales* required crews possessing considerable strength, powers of endurance and, above all, bravery. Moreover, operations of this kind required a special naval organization; in the case of the World War II Italian Navy the designated unit was *Decima Flottiglia Mas*, the 10th Light Flotilla. Known as *Decima Mas*, throughout its brief life it was an extraordinarily effective and very economical secret weapon[7].

*Decima Flottiglia MAS* (**Decima Flottiglia M**ezzi d'**As**salto)

Following the defeat of France and the entry of Italy into the war, it had become obvious to Britain's Mediterranean Fleet commander Admiral Sir Andrew Cunningham that Malta was too vulnerable to air attack from Sicily for it to remain his main fleet harbor. He therefore withdrew his main elements to Alexandria, well to the east.[8] *Decima Mas'* first wartime operations were directed at this important British naval base.

Two attacks by guided torpedoes were planned for the autumn of 1940, but both proved unsuccessful. The first, in August, was abandoned when British aircraft sank the submarine designated for the mission. Interviewed after the war, Lieutenant (by then Admiral) Gino Birindelli recalled being on the conning tower of the submarine *Iride* as she left the Gulf of Bomba, where it had picked up its *Maiales*. Three British torpedo-carrying planes attacked head on. There was no time to turn or dive, so the submarine's captain kept the boat head on to the approaching torpedo, hoping it would pass harmlessly by. However its magnetic warhead came close enough to set off the charge, sinking *Iride* and carrying all except the five men on her bridge to the bottom. After a long night's work six men were rescued from the aft torpedo room, and the precious *Maiales* were recovered from *Iride*'s deck, forty-five men and a valuable submarine had been lost, and nothing gained.[9]

The second attack, scheduled for a month later, consisted of a dual operation against Alexandria and Britain's other important Mediterranean naval base at Gibraltar, 2,000 miles to the west. Learning from past mistakes, *Decima Mas* installed cylinders on the foredecks of the two new submarines involved – *Gondar* and *Scire* – large enough to contain the *Maiales* and strong enough to restore full maneuverability to the parent submarine.[10]

The attack against Alexandria was cancelled when it was discovered that the intended targets had left port, but by that time *Gondar* had already been sunk. She had been detected by three Allied escort vessels that had carried out a relentless all night depth charge attack, eventually forcing the submarine to the surface, her batteries exhausted and close to uncontrollable. Flinging open the hatches, the crew threw themselves overboard, thankfully breathing fresh air into their oxygen starved lungs. All but one was rescued by the Australian destroyer HMAS *Stuart*, whose guns subsequently sank *Gondar*. Among *Stuart*'s captives was *Maiale* developer Elios Toschi.[11]

*Scire*, the submarine carrying the *Maiales* bound for Gibraltar, commanded by Lieutenant Commander Junio Valerio Borghese, was disappointed also. When only 50 miles from the British base, a signal from Rome ordered the boat to return home; the British fleet was at sea, at that moment attacking the French fleet in Dakar. There was no point in waiting, the vigil could prove indefinite.[12]

Back in Italy the remaining *Decima Mas* officers pondered the results to date. Two operations completed, two submarines and their crews lost, and no results to show for it. There was, Admiral Birindelli recalled, a lot to think about. The group concluded that despite the obvious risks, there was much to be gained from attacking major enemy warships in harbor, and that at least one more attempt should be made to test the concept. The target would once again be Gibraltar.[13]

The attack took place at the end of October. *Scire*, still commanded by Lt. Borghese, was able to approach close enough to release three *Maiales* and then escape safely. One of the torpedoes, manned by Sub-Lieutenant Luigi de la Penne with Petty Officer Diver Emilio Bianchi, lost power, then depth control, and finally sank. The two men got rid of their equipment and then had sufficient stamina to be able swim some two miles to the Spanish coast. The second *Maiale*, manned by Engineer Lieutenant Teseo Tesei with Petty Officer Diver Alcide Pedretti, had reached the harbor entrance when failure of the SCUBA gear and loss of depth control made it impossible to submerge. Tesei wisely decided to abandon the mission and steered his injured torpedo over to the Spanish coast. After he had scuttled his craft he and Pedretti made a pre-arranged rendezvous with the other crew and with *Decima Mas* agents who were able to return both teams safely to Italy.[14]

Lieutenant Gino Birindelli and Warrant Officer Paccagnini astride the third *Maiale* encountered considerable difficulty getting the torpedo out of the cylinder on *Scirè*'s deck and thus found themselves some fifteen minutes behind their companions. Although they too encountered trimming difficulties, they were able to penetrate the nets defending the inner harbor and approach close to the battleship *Barham*, at which point Birendelli lost control of his craft, which sank. Paccagnini came to the surface and was captured by the British.[15]

Birindelli's exploits over the next few hours were typical of the courage common to members of this elite group. Having failed to repair his torpedo, now lying on the seabed, he attempted to drag its 500 lb. warhead along the harbor bottom to a position underneath the *Barham*. Losing consciousness, he came to the surface, saw *Barham* a mere thirty yards off, and dived to make another attempt, only to find that he had lost the warhead. He then swam away, finally dragging himself exhausted onto the harbor mole. Slipping out of his wet suit, he walked along the jetty towards some neutral merchant vessels, passing several British guards who appeared to ignore him despite the fact that he was drenched to the skin and staggering with fatigue. Interviewed later he commented how much he appreciated the British sense of privacy. He was able to make his way aboard a nearby Spanish merchant ship, but there his luck ran out; he was seen by an alert British sentry and captured. After a difficult time persuading his captors that he was not a spy he was sent to a prisoner of war camp where he spent most of the next four years in hospital recovering from the effect of too much oxygen on his lungs, which were, he recalled, "full of holes."[16]

Just after his capture Birindelli's warhead exploded. Too far from *Barham* to do any damage, but it did alert the British to the existence of an underwater threat to Gibraltar. Italian agents in Spain reported increased nervousness among ships in harbor, and frequent dropping of depth charges.[17]

Birindelli's immediate concern after capture was how to tell his *Decima Mas* comrades that the mission contemplated was indeed possible; only mechanical failures had prevented a successful attack. However, he realized that only he knew this. His solution was a letter from prison camp in which he told his mother "Tell my friend GG (de la Penne) not to be afraid of the professors; keep on trying and he will succeed." His mother could make no sense of the message but decided to send it on to de la Penne anyway. De la Penne, now safely back in Italy, understood immediately, and it was on his recommendation that further operations were authorized.[18]

One of the two *Maiales* that never made it into Gibraltar harbor was washed up on the Spanish shore where British intelligence was able to study it. The Royal Navy then produced its own version of the weapon, but carrying the more grandiloquent name "Chariot." Although Chariots had limited success, one of them did sink an Italian cruiser. Others were sent across the North Sea to Norway in an early attempt to sink the German battleship *Tirpitz*, but without success[19] (See Chapter Six).

Clearly, although *Decima Mas* operations to date had demonstrated the practicality of bringing *Maiales* within striking distance of enemy bases, and then penetrating their inner defenses, mechanical problems had doomed the attacks to failure despite the skill and bravery of the crews. The torpedoes in use were essentially the same design that had been developed before the war by Tesei and Toschi. (One might ask whether the records of modern warfare disclose any other advanced weapons systems being taken into action so aggressively by their own inventors). Work had been started on an improved version of the *Maiale*, but in the meantime every effort was made to eliminate the material shortcomings in the existing weapons, including the use of better components and stricter testing. Nor had the enemy been asleep; now aware of *Decima Mas'* activities the British had increased patrol boat activities, particularly around the harbor entrances, they started dropping depth charges systematically along likely approach routes, and laid listening devices on harbor bottoms.

Two subsequent *Maiale* attacks on Gibraltar proved disappointing: the first, in May 1941, again found the expected major vessels absent; while the second, in September of that year, although sinking 30,000 tons of shipping, including two oil tankers carrying fuel desperately needed by the British, failed to garner the rich naval prizes so eagerly sought by *Decima Mas* command. Nevertheless, the equipment, formerly the weakest element in the attacks, now appeared to be working well, while the crews had demonstrated the ability to overcome the best defenses the British were able to deploy. *Decima Mas'* newfound confidence was to be fully tested in December 1941, when the underwater team carried out its most successful and daring undertaking.[20]

1941 had been a disastrous year for Britain's Mediterranean Fleet; losses, including those incurred during the evacuation from Crete, were one battleship sunk and four badly damaged, one carrier sunk and two damaged, seven cruisers sunk and ten damaged, sixteen destroyers sunk and twelve damaged, one monitor sunk, and five submarines sunk and three damaged. In November alone the veteran carrier *Ark Royal* had capsized and sunk, victim of a torpedo from German submarine *U-81*, while ten days later Mediterranean Fleet commander Admiral Sir Andrew Cunningham had watched helplessly from his flagship *Queen Elizabeth* as the battleship *Barham*, torpedoed by German submarine *U-331*, exploded with the loss of 850 men. The Italian Navy surmised, correctly, that the Royal Navy would seek to protect its few remaining capital ships, and that

Alexandria probably represented the safest place for them to be.

The attack against Alexandria was scrupulously planned, air reconnaissance and agents in the port city delivering accurate information about the state of British harbor defenses.[21] On December 18, 1941, Lt. Commander Borghese, in command of *Scire*, had been able to bring his boat undetected over 1,700 miles from Port Lago on the island of Leros to within a mile of the entrance to Alexandria harbor. During his approach he had managed to evade minefields, detector cables and net barriers. Lying on the bottom, he waited until nightfall, and then at 8:45 P.M. surfaced while the three crews, assisted by the reserve crew, opened the doors to the containing cylinders and carefully checked their *Maiales*. *Scire* submerged again, allowing the three torpedoes to float off the foredeck, each with its crew sitting astride. Reports received just before launching the torpedoes indicated that the battleships *Valiant* and *Queen Elizabeth* were still moored inside, together with *Sagona*, a large tanker.[22]

Engineer Captain Antonio Marceglia and *Scire*

Waiting until all three were safely on their way, Borghese turned his vessel towards the west and the safety of home. Mounted on the three torpedoes were Lieutenant Luigi Durand de la Penne assisted by diver Emilio Bianchi, Engineer Captain Antonio Marceglia with diver Spartaco Schergat, and Marine Captain Vincenzo Martellota with his diver Mario Marino. De la Penne, the commander of the three teams, was a big, good-looking Ligurian. Born in 1914, he graduated from the Naval Academy in Leghorn in 1934 and after a tour in destroyers joined the *Decima Mas* Squadron in Spezia in 1936. De la Penne and Bianchi were the reserve crew for the aborted 1940 Alexandria attack, designated for one of the attacking torpedoes in the September, 1940 sortie against Gibraltar and, as noted, strong and resourceful members of the team whose equipment had failed after penetrating Gibraltar harbor the following month. They were the most experienced members of the group. Their target was *Valiant*.

Marceglia, born in 1915, graduated from the Naval Academy in 1936, spent two years in submarines, and joined *Decima Mas* in 1940. He and Schergat had been the reserve crew for the attack on merchant shipping off Gibraltar the previous month. Their target was *Queen Elizabeth*.

HMS *Queen Elizabeth* in Alexandria harbor surrounded by anti-torpedo nets

Martellota, born in 1913, graduated from the Naval Academy in 1934 and, after taking special courses in naval construction and armaments, spent two years working on torpedoes. He joined *Decima Mas* in 1940. This mission appears to have been his first operational sortie. He and Marino were originally supposed to attack the carrier *Eagle* but, in her absence, had been instructed to seek out any large oil tanker.

The day before *Scire*'s arrival Cunningham had issued a general warning in which he said: "Attacks on Alexandria by air, boat or human torpedo may be expected when calm weather conditions prevail. Lookouts and patrols should be warned accordingly.[23]" Despite this, however, little attempt seems to have been made to control access into this strategically vital harbor. Two Royal Navy corvettes were patrolling the entrance to the harbor, dropping depth charges at random, but half an hour after midnight the anti-submarine boom was opened and the entrance lights turned on to permit the Royal Navy's 7th Cruiser Squadron to return to port. Taking advantage of this illumination and the open barrier, the Italians were able to slip through.

In contrast to previous *Decima Mas* operations, the attack on Alexandria was nearly faultless. Only de la Penne and Bianchi encountered any serious problems. After successfully floating their *Maiale* over *Valiant*'s protective netting, Bianchi was knocked off his seat and, finding his breathing apparatus no longer working, swam to a nearby buoy. De la Penne continued, but a short distance from the battleship his torpedo's engine stopped and the weapon dropped to the harbor bottom. He dived and was able to locate it, but was unable to restart the motor; a steel wire was wound around its propeller. Alone, de la Penne had to struggle to drag the warhead's dead weight along the seabed but, his visibility hampered by the mud he was stirring up, he lost any sense of direction. Then, miraculously, he heard the steady beat of ship's pump that guided him like a beacon to where he was able to leave the warhead resting on the harbor bottom some five feet beneath *Valiant*'s hull. Setting the fuse he surfaced and swam over to join Bianchi. It was 3:30 A.M. when John Knight, a signalman on *Valiant*'s bridge, received a call from the quarterdeck: "Shine your light on the port torpedo netting." Switching on the searchlight he saw a man clinging to one of the glass globes that held the netting up. A nearby sentry fired a burst from his machine gun, and a voice cried: "There's another one on the buoy!" A ship's boat quickly brought the two men on board, where they were separated.[24]

Marceglia and Schergat came through the harbor entrance together with de la Penne and made their way to the starboard side of *Queen Elizabeth*. They felt their way along the protective netting until they found an opening and then, close to the bow, dropped to the bottom. Guided by the sound of the ship's machinery, they made their way under the hull where they blew the *Maiale*'s ballast tanks. The torpedo rose so rapidly to the surface that it struck the battleship's bottom. Detaching the warhead, Marceglia secured a line to the starboard bilge keel and then sent Schergat to fix the other end to the port side. Schergat, however, was overcome by breathing pure oxygen for too long, so Marceglia completed this task, all the time working in the pitch darkness under the ship's hull. The explosive charge finally secure and the fuses activated, the two men remounted their torpedo, took it down to the bottom and under the netting, and then up to the surface, heading for shore. On their way they released incendiary flares timed to go off shortly after the main explosion so as to set fire to any spreading oil. While still in deep enough water they sank their equipment and started machinery designed to destroy their torpedo. At 4:30 A.M. they walked ashore, changed into civilian clothing and began their planned escape.[25]

Martellotta and Marino had as their intended target the aircraft carrier *Eagle* but, seeing no sign of her (she was away at sea) they headed for their secondary target, which was any large oil tanker. On his way to the tanker anchorage Martellotta nearly ran into a large warship that he took to be an enemy cruiser; to his consternation a sentry on board shone a flashlight directly at him. The vessel was in fact the French battleship *Lorraine*, interned in Alexandria by the British following the French surrender the previous year. To the Italian's surprise the sentry pointed in the direction down the harbor where the battleships lay. (Some accounts claim that Martellotta surfaced next to *Lorraine* and shouted to the sentry "*Valiant?*" and that the Frenchman kindly pointed the way). By now Martellotta was beginning to feel dizzy; he realized that his nose clip had fallen off and that he was inhaling carbon dioxide. Proceeding on the surface they found the tanker *Sagona*, fixed their warhead to her stern, distributed their incendiary flares, and then headed for a coaling pier where they jettisoned their equipment, set the self destructing mechanism on their torpedo, and waded ashore.[26]

Admiral Cunningham took up the story in his memoirs:

> "At about 4 A.M. on December 19 I was called in my cabin on board the *Queen Elizabeth*, with the news that two Italians had been found clinging to the bow buoy of the *Valiant*. They had been taken on board and interrogated; but had vouchsafed nothing and been sent ashore under arrest. I at once ordered them to be brought back to the *Valiant* and confined in one of the forward compartments well below the water line. The boats of all ships were also called away to drop small charges around them, while the ships' companies were turned out of their hammocks below and chain bottom-lines were dragged along the ships' bottoms."[27]

The first explosion occurred at 5:47 A.M. under the stern of *Sagona*. It caused a serious hole in her hull, and damaged her rudder and propeller shafts. The destroyer *Jervis*, lying alongside the tanker, was also damaged and required a month in dry-dock for repairs.[28]

De la Penne calculated that *Valiant*'s anchor cable locker, where he was confined, was just about over the spot he had dropped the torpedo's warhead. When he reckoned there could not be more than ten minutes before his warhead would go off, he asked to see Captain Charles Morgan, RN, the battleship's commanding officer, telling him that he had but a few minutes to save his crew. When de la Penne again refused to say where the charge had been placed, he was taken back to the cable locker, but Morgan did bring all his ship's company up from below. Midshipman Adrian Holloway, who was standing on the quarterdeck at the time, later recalled that the Officer of the Watch berated the ship's bugler for a poor rendering of the required bugle call: "How dare you make such an appalling mess of sounding off "Clear lower deck" . . . don't you know there are foreign officers on board?" As the sailors were climbing out of their mess decks there was a tremendous explosion from the forward end of the ship. De la Penne recalled that the ship was violently shaken, all the lights went out and the cable locker filled with smoke. There were no casualties, but *Valiant* settled heavily by the bow.[29] De la Penne, realizing that his chances of survival locked in a steel box below the water line were slight, frantically sought a way to escape. The porthole proved too small, the hawse pipe too hard to access. Finally he pushed against the door and found to his astonishment that it had been left unlocked, whether by accident or an act of compassion is unclear. He made his way up on deck and back aft where he found the ship's Captain and demanded to know where they were keeping Bianchi. Not surprisingly his question was unanswered, so he made his way further aft to a point from where he could see *Queen Elizabeth*.

Some five minutes later there came a second explosion, this time under *Queen Elizabeth*. Cunningham, who was standing right aft by the ensign recalled later: "I felt a dull thud and was tossed about five feet into the air by the whip of the ship . . . I saw a great cloud of black smoke shoot up the funnel and from immediately in front of it and knew at once that the ship was badly damaged."[30] The blast, which killed nine seamen, blew two large holes in her hull, caused flooding in her boiler rooms and cut off light and power. A sharp list to starboard was countered by flooding port side compartments. De la Penne was escorted below to the wardroom where he found Bianchi. Both were shortly taken back ashore.

De la Penne spent several hours in British naval custody, much of it on board the ship he intended to sink. Yet throughout the time he demonstrated remarkable composure for someone who, not unreasonably, might have been shot as a spy or saboteur. Biding his time until the very last moment before disclosing that he had in fact placed an explosive charge under the ship within a few feet of where he was confined, striding up to the captain and demanding to know the whereabouts of his fellow diver, refusing at all times to provide any details about his mission; all this is evidence of a remarkably self-assured and very brave individual. Moreover, several contemporary accounts indicate that when he was taken ashore for the first time, he tried to warn his captors not to return to their ship which would, he assured them, soon go "Phoom[31]."

Martellotta and Marino enjoyed a very brief period of freedom ashore in Alexandria. They landed near one of the port's coaling piers and headed for the nearest gate. The guard at the gate was surprised to see two men coming towards him dressed in blue one-piece suits and rubber boots, both of whom were soaking wet. Suspecting they might be Italians, the guard arrested them. They carried identity cards with their real names and photographs, and claimed they were Italian sailors who had survived the sinking of their ship and swum ashore.

The guard took them to 2nd Lieutenant Mahmoud Fouad el Sayed, the officer in charge of the post, who searched them and turned them over to the British Army. At all times the two were quiet and made no attempt to escape or resist. Among Martellotta's possessions were two cans of cigarettes, in one of which was some sugar wrapped in a piece of paper on which was typed the course and distances needed to take them from their launching point to their target.[32]

Escape plans for the frogmen involved an Italian submarine waiting at prearranged times off the coast near the town of Rosetta. Pretending to be French sailors Marceglia and Schergat were able to leave the harbor, walk into the city, and make their way to the railroad station. Here poor preparation by *Decima Mas* staff nearly led to their discovery; they had been given British pound notes to use while in Egypt, unaware of the fact that only the Egyptian pound was acceptable at that time. Amazingly, a passing British army officer, sympathizing with their difficulties, offered to change their money for them. However, the transaction took some time, causing them to miss their train. Concerned that their luck might run out, they started towards Rosetta on foot. One Egyptian police patrol stopped them, but then released them. Later they were less fortunate.

Marceglia and Schergat arrived in Rosetta at 7 P.M. in the evening of December 19 and made their way to the Hotel Farouk el Awal where they registered under the names Antonio Doradin and Emile Rabat, giving their nationality as French and stating that they were seamen from Alexandria. They spent the night at the hotel and then set off down the banks of the Nile towards the sea. By 3 P.M. they had covered about 7 km and were some 10 km from the coast. Approaching the Burg Raschid pumps they were spotted by a police corporal who asked them what they were doing there. When Marceglia responded in Italian, and failed to provide any account as to why he was in Rosetta, the Corporal arrested them both. And took them to Captain Amin Mohamed, the officer in charge of the local police detachment. Marceglia admitted to Mohamed that they were

Italians, but claimed that he was an army officer who was in Rosetta hiding from the British. He then requested that they be handed over to the British and refused to tell the Egyptians anything more. Mohamed's report indicated that Marceglia appeared quite cheerful and at the end of the interrogation said he was very glad the war was finished for him.

Investigation in the days following the attack showed that *Valiant* had underwater damage extending for over 80 feet. She was taken into the Royal navy's only available large floating dock where she required two months for temporary repair and three more before she could be ready for action again.[33] *Queen Elizabeth* too required dry-docking, but could not be accommodated until *Valiant* was clear.[34]

Noting that there had been no news from Rome regarding damage to his battleships, Cunningham hoped to bluff the Italians into believing the attack had failed. Believing, rightly, that all the frogmen were in custody, he ordered them held incommunicado for at least six months, hoping to give the impression they had perished in an attempted attack. Power was provided to *Queen Elizabeth* by two submarines brought alongside for that purpose, Cunningham occupied his normal quarters, and parades were held on deck with guards and the ship's band. The admiral even had a false waterline painted to give the impression she was floating normally. Nothing could be done, however, to disguise the fact that *Valiant* was in dry-dock.

Britain's strategic position in the Mediterranean had been considerably improved by the capture of the whole coastline of Cyrenaica, providing useful airfields for the Royal Air Force. This favorable position was, however, largely offset by two events: the damage to *Queen Elizabeth* and *Valiant* and, on the same day, serious losses to naval forces based in Malta. Force "K," consisting of three cruisers and four destroyers, while seeking to intercept an important enemy convoy, ran into a newly laid minefield. One cruiser was lost and two damaged, as was one of the destroyers. In the words of the Mediterranean Fleet December, 1941 War Diary, "The striking power of the fleet was thus seriously reduced just at the time when we had at last reached a position to operate offensively in the Central Mediterranean."[35]

# 3 THE CHANNEL DASH

*[This was the first of my naval history articles to be published (Military History Quarterly, Summer, 1995). It was later anthologized in the collection, No End Save Victory, Putnam & Sons, 2001). My principal reasons for researching the event were amazement at the universal applicability of Murphy's Law (if things can go wrong they will, and at the worst possible time), and a serendipitous postal relationship I developed with Edgar Lee, one of the few survivors of the disastrous Swordfish attack on the German squadron, a relationship that continued until his death (natural causes) some seventy years later.]*

British naval planning for war against Germany traditionally relied heavily on the Royal Navy's demonstrated ability to control its enemy's only exits from the North Sea: the English Channel and the narrow passage between Scapa Flow and Norway. For a few fleeting hours during the winter of 1942, however, Great Britain lost command of the Channel. In a daring maneuver, the German battle cruisers *Scharnhorst* and *Gneisenau* and heavy cruiser *Prinz Eugen* steamed in broad daylight through waters the British had always deemed their own.

The German battle cruisers *SCHARNHORST* and *GNEISENAU* travel in a line with their guns firing, allegedly taken during their escape from Brest on 12 February 1942.

In London shortly after the incident, a *Times* editorial thundered:

> *Vice Admiral Ciliax has succeeded where the Duke of Medina Sidonia failed: with trifling losses he has sailed a hostile fleet from an Atlantic harbour up the English Channel and through the Straits of Dover to safe anchorage in a North Sea port. Nothing more mortifying to the pride of sea power has happened in home waters since the seventeenth century.*

Naval air power was also affected. After the potential of naval aircraft was first demonstrated in World War I, there was considerable dispute during the interwar years regarding proper control over the new weapon. Advocates of an independent air force argued that the air was indivisible, while navies insisted that they retain command of all maritime activities. In the United States and Japan, the admirals were successful in preserving their air arms; in Britain, the Royal

Navy lost control of all aviation to the new Royal Air Force, and it was not until 1937 that it regained only the shipborne portion. However, it took the German navy's 1942 "Channel Dash" to demonstrate convincingly the folly of dividing command of maritime aviation.

Germany's 1940 occupation of Norway and defeat of France greatly reduced Britain's natural geographic advantages, since the choke points that for so long had frustrated Germany's ability to wage war in the world's oceans were suddenly unblocked. Brest and Saint-Nazaire provided access to the Atlantic, while the fjords of Norway furnished surface-vessel and submarine bases well outside the North Sea. A major German victory on land had inflicted a significant setback on Britain's position at sea.

Nevertheless, it was not until the beginning of 1941 that the *Scharnhorst* and *Gneisenau*--fast, modern, 32,000-ton battle cruisers each carrying nine eleven-inch guns and numerous smaller weapons--were able to evade the Royal Navy's arctic patrols. For two months they menaced British shipping in the North and South Atlantic. Then, in late March, their initial mission completed, the two ships entered Brest.

Significant as access to a French Atlantic port may have appeared to German naval planners, the ability of the RAF to subject it to constant air attack greatly reduced the effectiveness of the Brest-based squadron. In addition, destruction of most of Germany's Atlantic supply vessels significantly restricted the big ships' range. These factors, together with maintenance problems, would keep the *Scharnhorst* and *Gneisenau* close to Brest for the rest of 1941. Even so, the two battle cruisers, joined in June by the *Bismarck*'s consort *Prinz Eugen*, remained a constant threat to Britain; never sure when they might sortie into the Atlantic again, the Admiralty had to maintain significant naval strength at Gibraltar and Scapa Flow in readiness.

Aerial photograph taken during a daylight attack on German warships docked at Brest, France. Two Handley Page Halifaxes of No. 35 Squadron RAF fly towards the dry docks in which the battle cruisers *SCHARNHORST* and *GNEISENAU* are berthed (right), and over which a smoke screen is rapidly spreading.

During the second half of 1941, the disposition of the large surface ships became a frequent topic of discussion between Adolf Hitler and his naval commander, Grand Admiral Erich Raeder. The fuehrer, concerned abut the battle cruisers' vulnerability in Brest, felt they would be of more use in Norway, where they could deter a feared British attack against that country, while threatening Allied convoys supplying the Soviets via Murmansk. Raeder, on the other hand, argued that by remaining in Brest the squadron represented a continuing menace to vital British routes to the south.

In Hitler's opinion, however, the squadron was like a cancer patient whose life can be preserved only by major surgery, however risky. It was his threat to order the idle ships decommissioned and their guns and crews used in defense of Norway that finally persuaded the admirals to chance the surgery; by the end of the year, discussion was focusing on the route to be taken.

Raeder recommended a breakout to the north around Scotland, telling Hitler that the shorter Channel route was too risky. His operational commanders, including Vice Admiral Otto Ciliax, who would command the squadron during the passage, did not share Raeder's pessimism. The Channel route was preferable; they persuaded Hitler, pointing out that it was shorter and that escort by small vessels would be possible, air cover available, harbors of refuge nearby, and the enemy battle fleet far away.

On January 12, 1942, the German navy presented Hitler with its plan for the big ships' passage through the Channel, which depended on three principal elements: careful clearing of British mine-fields, high-density air cover, and surprise. Mines had always ranked high on the list of reasons that heavy naval units could not force their way through the Channel. Still, Commodore Friedrich Ruge, the minesweeper commander (see also Chapter Five), was unexpectedly optimistic. Absolute safety could not be guaranteed, but he felt that a deepwater passage could be cleared without attracting too much attention.

Readily understanding the need for effective air cover, Hitler directed the Luftwaffe to do everything it could to ensure the safety of the ships. Despite pressing demands on its strength from other theaters, the Luftwaffe proved surprisingly cooperative, possibly recognizing that removal of the battle squadron from Brest would reduce the intensity of RAF attacks on the Atlantic ports and therefore the associated air-defense requirements.

Hitler also seized on Ciliax's idea of a nighttime departure, essential if surprise was to be maintained as long as possible. He countered the arguments of his advisers, who feared annihilating daytime air attacks in the Straits of Dover, by saying that past experience indicated the

British were incapable of making and executing lightning decisions. In this case at least, the fuehrer knew his enemy better than many of his admirals did.

Information from U-boats in the North Atlantic indicated that good weather conditions would be likely in mid-February: little moonlight and low clouds, resulting in poor visibility. Tides and currents also would be favorable then. The ships would leave Brest on the evening of February 11, pass Dover at noon the following day, and arrive in Germany's North Sea ports twenty-four hours after departure. As the *Times* would later comment, "The German plan combined audacity in action with accurate and patient organization in advance."

Surprise was, in the final event, tactical rather than strategic. As early as April 1941, an RAF analysis of possible enemy naval movements had predicted an attempt by the *Scharnhorst* and *Gneisenau* to reach Germany via the Channel, and a plan for opposing action by bombers, torpedo bombers, and light surface craft had been prepared and circulated. Crucially, the plan, code-named Fuller, assumed a night passage through the Channel's narrow waters. Regular photoreconnaissance of Brest began, and several submarines were stationed off the harbor to report any movements. Unfortunately, requirements in other theaters caused these to be reduced to one by year's end.

All intelligence available by late January pointed toward the likelihood of a breakout in the near future. A British Admiralty "appreciation" on February 2 stated in part, "We might well . . . find the 2 battle cruisers and the 8-inch cruiser with 5 large and 5 small destroyers, also, say 20 fighters constantly overhead . . . proceeding up Channel." It added, "Our bombers have shown that we cannot place much reliance on them to damage the enemy, whilst our Coastal Command T/B [torpedo/bomber] aircraft will not muster more than 9." The following day, the Admiralty warned its various operational commanders and the RAF's Bomber, Fighter, and Coastal commands that a breakout was likely and requested all commands to bring the Fuller arrangements into force.

By February 7, six destroyers, ten torpedo boats, over thirty minesweepers and numerous smaller vessels had reinforced German naval forces already in the Channel. The next day, the RAF's Coastal Command determined that weather and tidal conditions favored a movement anytime after February 10, with the Channel the likely route. At this time, therefore, the British could assume with some confidence that the German fleet would soon break out, and that it would move through the Channel; the only uncertain element was the precise time of departure. Nevertheless, both the Royal Navy and the RAF had become convinced that the ships would try to pass through the Straits of Dover at night, which argued for a daytime departure from Brest. Reports from an agent in that port, warning urgently that the likeliest time of departure would be around 11:00 P.M. during a new-moon period, either were never seen by the Admiralty or were disregarded.

Coastal Command, whose torpedo bombers probably represented the greatest threat to the German fleet, did very little other than institute night patrols by radar-equipped aircraft over the western approaches to the Channel. A squadron of Beaufort torpedo bombers was ordered to move south from Scotland, but it was unable to do so because of bad weather. None of the other anti-shipping squadrons were moved nearer to Dover, and, in view of the high level of secrecy surrounding Fuller, none of the pilots concerned were told about the possibility of a breakout or the ships they might encounter.

Bomber Command, normally unwilling to divert resources from its strategic offensive against Germany, reluctantly designated a strike force to prepare for action against the battle cruisers; but on February

10, without telling anyone, it ordered half of the strike force to stand down and extended the remainder's notice from two hours standby to four. Significantly, however, it did arrange to lay ninety-eight magnetic mines off the Dutch coast, in what Enigma decryptions and captured enemy charts indicated were the paths just swept by Ruge's coastal forces.

The Admiralty, its capabilities stretched to the limit, took what minor defensive measures lay within its means. Vice Admiral Sir Bertram Ramsay, commander in chief at Dover, was placed in tactical command of a skimpy fleet consisting of two fast minelayers at Plymouth and Portsmouth, eight motor torpedo boats (MTBs) at Dover and nearby Ramsgate, and half a dozen elderly destroyers based at Harwich. At Ramsay's request, these surface forces were augmented by six naval Swordfish torpedo planes. These obsolescent biplanes were moved to an RAF fighter field at Manston, near Dover, and placed under joint RAF-navy command. The mine-layers sowed new fields off the French coast, but Ruge's forces discovered and swept them just before the heavy ships passed through. Because of the continuing threat represented by the German battleship *Tirpitz*--which had been moved north to Trondheim in mid-January and was thus ideally situated to attack Soviet-bound convoys--and the Admiralty's quite logical unwillingness to subject an already badly stretched fleet to the risk of German air attack, the British did not shift any major units based at Scapa Flow. Such concern would have been heightened by the recent destruction of the capital ships *Repulse* and *Prince of Wales*. Fast, modern naval aircraft, manned by well-trained Imperial Japanese Navy crews, had taken less than two hours to sink two of the Royal Navy's most powerful ships.

In essence, therefore, it was the RAF, strongly resenting any diversion of resources from its strategic-bombing mission, that had the primary obligation to detect any movement of the German squadron, and that would play the most important role in stopping it if it did move. The Royal Navy's role was effectively to act as the goalkeeper: to provide what force it could to prevent the enemy ships from passing through the narrow portion of the Channel, by which time any breakout would be more than half completed. No one person was in charge of British defenses; indeed, it would have been hard to divide responsibility better if that had been the intention.

The breakout, which the Germans code-named Operation Cerberus, began on the evening of February 11. Just as the ships were about to put to sea, a major RAF bombing raid began. The Germans were extraordinarily lucky. Not only did the bombs cause no damage, but more importantly, the returning bomber crews confirmed that the ships were still in harbor, presumably for the night. At 10:45 P.M., the three heavy ships and six escorting destroyers cleared the Brest breakwater and headed into the Atlantic, before entering the English Channel.

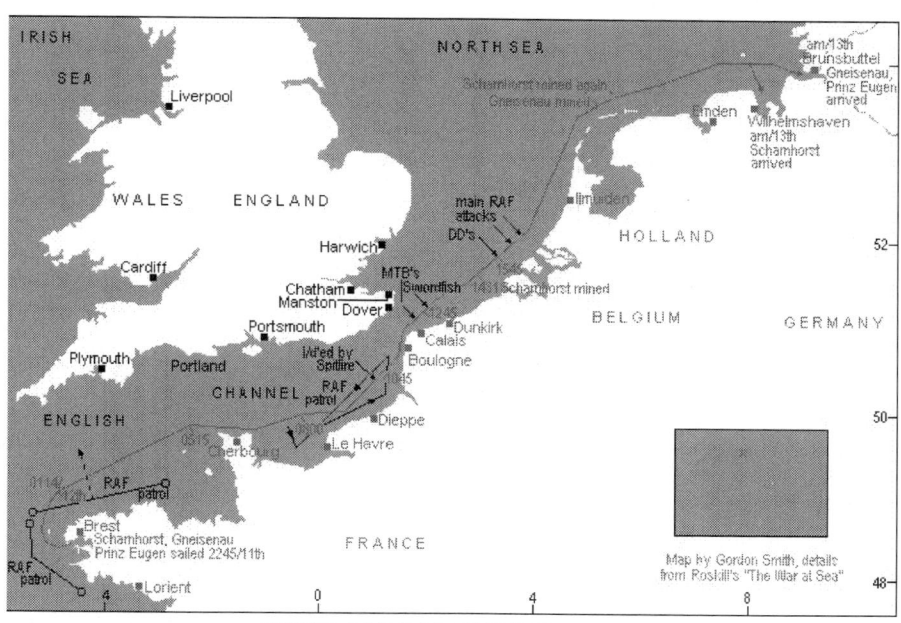

## OPERATION CERBERUS
(Map courtesy Naval-history.net)

Already off Cherbourg by 6:30 A.M., still in the dark, the squadron was joined by an additional escort of E-boats, which would be relieved at intervals throughout the day. About an hour later, the first of the escorting fighter aircraft, Messerschmitt Bf 109s and 110s, and Focke-Wulf 190s, arrived.

General Adolf Galland, Germany's veteran fighter leader, had meticulously prepared air cover for the operation. More than 250 day and night fighters controlled by flexible, on-the-spot command arrangements and supported by sophisticated communications, were dedicated to the naval squadron's safety. Some sixteen fighters would be over the warships at any one time, keeping as low as possible to avoid detection by British radar. Other aircraft were kept on immediate alert at various bases along the French coast. Crucial to the whole plan were Luftwaffe pilots and communications specialists aboard the ships, in constant contact with Galland's command post ashore, to give local direction to the fighter effort.

The German air-defense plan also involved secret and relatively untried electronic countermeasures designed to jam British radar. Beginning several weeks before the breakout, in order to reduce suspicion, the interference gradually increased so that by early February it had become a daily phenomenon, which the RAF assumed was a result of atmospheric disturbances. These countermeasures greatly reduced British ability to detect the ships as they entered the narrow portion of the Channel.

As dawn broke over the German capital ships, at 8:20 A.M., Admiral Ciliax could not believe that he had gotten so far undetected. A number of factors had combined to frustrate early discovery, evidence either of German good fortune or of poor British planning. First, with the assumption that no movement was likely that night, HMS *Sealion*--the lone submarine covering the entrance to Brest--had withdrawn to recharge her batteries. If the British air raid had not delayed the squadron's departure, the *Sealion* might well have reported its movement.

Admiral Ciliax inspecting men on *Scharnhorst*

Enigma, normally such a reliable source of information on the movement of German surface vessels, also failed to provide timely intelligence. Traffic decrypted through February 10, while indicating that departure was probable, had given no precise indication of timing. Unexpected decoding delays then caused a backup so that signals received February 10 through 12 were not available for three crucial days, by which time the German ships were safe in their home ports. As noted earlier, vital human intelligence also never reached its proper destination or was disregarded.

Coastal Command's plan to detect any movement of the German fleet called for nightlong patrols along three lines: Brest to Ushant, that island to LeHavre, and LeHavre to Boulogne. On the night of February 11, the air-to-surface vessel (ASV) radar of two of the night patrols, never very reliable at the best of times, failed just at the moment the German squadron was passing the respective patrol lines. The third patrol was recalled due to weather conditions. By the time the various commands became aware that coverage of the western Channel had been seriously compromised, it was too late. Adding to British misfortunes, photoreconnaissance of Brest at dawn on February 12 was hampered by low clouds and thus unable to discover that the ships had departed.

Responsibility for air coverage of the Channel now shifted to Fighter Command's morning Spitfire patrols. The pilot of the first of these sorties caught sight of a number of small craft leaving Boulogne, but lowering clouds made visibility so bad that he returned home, assuming the ships he had faintly seen were a routine coastal convoy. The German squadron moved on, unseen, just below him. After this first patrol came two more pairs of Spitfires, one on routine reconnaissance, and the other investigating extensive enemy fighter activity over the Channel. Both sorties spotted the enemy squadron, but neither fully understood its significance. Slavish adherence to radio silence meant that not until the planes landed, soon after 11:00 A.M., did Fighter Command realize that the German capital ships were not only at sea, but already fast approaching the Straits of Dover.

About twenty minutes elapsed before the Spitfire reports had traveled up the chain of command to Fighter Command headquarters, thence to the Admiralty, and finally to Ramsay's command at Dover. The Fuller plans—calling for coordinated attacks by aircraft, surface vessels, and shore batteries, all well supported by the RAF's 550 available fighters—were then finally set in motion.

Meanwhile, in spite of effective enemy jamming, as early as 9:30 A.M. British coastal radar had picked up plots of circling aircraft near the

French coast and moving slowly eastward. Amazingly, in view of the known possibility of a breakout, no alarm was sounded. It was not until after 10:00 A.M. that fast-moving, large radar echoes, surrounded by smaller, faster blips, provided unmistakable evidence that major surface vessels with substantial fighter escorts were moving up the Channel. Then difficulties finding a secure telephone delayed getting this information to Ramsay's Dover command for another forty minutes. Even so, despite the lack of any official confirmation, Ramsay alerted his scanty surface forces and the six Swordfish at Manston, informed the army-manned shore batteries at Dover, and—without authority to give orders to the RAF—suggested that the Coastal Command bring its own torpedo bombers to readiness.

Even so, it was past noon on February 12 before Admiral Ciliax first heard the sound of British gunfire as shore batteries engaged his ships in the narrowest part of the Channel. The firing was uneven, impeded by reduced visibility and German evasive action. Thirty-three rounds were fired, but there were no hits.

Surface forces most immediately available to Ramsay were the five motor torpedo boats based at Dover, commanded by Lieutenant Commander E.N. Pumphrey. He left harbor just before noon. With the uncooperative Germans appearing from nowhere in broad daylight, Pumphrey hastily abandoned complex plans for a coordinated night attack by his MTBs and the Manston Swordfish. Once clear of the narrow waters, Ciliax had increased speed to close to thirty knots, so that Pumphrey had to coax the maximum performance from his little fleet. The first enemy sighting was the E-boat escort and then, as the German smoke screen momentarily cleared, the massive gray shapes of the three heavy ships.

With one of his boats already out of action from engine failure due to the high-speed chase, Pumphrey determined he would be unable to pass ahead of the enemy and must attack through the E-boat screen.

Torpedoes were fired at a range between 4,000 and 5,000 yards, but because of weapon malfunctions and Ciliax's evasive maneuvers, none found their mark. Then, assisted by two accompanying motor gunboats that laid a protective smoke screen of their own, all the MTBs withdrew to Dover, suffering superficial damage and no casualties. Meanwhile, the three MTBs from Ramsgate had also put to sea, but they never caught up with the Germans.

At the Manston RAF base, Lieutenant Commander Eugene Esmonde, commanding the six Swordfish torpedo bombers of the Royal Navy's 825 Squadron, had previously been told to prepare his planes for a night strike as the German ships passed by Dover. Such an attack, though dangerous, was within the elderly biplanes' capabilities. Indeed, British naval aviators were given extensive training in night torpedo attacks, despite their difficulty, because of the operational limitations of their aircraft. On the other hand, a daylight attack against heavily armed battle cruisers with substantial fighter cover would be extraordinarily risky. Esmonde, however, was a particularly experienced pilot. It was he who had led the final and successful air attack on the *Bismarck,* an operation for which he had recently been decorated.

Just before noon, a message from Ramsay at Dover informed Esmonde that the *Scharnhorst* and the *Gneisenau* were approaching the straits. At the same time, the alert reached the five RAF fighter squadrons designated to escort the Swordfish, but this was amid great confusion because the officer with the Fuller plans had locked them in his safe and had gone on leave. Adding to the chaos was incorrect information that the German ships were traveling at only twenty-one knots.

Even so, it would take the Swordfish, flying at ninety knots, their maximum speed when armed with a torpedo and carrying a crew of three, a dangerously long time to catch the enemy as he headed eastward. Told that some of the fighter escort might be late, Esmonde decided to take off at 12:20 P.M. and circle over the coast for a few minutes while awaiting them. Just as he was about to start his engine, he was told that the enemy's speed was now estimated to be twenty-seven knots. Haste was therefore, essential. Over the coast five minutes later, with still no sign of his escort, Esmonde was becoming desperate when at last ten Spitfires appeared.

The fighters, from the RAF's 72 Squadron, were the only ones to rendezvous with Esmonde that day. The pilots, told only to escort some Swordfish, knew nothing of this engagement going below in the Channel. Esmonde circled for a few more minutes; then, realizing there would be no more escorts, he dropped down to fifty feet to cover the twenty-three miles separating his planes from the enemy ships. The weather was closing in, and a lowering cloud base and poor visibility hampered coordination between the Swordfish and their escorting Spitfires, already complicated by the big difference in the speeds of the two aircraft. Moreover, the lack of radar in any of his planes meant that Esmonde could not use the clouds as cover (as he had during his 1941 attack on the *Bismarck*) without running an unacceptable risk of losing his targets.

The planes soon came into contact with the Luftwaffe screen. Outnumbered and, in the case of the Fw 190s, out-classed, the Spitfires fought valiantly but could not prevent the German fighters from attacking the Swordfish. Esmonde's planes, now committed to their torpedo runs, made easy targets as they flew straight and level just above the waves.

Soon they were over the E-boat and destroyer screen and had to face intense fire from the entire German fleet. The battle cruisers' eleven-inch guns aimed their heavy projectiles into the sea ahead of the Swordfish, creating lethal walls of water through which the badly damaged craft had to fly. The tail of Esmonde's aircraft was on fire and half his lower wing shot away. Finally a German fighter blew away his top wing, and his plane, out of control, crashed into the sea--though not before he dropped a torpedo aimed at the *Scharnhorst*. However, it did not strike its target.

So died Eugene Esmonde, who had flown against the Germans in France and Norway, had led the first torpedo attack on the *Bismarck*, and had survived the sinking of the *Ark Royal*. A citizen of the Irish Republic, he had owed no allegiance to Britain or to its king. His mother received his posthumous Victoria Cross at a Buckingham Palace investiture on St. Patrick's Day.

As the second plane passed over the destroyer screen, its gunner was killed by an enemy fighter. Sub-Lieutenant Edgar Lee, the observer, tried to take over the gun but was unable to move the gunner's body. His pilot, Sub-Lieutenant Brian Rose, managed to drop his torpedo about 1200 yards from the *Prinz Eugen*, despite severe wounds from shell splinters. His engine failing and his main tank losing fuel rapidly as a result of cannon fire, he turned away astern of the enemy ships before crashing into the sea some 500 yards beyond the screen. Lee managed to get Rose out of the plane and into a life raft, from which they were later rescued.

The third Swordfish--its three crew members all wounded, its engine missing two cylinders, and its top wing on fire--astonishingly attempted two attacks. Although injuries caused the pilot, Sub-Lieutenant C.M. Kingsmill, to abandon his first run on the *Scharnhorst*, he recovered and was able to alter course and aim his torpedo at the *Prinz Eugen* before crashing into the sea. British MTBs rescued all three crewmen. The remaining three Swordfish were last seen attacking against continuous heavy ship and air defense. Nothing more is known of them; none of the nine crewmen survived.

The attack was over at 12:45 P.M., twenty minutes after Esmonde's planes took off. None of the torpedoes had found their targets. Only five of the eighteen men who set out survived, three of them badly wounded. Fifteen minutes later, two more Spitfire squadrons arrived over the scene, having taken off too late or lost their way. By then, that phase of the battle was over.

More than an hour and a half after the abortive Swordfish attack, Ciliax received his first setback. At 2:30 P.M. a heavy shock from an underwater explosion rattled the *Scharnhorst*. Her lights fading slowly, the ship gradually came to a standstill as the *Gneisenau* and *Prinz Eugen* roared past. The *Scharnhorst* had hit a mine laid by Bomber Command. In such an event, the breakout plan called for Ciliax to transfer his flag, together with his Luftwaffe liaison team, to an attendant destroyer. Jumping onto the heaving deck of the escort vessel, the admiral and his staff raced off in pursuit of the rest of his squadron. The crew of the *Scharnhorst* rapidly repaired the damage, and the ship soon was able to resume full speed. She overtook the other ships before long, though Ciliax would not return to the *Scharnhorst*'s deck until dawn on February 13.

Six destroyers commanded by Captain C.T.M. Pizey now represented the Royal Navy's last hope of intercepting the Germans. In the words of a survivor, they were "ancient destroyers, really only junk for the scrapyard, on their way to meet the most powerful and modern naval squadron of all." Already at sea in exercises off Harwich, Pizey's squadron set course at noon, believing there was ample time to intercept the Germans, whose speed was assumed to be only twenty knots. Learning at 1:00 P.M. that the enemy was actually making twenty-eight knots now, Pizey realized that he would be unable to catch the ships unless he moved at full speed along the most direct route--which lay right through a known minefield. Shortly after the course alteration, one of the destroyers had to return to Harwich with engine trouble. From 1:30 P.M. on, the little fleet was shadowed by a German reconnaissance plane and subjected to several bombing attacks. RAF fighters detailed to escort Pizey's force failed to find it.

At about 3:15 P.M., when Pizey's destroyers were twenty-two miles west of the Hook of Holland, his radar picked up three large echoes some ten miles to the southeast. Deteriorating weather and particularly low visibility helped cover his approach as he turned on a course to intercept. Large numbers of aircraft from both sides were now appearing in and out of the clouds in the vicinity of the German squadron. Several German aircraft assumed Pizey's ships were friendly and fired their recognition signals, while some of the British planes mistook them for the Germans and attacked them.

Sighting the enemy at 3:42 P.M., Pizey immediately turned to attack. The three destroyers of the first division – the *Campbell*, *Vivacious*, and *Worcester* -- approached to within just over a mile and a half, under a hail of fire from the German battle cruisers and destroyers, before the *Campbell* and *Vivacious* turned to launch their torpedoes at the *Gneisenau*. The *Worcester*, failing to see the *Campbell*'s turn, came in even closer, under heavier and more concentrated fire, before launching torpedoes at the same target. By this time the battle cruiser was turning away, and all three sets of torpedoes missed. Hit in both boiler rooms, the *Worcester* came to a standstill right under the muzzles of the enemy guns.

The second division--the destroyers *Mackay* and *Whitshed*--attacked the *Prinz Eugen*, which in turn was taking radical evasive action to avoid bombing attacks. Neither ship's torpedoes found their target, and the two vessels then returned safely to Harwich.

A further decrease in visibility helped shield the *Campbell* and *Vivacious* as they disengaged from the enemy, exchanging gunfire with some of the escorting destroyers. As they withdrew, they came upon the *Worcester* drifting in the water, badly flooded and on fire. The *Campbell* stopped to pick up survivors and tried to take the damaged ship in tow, while hampered by attacks from friendly as well as hostile aircraft. By this time, however, the *Worcester* had managed to raise steam in one boiler. Pizey took his two undamaged ships back to Harwich to replenish their ammunition. The *Worcester* limped home, arriving in port at dawn the following day.

While Pizey's destroyers were making their gallant but abortive torpedo attacks, the RAF was also throwing most of its available strength into attempts to halt Ciliax. His chief of staff, Captain H.J. Reinecke, later recalled that the British seemed to be using anything with a propeller that could carry bombs. These air attacks lasted from about 2:45 to 6:15 P.M. Although 242 Bomber Command aircraft and 28 torpedo bombers of Coastal Command took part, escorted by 398 fighters, only 39 bombers and 16 torpedo bombers were able to locate the enemy. By early afternoon, pilots were reporting ceilings of 1,000 feet or less and visibility less than 1,000 yards, conditions that contributed greatly to the difficulty of finding and attacking the German squadron. As visibility worsened, aircraft that were able to spot the enemy tried to gain enough height to make effective attacks, only to find themselves in the clouds, unable to see their targets. Armor-piercing bombs designed to be dropped from a high altitude had little effect on the heavily armored warships when released below the cloud base.

Several factors other than weather also accounted for the RAF's failure to mount an effective attack: lack of training in anti-shipping work, delays in getting the bomber force airborne, and communications errors. In addition, many of the bomber crews had not been told the importance of the targets they were going after-- indeed, what the targets actually were. Those who did find the enemy attacked "incessantly and with tenacity," according to General Galland. However, only two of the smaller German escort vessels suffered any damage. The torpedo bombers fared no better: Thirteen torpedoes were dropped but no hits resulted. Summarizing the air attacks after the event, Galland noted that the RAF had been sent into action without sufficient planning, a clear concept of the attack, or systematic tactics. The obsessive secrecy that surrounded the Fuller plans certainly had a price.

As dusk fell and the air attacks gradually petered out, Ciliax and his staff began to relax for the first time since they had left Brest. The peaceful interlude was brief. At about 8:00 P.M., while just north of Vlieland, the *Gneisenau* hit a mine. Damage was only slight, however, and she was able to continue in the company of the *Prinz Eugen*, with only a slight reduction in speed.

Worse damage occurred an hour and a half later, when a massive underwater shock indicated that the *Scharnhorst* had struck a second mine, which inflicted more serious damage than did the first. With her engines stopped, the huge vessel drifted in the dark waters off the Dutch coast. It took nearly an hour for her crew to get two of her three engines working, and then she was able to limp along at only twelve knots, with her fire-control apparatus and important navigational equipment out of order, and over 1,000 tons of water in her bilges. Unfortunately for the British, they had lost contact with the enemy squadron and, in any event, had exhausted their available resources. As dawn broke and the German coast came in sight, Ciliax and his staff rejoined the *Scharnhorst* as she came slowly into Wilhelmshaven; at about the same time, the *Gneisenau* and *Prinz Eugen* entered the mouth of the Elbe.

In the eyes of the admiral and his subordinates, the operation appeared a complete success. German casualties were minor, while it was estimated that the British had suffered a badly damaged destroyer (the *Worcester*) and lost over sixty aircraft. Captain Reinecke recalled, "We knew we had twisted the lion's tail, and that the British didn't like it."

Indeed, the British did not like it. The writer Harold Nicolson, a Member of Parliament, recorded in his diary that people were more distressed about the Germans' exploit than they were about the loss of Singapore two days later. Responding to criticism in the House of Commons, Prime Minister Winston Churchill took the position that although the breakout was a tactical success for the enemy, the abandonment of Brest by the German capital ships represented a strategic gain for the British. Subsequent events largely confirmed this analysis, but the *Times* refused to accept it, instead questioning whether a chance had been missed to send something like a quarter of the German navy to the bottom of the Channel, "where its effectiveness in the battle of the Atlantic would need no dialectical estimation."

As frequently happens when a British government has to explain an embarrassing event, an eminent jurist was asked to convene a Board of Enquiry. The resulting report by a High Court judge, A.T. Bucknill, implied that the main blame for the fiasco lay with the Germans, for choosing to make the passage by daylight when they were expected at night. The report also concluded that the forces available to the British were, even with adequate warning, insufficient to cripple the German squadron. In fact, any rational analysis would have determined that the chances of sinking the three ships in the Channel were remote. The sustained fire-power of two British battleships and two cruisers with eight-inch guns had earlier proved insufficient to sink the *Bismarck*, which was finally scuttled. The *Scharnhorst* and *Gneisenau* were horses from the same design and construction stable. As for British bombers, their crews were trained to bomb cities at night from high altitude, not fast-moving ships at sea--unlike the specially trained Japanese crews who had made the lethal attack on the *Repulse* and *Prince of Wales* off Malaya.

Nowhere did the report seriously question the divided-command arrangements, under which the navy could only suggest to the air force that it bring its planes into readiness. But as Stephen Roskill pointed out after the war in his official history, "the organization for the control of all the various sea and land forces involved did not prove adequate to the occasion. . . . A specially created command was essential to the efficient and flexible control of all our forces."

Although the Bucknill Report covered the immediate and obvious reasons for the debacle of February 12, 1942, it failed to deal with more fundamental historical causes. It wasn't long before the outspoken Admiral of the Fleet, Sir Roger Keyes, drew attention to the more basic structural flaws that had permitted the German success. The event, he said, was a cruel humiliation that emphasized the folly of those who twenty-four years earlier had deprived the navy of its large and highly efficient air service and who still tolerated dual control of naval air power. "Aviation," said Keyes, "is of vital importance to the Navy. . . . There should be no dual responsibilities . . . . The Navy must be left free to develop, train and control the naval air service it needs." The Channel Dash did indeed have at least one positive impact: From 1942 onward, the Fleet Air Arm was largely reequipped, mostly with American-made aircraft.

As it turned out, Churchill's assessment was probably right: The passage of the enemy battle squadron, though a tactical success, resulted in a strategic gain for the British. Back in their home waters, where the Royal Navy had always preferred to contain a German fleet, the three ships proved to be much less of a threat than they had been on the French Atlantic coast.

As early as the night of February 26-27, an RAF bomber raid inflicted heavy damage on the *Gneisenau*, which was subsequently withdrawn from service. Scuttled at the end of the war to block the approaches to the harbor at Kiel, she was later used as scrap steel by the Soviets.

The *Scharnhorst* eventually reached Norway, where she joined the battleship *Tirpitz* and remained a threat to convoys to the Soviet Union. On December 26, 1943, she was sunk by the Royal Navy's battleship *Duke of York* during the Battle of North Cape, the last gunnery duel between battleships in European waters (see Chapter Five). It took the *Duke of York* and her consorts more than two hours to sink the German vessel, during which time she survived direct hits from over a dozen fourteen-inch shells, many eight-inch and six-inch salvoes, and some eleven torpedoes. Only 36 of her crew of nearly 2,000 were saved.

On her way to Trondheim, the *Prinz Eugen* was torpedoed by a British submarine. She managed to return to Kiel and, following repairs, spent the rest of the war in German waters, lending gunnery support to the German army against the Soviets in 1945. Ceded to the U.S. Navy at the end of the war, the *Prinz Eugen* went to San Diego; on board was the same Captain Reinecke who had helped Admiral Ciliax manage the breakout four years earlier. She was subsequently used as a target during atomic bomb tests at Bikini Atoll.

What happened on February 12, 1942, can be summarized as follows: For thirty years, the admirals respectively responsible for British and German naval strategy had assumed it would be impossible for a German battle fleet to pass through the English Channel. It took an Adolf Hitler, essentially a land person, to challenge that assumption, while an accumulation of British political and strategic errors created the circumstances that permitted the challenge to succeed. The Royal Air Force had most of the skills but few of the tools; more important, it lacked the command authority to conduct a unified defense of Britain's vital maritime approaches.

## 4 SICILY, 1943

How 50,000 Axis troops, pursued by superior Allied forces, were allowed to escape across the Straits of Messina

*[A condensed version of this article was presented at King's College London on May 3-5, 2012 as part of the program "Global-Regional Nexus: The Sea and the Second World War." The author wishes to thank Dr. H. P. Willmott who kindly read a draft version of this article, and made many invaluable suggestions, and Dr. Marcus Faulkner of KCL's Department of War Studies who provided important assistance in solving many of the logistical problems associated with transatlantic research.]*

The 1943 campaign in Sicily involved four navies, four armies, and three air forces, all fighting in and around a Mediterranean island some 175 miles by 100 miles. Fighting went on for thirty-eight days at the end of which nearly half a million Anglo-American troops, despite having near total air and sea superiority, failed to prevent the 50,000 German defenders from escaping across the Straits of Messina, taking most of their equipment with them. Historian Samuel Eliot Morison has described this as "an outstanding maritime retreat of the war, in a class with Dunkirk, Guadalcanal and Kiska[1]". However, he was also unusually critical of the Allied navies' failure to prevent the Axis escape, saying: "The employment of (Allied ships) during the fortnight when the Strait was swarming with evacuation craft seems, in retrospect, to have been nothing short of frivolous.[2]"

This article describes what happened and suggests the key factors that enabled the Germans to withdraw from Sicily so successfully. The author argues that better use of the available naval and air assets, starting shortly after the invasion, might have disturbed or even prevented the Axis retreat, and suggests that Morison's characterization of the employment of Allied ships as "nothing short of frivolous," is much less nuanced than the evidence requires. For much of the time period covered by this work the Italian Government was negotiating an armistice with the Allies. Although many individual Italians and their units fought bravely during the campaign, and their subsequent evacuation from Sicily was executed almost as well as the Germans', the Italian army that fought in Sicily was most notable for surrender en masse. As a result, when considering the Axis armies, this article focuses almost entirely on the German formations involved.

## Prelude

The meeting at Casablanca in January 1943 between President Roosevelt, Prime Minister Churchill and their respective Chiefs of Staff, was designed to answer the question "where do we go from here?" following the successful invasion of North Africa the previous November. However, it also illuminated the significant strategic differences developing between the British and American Allies. The British leaned strongly towards a "Mediterranean strategy" whose many rewards they believed would include: reopening the direct sea route through the Mediterranean, eliminating Italy from the war, diverting German pressure on the Russian front, and reduction of Axis air power in southern Europe[3].

The Americans, on the other hand, and particularly Army Chief of Staff General George Marshall feared that the Mediterranean, particularly Italy, would become a "black hole," sucking Allied resources into actions which many Americans believed were designed more to further British post-war imperial ambitions than to bring the war to a rapid conclusion.

Failure to reach agreement on alternatives meant that the only Mediterranean operation approved at Casablanca was the invasion of Sicily (operation "Husky"). American General Dwight Eisenhower was designated Supreme Commander of the Allied forces involved (Army, Naval and Air), with British General Harold Alexander as his deputy and operational commander of the two invasion armies (British 8th and American 7th).[4] The final Casablanca report made no mention of invading Italy proper, although anyone in possession of a map would have noticed that the three mile wide Straits of Messina were all that separated Sicily from the Italian mainland. Significantly, and most likely to avoid inter-Allied disagreement, no decision was made about what the Allied armies would do if and when they reached the Straits. It appears clear that an important reason for this planning failure was Marshall's fear that any step further into the Mediterranean would lead the Allies closer to the Balkans and further from Normandy[5]. As an Eisenhower biographer notes: "What they were to do after Sicily remained hidden in a closet, an unwanted guest at a banquet of accord[6]".

When the Allied leaders met again, this time in May 1943, in Washington, DC ("Trident") the situation in the Mediterranean had changed greatly to their advantage. The campaign in North Africa had concluded when Axis armies in Tunisia retreated onto the Cape Bon peninsular where, on May 13, 1943, a quarter of a million men ("most of Rommel's veterans and the pick of the Italian army") with more than a thousand guns and several hundred tanks, had surrendered to the Allied armies[7]. Their backs to a sea dominated by the Royal Navy, there had been no possibility of flight: a bare seven hundred Axis troops, mostly by air and at night, made good their escape. The Germans, referring to this defeat as "Tunisgrad," vowed not to allow a repeat[8]. However, uncertainty still continued as to what the Allies should do after conquering Sicily, although by that time there would be two armies on that island and one in Algeria impatiently awaiting further direction[9].

The events in Tunisia on May 13, 1943 provide essential background for any analysis of the German conduct of the Sicilian campaign. For Germany's Field Marshal Albert Kesselring (Commander in Chief of Hitler's Air and Ground forces in Southern Europe) and his superiors, the appalling losses in North Africa created a determination that no further experienced manpower would be sacrificed in vain in Sicily. By mid-July, only a few days after the Allied invasion, the German High Command (OKW) had accepted the inevitability of evacuation from the island; OKW orders were explicit: at the very minimum, they said, "our valuable human material must be saved[10]". But to illustrate the conflicts within the German high command we should note that two days after the Allied invasion Hitler decided to reinforce Sicily, crucially sending there two Panzer divisions from mainland Italy and an airborne division from France[11].

## Planning and Preparation

Allied planning for Husky was complicated by the fact that the Supreme Commander and the three Commanders in Chief had chosen widely separated headquarters: Eisenhower was in Algiers; Alexander and Air Marshall Arthur Tedder (commanding the Allied air forces), in Tunis; naval commander Admiral of the Fleet Sir

Andrew Cunningham in Malta, all 600 miles apart and thus violating one of the basic principles of combined operations[12]. The Commanders in Chief were reluctant to combine their activities into one location, and Eisenhower's unwillingness to order them to do so was symptomatic of future command problems[13]. Writing in early 1946, regarding preparations for Husky, Cunningham recalled: "I was not conscious of Eisenhower ever having stated any requirements of me or having asked my opinion[14]." Moreover, the respective land commanders, preoccupied by the ongoing campaign in Tunisia, were also unable to focus on planning for Sicily. However, in Eisenhower's defense, it must be recognized that no one involved was yet totally comfortable with the concept of inter-Allied command, and that whereas each respective Commander in Chief already had significant experience of combat in World War I and high command in World War II, their Supreme Commander had yet to hear a shot fired in anger and had never commanded anything larger than a battalion. As historian Basil Liddell Hart has suggested, Eisenhower's tactful deference resulted in strategic unreadiness[15] but, as General Sir Alan Brooke (Chief of Britain's Imperial General Staff) pointed out later, by appointing Alexander as Eisenhower's deputy, "we were pushing Eisenhower up into the stratosphere where he would be free to devote his time to the political and inter-allied problems, whilst we inserted under him one of our own commanders to deal with the military situations and to restore the necessary drive and coordination which had been so seriously lacking.[16]" Clearly, in Brooke's eyes at least, there should always be a seasoned Briton to take over if the American showed evidence of his inexperience.

Alexander's ground commanders for Husky were Generals Montgomery (British) and Patton (American), each with important ideas of his own as to how the forthcoming battle should be fought. Montgomery came to the table with supreme confidence based on his own record in North Africa. Arriving late into the Sicily planning process, he seized control of the debate, virtually insisting that his 8th

Army would undertake the brunt of the attack, on a fifty mile front in southeast Sicily, while Patton's U.S. 7th Army guarded his flank to the west. Alexander was suspicious of Americans' fighting ability following their demoralizing defeat at Kasserine Pass, and such suspicions dissipated slowly[17]; Patton on the other hand was determined to reverse this impression. Eisenhower, however, liked Montgomery's plan, Alexander acquiesced, and Patton, uncharacteristically, went along with it - for the time being[18]. Even so, the seeds of future rivalries had been sown.

The final plan was well designed to achieve the occupation of Sicily, the sole objective set by the Combined Chiefs[19], but, as Alexander's biographer pointed out: "trapping the Germans in Sicily was not part of it; it was left to Eisenhower to exploit a Sicilian victory as he felt best[20]." A contemporaneous Allied landing in Calabria represented the Germans greatest fear: they were convinced such action would catch their forces on the wrong side of the Straits of Messina and result in another overwhelming Allied victory[21]. A similar plan had earlier been advanced by Alexander and endorsed by Churchill, but was never fully supported by their American allies. By mid-August, however, Eisenhower was confiding to his Naval aide that not landing on both sides of the Straits had been one of his major mistakes[22].

To anyone studying the Sicily campaign today, the key unanswered question regarding the Allies' intentions would appear to be: were they invading the island to occupy Italian territory, or to destroy the Axis defenders? Logic would indicate that if the defending armies were destroyed, the territory would fall into Allied hands, while if the Allies focused on territory, the enemy armies could survive to fight another day - which is exactly what happened[23]. When considering strategic alternatives it often makes sense to consult Clausewitz, and on this question the great strategist is quite clear: "Direct annihilation of the enemy's forces must always be the dominant consideration.

The preservation of our own military power, and the diminution or destruction of that of the enemy, take precedence in importance over the occupation of territory, and, therefore, is the first object which a general should strive for[24]." Patton held the same beliefs: "To conquer we must destroy our enemies. We must not only die gallantly; we must kill devastatingly[25]". Joseph Stalin, looking at the Allies' plans for Italy (which must have seemed puny compared with the massive battles then being conducted by the Soviet armies) appeared to be in agreement with Clausewitz, writing to Churchill before the invasion of Sicily: "I wish you to kill the enemy and capture as many prisoners and trophies as possible.[26]"

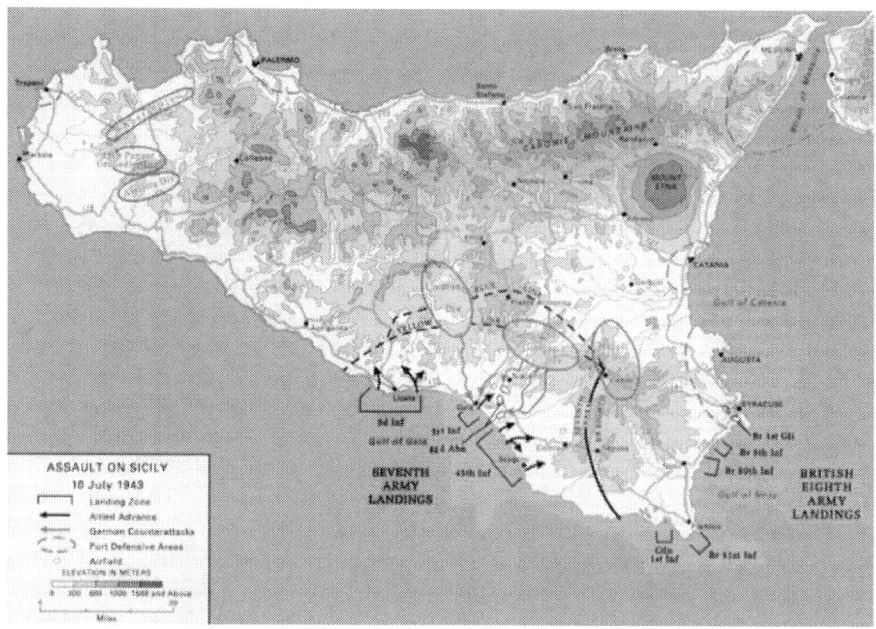

Assault on Sicily, 1943[27]

# The Invasion; the Naval Contribution

The invasion of Sicily was at the time the largest amphibious operation ever undertaken, outclassed later only by the 1944 landing in Normandy[28]. The initial assault force consisted of 3,000 ships (including landing craft), 160,000 men, 14,000 vehicles, 600 tanks, and 1,800 guns[29]. Thanks largely to terrible weather and a brilliant deception plan[30], the Allied landings on the southern shores of the Island on July 10, 1943 were to a great extent unexpected by the enemy and thus took place very much as planned, though the airborne component suffered significant losses due to higher than projected winds, and inexperienced aircrew.

Allied Naval forces were under the command of Britain's Sir Andrew Cunningham. The Western Task Force under Vice Admiral H. K. Hewitt USN supported the American landings on the south coast, while Admiral Sir B. H. Ramsey, RN commanded the Eastern Task Force supporting the mostly British and Canadian landings on the southeast coast. Fortunately Ramsey, a masterly planner of amphibious operations, was in general agreement with Montgomery's late revisions to the invasion plan[31]. Although the United States Navy's presence during Husky was by no means insignificant, the Royal Navy provided the lion's share of the support and covering forces for the operation.

At the time of the invasion the Italian Navy still represented what in theory was a formidable[32] "fleet in being," (see Chapter Six) despite the fact that it was dispersed between Genoa and Spezia to the north, and Taranto in the southeast of Italy. However, although the fleet, which included three modern 15-inch gun fast battleships, appeared strong on paper, it had some severe weaknesses including lack of radar, fuel oil, and naval aviation[33]. Nevertheless, while it was still in being, Cunningham's planners deemed it necessary to maintain strong cover capability: Force H, positioned in the Ionian Sea, a balanced battle fleet that included two fleet carriers, protected the invasion's eastern flank; Force Q, the six-vessel 12th Cruiser Squadron covered the west flank, while Force Z (two battle ships and two cruisers) was held in reserve in the Western Mediterranean. The two fleet carriers appear to have played no supporting role at all in the Sicily campaign other than occasional CAP[34]. Apart from causing wide dispersion of considerable numbers of large Allied warships and their valuable escorts, Axis naval forces did little to interfere with Husky, notes the official naval account of the invasion[35].

In addition to the six cruisers and numerous destroyers and smaller support vessels accompanying the invasion fleet, Forces H and Q were available to provide shore bombardment as needed following establishment of the beachheads. It is noteworthy that there appeared to be some resistance at the higher levels of the Royal Navy to employment of its heavy vessels in shore bombardment duties: "it is disturbing to realize," wrote the First Sea Lord (Admiral of the Fleet Sir Dudley Pound) to Cunningham on July 3, 1943 "how much dependence is put on naval gunfire.[36]" Indeed, neither the British or the American bombardment organizations contemplated supporting fire being needed after the initial assaults[37]. The Force H battleships could only be used for bombardment by order of the C-in-C, and in fact only the veteran *Warspite*, long Cunningham's favored flagship, was so used. Probably with the 1941 sinking of *Prince of Wales* and *Repulse* by Japanese aircraft off Malaya very much in mind, Pound had earlier reminded the C-in-C that he was "all against putting battleships and aircraft carriers within range of shore-based aircraft.[38]" However, on the subject of shore bombardment Admiral Hewitt politely disagreed: "The old fashioned military concept that naval guns are unsuitable for shore bombardment needs revision. Modern naval guns in cruisers and destroyers are high angle weapons capable of ranging on reverse slope targets far in the interior in support of seaborne landings. *The firepower in the vessels assigned to gunfire support (of Patton's Army) exceeded that of all the artillery landed in the 7th*

*Army assault.*(emphasis added)³⁹" The Germans provided their own evidence as to the effectiveness of naval bombardment: a captured German sergeant asked his interrogator: "what is your new secret weapon that you used against our tanks?⁴⁰" General von Senger und Etterlin, later the defender of Monte Cassino, wrote after the war about "the opportunity presented to the invader of keeping down the enemy on land by means of ship's gunfire. The caliber of ships' guns is always heavier than that of an army in the field . . . the ship's artillery is more mobile than that of the defenders.⁴¹" After the event, the Royal Navy's report recognized the value of naval gunnery, suggesting that in the future greater use would be made both at the time of landing and during subsequent advances along the coast⁴².

## The Initial Landings

The invading British and American troops (Britain's 8th Army and the United States 7th) faced the Italian 6th Army, consisting of ten divisions (including six coastal defense units of low quality), and the German Herman Goering and 15th Panzer Grenadier Divisions. The landings were virtually unopposed.⁴³ The coastal defenders, the majority of them poorly equipped Sicilians who hated the Germans almost as much as they did the war, surrendered in large numbers⁴⁴.

On the following day (July 11) tanks of the Herman Goering Division made a determined counterattack on the American 1st Infantry Division that nearly succeeded in penetrating to the beaches. Hard fighting and direct fire from naval vessels offshore repulsed this thrust and by the end of the day landing strips were in use and a solid bridgehead established⁴⁵. Over two days the Allies had landed 80,000 men, 7,000 vehicles, 300 tanks, and 900 guns.

The Allies appear to have been surprised by the success of the landings, and it took them a few days to get organized for what promised to be a fast movement inland although, other than occupying the island, they still lacked any clear tactical objective for the rest of the campaign. Palermo and Messina, the ports at either end of the Island, did provide fairly logical goals, but Palermo was only a harbor, albeit a useful one, whereas Messina represented for the Allies access to Italy, if they wanted it, and for the Germans ultimate escape from that inhospitable island if, as appeared increasingly likely, they needed it.

The Germans, rapidly recovering their confidence and reinforced by an air drop of six battalions of combat hardened paratroops, withdrew to a strong defensive position around Catania, forcing Montgomery into a series of tough but inconclusive battles, while Patton's 7th Army found itself relegated to guarding the British left flank. Cunningham watched all this with frustration: he had ample heavy ships available to provide gunfire support, and landing ships ready to move, if 8th Army wanted to leapfrog Catania and be carried further up the coast, possibly as far as Messina where they should have been able to cut off a large number of the enemy, but the army command appeared uninterested[46]. This writer can find no evidence that Cunningham ever suggested such a movement directly to Alexander, nor any suggestion that Montgomery ever asked for it[47]. Yet in fairness, army calls for naval gunfire were acted upon effectively, and at one point *Warspite* came hurrying north from Malta in response to a request for help, and fired 57 15-inch shells, each weighing 1900 lbs., at German batteries defending Catania. However, the Germans manning them held on stoutly throughout.

Writing later, Cunningham commented rather bitterly on Montgomery's decision not to leapfrog Catania: "There were doubtless sound military reasons for making no use of this…priceless asset of sea power, and flexibility of maneuver, but it is worth considering whether much time and costly fighting could not be saved by even minor flank attacks, which must necessarily be unsettling to the enemy. It must always be for the General to decide.

The Navy can only provide the means, and advise on the practicability . . . of the projected operation. It may be that, had I pressed my views more strongly, more could have been done.[48]"

There appears to be considerable agreement (at least among American participants) that if Montgomery had been less conservative, more mobile, and more willing to take risks, he might have been able to take Messina in the first week of the campaign, thus trapping the Axis armies[49]. American sources also suggest that Brigadier Kenneth Strong, Eisenhower's British G-2 for the remainder of the war, concurred with this view[50].

Finding that the enemy had blocked the eastern coast road to Messina, Montgomery decided to try going round the west side of Mount Etna, although this road had previously been assigned to Patton's 45th Division. Alexander granted Montgomery's request that it be reassigned to him; Patton, seeing a tempting opening to the west, appeared at first to take this calmly, despite enraged objections from his II Corps commander, Omar Bradley, who was already well established on the disputed road[51]. After further thought Patton understandably objected to his 7th Army being given a subordinate and passive role guarding the British left flank, and tensions between the American general and Montgomery continued throughout the campaign[52].

After receiving a visit from an irate Patton, Alexander recognized the inter-Allied problem he had unthinkingly caused and authorized the Americans to strike off to the west on a "reconnaissance in force". Thus unleashed, the 7th Army's right wing sliced through the island from north to south, while the left occupied Palermo on July 22. Considering the fact that, without a viable port, Patton's army had been supplied across beaches, his progress in the days after Alexander let him loose was truly remarkable. Moving mostly on foot, under the hot summer sun, his infantry took 36,000 prisoners.

On July 28 the first supply ships berthed in Palermo[53].

Meanwhile, Cunningham had established an Inshore Squadron, under the orders of the newly designated Flag Officer Sicily, Rear Admiral Rhoderick McGrigor. The Squadron, consisting of two 15-inch gun monitors, two destroyers, and various smaller vessels, was to act in support of the army as it advanced towards Messina along the southeast coast of Sicily. For the next week the Inshore Squadron answered calls from 8th Army and bombarded enemy positions along the coast as far east as Catania, engaging enemy troop movements artillery, and communications.

At the time Palermo fell, Montgomery had written: "In ten days we have captured the whole of Sicily, and the enemy is now hemmed in the NE corner, rather like the Cape Bon Peninsular.[54]" But Montgomery was overly optimistic: his 8th Army, confronting strongly reinforced German units and despite the addition of naval fire power[55], remained stalled in front of Catania while suffering heavy losses. Any thoughts of a rapid dash 60 miles up the coast to Messina were now unrealistic. Nevertheless, only two weeks later, he was writing to Major General John Harding "The Bosche is getting very stretched. And he cannot possibly stand up to my thrusts." Prudently, however, he hedged his opinion by adding: "The enemy is well posted, and in ideal defensive country, advance only possible on a one tank front, and it is necessary to pause and regroup[56]". Writing to the Combined Chiefs of Staff on August 2, Eisenhower was more circumspect. Pointing out the "unbelievably difficult" nature of the road along the north coast, and the need for small landing operations to advance and supply 7th Army, he expressed the hope that 8th Army, supported by naval gunfire would be able to "cut off a large part of the German garrison[57]." This is the first specific reference that this writer has found indicating that cutting off the German garrison had become an objective of the campaign in Sicily.

Sicily, separated from mainland Italy by only the Straits of Messina

Montgomery's casual equating of Cape Bon with Messina reinforces the impression that maps may have been read somewhat casually during the Sicilian campaign: in Tunis the Allies had pushed the Axis armies before them until, surrounded on Cape Bon, they had nowhere left to go: Italy was the nearest dry land, some 100 miles away across the British controlled Mediterranean. In Sicily the Germans, and what was left of the Italians, were being hemmed into a peninsular whose adjacent waters represented a small barrier between them and the safety of Calabria; possibly their strongest swimmers would not even need boats to get across. Underestimating Axis capabilities, and with little appreciation for their intentions, Alexander and his generals appear to have assumed that if they kept on pushing the enemy back, they would eventually enjoy another "Tunisgrad."

Sicily west of Mt. Etna provides reasonable terrain for a war of movement, and was well used for such by both Axis and Allied armored units. Etna and its centuries of lava run-off, however, do provide a formidable barrier to movement further east, the only practicable lines of advance from that point being along the north and south coastal roads, plus some use of a more central road among the foothills. Had the Allied command anticipated an Axis retreat, it would have made sense to plan to block the coast roads early on by naval gunfire or naval assisted "leapfrogging" operations. Only by getting ahead of the Germans could they be stopped, and it seems that the army command only contemplated such as a last resort.

On July 29 Alexander (now established in Sicily, having moved his headquarters there the day before[58]) ordered Patton to swing to the east along the northern coast road, while Montgomery's left wing would attack through the center of the Island. But the Axis (by now essentially a German command[59]) had already established themselves in a formidable position based on the commanding foothills of Mount Etna, and controlling the entire northeast of the Island. Moreover, there were only three roads leading to Messina, and Alexander had allocated two of them to the slow and deliberate Montgomery, at a point in the campaign when Patton's dash and flair might have proved more effective in heading off the Germans[60]. Unfortunately national and personal rivalries had intruded on the battlefield and the advance to Messina thus became a contest between Montgomery and Patton as to who could reach that city first, rather than a struggle between the Allies and the Germans for the same goal.

On August 5 Catania fell and by August 8, the Allies were advancing slowly towards Messina, Patton's 7th Army on the north side of the peninsular, Montgomery's 8th on the south. But, as Montgomery wrote later, "I was fighting my own battle and the Seventh American Army was fighting its battle; there was no coordination by 15th Army Group (Alexander)[61]". The fighting was bitter, involving most difficult terrain. For those visiting Sicily today, not much has changed: the entire area is dominated by Mt. Etna, whose heavily eroded foothills are littered with large chunks of black basalt rock: definitely not "tank country."

Fearing that stiff Axis resistance would significantly delay his progress, Patton on July 25 suggested to Hewitt that the Navy should undertake a series of amphibious landings in the enemy's rear. Hewitt agreed and created Task Force 88 under the command of Rear Admiral Lyal Davidson USN whose mission was to support the coastal advance of 7th Army by means of naval gunfire and by effecting advanced "leapfrog" landings by ground forces. Task Force 88 originally consisted of a cruiser division, ten destroyers, and various LST's, LCI's and LCT's[62].

From July 30 through August 8, Task Force 88 operated in support of the army's eastward movement with intensive gunfire directed at enemy road traffic on the north coast highway. However, on August 4, despite covering naval gunfire, heavy enemy artillery fire on the coast road slowed the advance while the point units sought a more favorable route over the Furiano River. Later the same day landing craft transported a Regimental Combat Group with its artillery to reinforce the advance. The task force continued to provide significant gunfire support, but strong Axis resistance and determined counterattacks still slowed progress to a crawl[63].

## The German Retreat

At the time of the Allied invasion, the German army on Sicily was commanded by the legendary General Hans-Valentin Hube, a one armed veteran of Verdun, who two decades later commanded a Panzer division during the German invasion of Russia. Surrounded in Stalingrad, he was forcibly evacuated by his own troops following Hitler's personal intervention. After Stalingrad, Hube was sent to Sicily, with responsibility for its overall defense, and the subsequent Axis evacuation to the Italian peninsula[64].

General Hans-Valentin Hube

Experts at highly disciplined withdrawal, Hube's troops made skillful use of mines, every piece of high ground, every rock and every natural obstacle to delay the Allies. Bridge, road and culvert demolition were ubiquitous. Devastating counterattacks came when least expected. One has to believe that Hube was familiar with Clausewitz' writings about an army in retreat:

> "In order to keep morale as high as possible, it is absolutely necessary to make a slow fighting retreat, boldly confronting the pursuer whenever he tries to make too much of his advantage. The retreats of great commanders and experienced armies are always like the retreat of a wounded lion . . . . The means of putting the above mentioned principle into practice consists of a number of factors: a strong rear guard made up of the best troops, led by the

most courageous general, and supported at crucial moments by the rest of the army; skillful use of the terrain; strong ambushes wherever the daring of the enemy's vanguard and the terrain permit. In short it consists of planning and initiating regular small-scale engagements[65]."

Descriptions of the German withdrawal across eastern Sicily convey an image of General Hube directing the battle with a copy of Clausewitz' instructions grasped in his one remaining hand. The General's plan of retreat involved brilliant use of the geometry of the triangular northeastern corner of Sicily[66]. German defenses east of Mt. Etna had focused on three well prepared lines running from the southeast to the north coasts of the island. Once Kesselring had definitely decided to evacuate, movement focused on three phase lines that, as the coast lines converged towards Messina, became progressively shorter, permitting successive groups of troops and related equipment to be sent to the embarkation points for shipment to Calabria. Each line was thus, to the end, appropriately manned relating to its length. Advancing Allied lines, on the other hand, would become overcrowded as commanders tried to determine whether the time had yet arrived to withdraw troops from the battle line.

As Eisenhower's biographer Stephen Ambrose put it, "The Americans were getting closer to Messina, but they were getting there on German terms, not their own.[67]" By this time Mussolini had fallen from power, and Italian interest in the war and their German allies was crumbling fast. The Axis army on Sicily had become de facto German: the 14th Panzer Corps and, although Alexander's two armies were under the impression that they were forcing the Germans inexorably into the sea, the enemy was in fact conducting a spectacularly successful retreat designed to withdraw from Sicily as many as possible of his soldiers, and as much equipment as could be moved.

The pace of Allied advance did improve at dawn on August 8 when, at Patton's request Task Force 88, known by then as "Patton's Navy," landed a battalion of infantry, a tank platoon, and two batteries of field artillery about six miles south of Cape Orlando. Task Force 88 supported the operation with fire control parties directing gunnery from ashore. The Germans were taken by surprise, their line broken, and many prisoners and much equipment taken[68].

Before dawn three days later a second amphibious landing succeeded in breaking strong enemy defense lines along the Cape Orlando ridge. A German counterattack threatening the beachhead was broken up by cruiser *Philadelphia*, which later went on to expend over 1,000 rounds of 6-inch ammunition shelling the adjacent coast road[69]. However, few German troops were trapped by either of these landings. Later, German Admiral Friedrich Ruge wondered why the Allies had not done more operations of this kind, and in greater strength[70].

At Cape Orlando the road went through a long tunnel at the end of which Patton's troops found their way blocked by a large crater in the road. The excitement of the chase, and probably fear of Patton's anger if 8th Army got to Messina first, goaded 3rd Division and Task Force 88 into increased efforts, embarking troops, vehicles and artillery into LCT's and ferrying them around the Cape. 3rd Division gave the enemy no respite; the narrow road invited enemy traffic jams and, as they occurred, Task Force 88 was merciless[71].

## The Royal Navy Inshore Squadron[72]

Starting August 4 the Inshore Squadron continued its attempts to prevent German evacuation by the south coast road. Its main focus was the holiday resort of Taormina, a small town located some 1,000 feet above sea level, and approachable only by zigzag roads, seemingly an ideal place to block a retreating enemy. The 15-inch gun monitor *HMS Roberts*, assisted by two Spitfires for spotting, fired over fifty 15-inch shells at the undercliff road and the railway tunnel. Two days later a follow up night bombardment was carried out by three destroyers, designed to block the other end of the tunnel. Follow up naval reports indicated that "a good proportion of the 300 rounds fired fell close to the target," but in this case maybe close wasn't quite good enough. A further two days later the same three destroyers fired another 150 rounds, a "number of which fell close to the target". Subsequent German reports noted that the main coast road was never blocked, "even by the repeated bombardments at Taormina.[73]"

## The "Race" to Messina[74]

Much has been made of the so-called "race" between Patton and Montgomery with Messina the prize. Indeed, at times it appears that such a contest was the entire tactical objective. "Patton and Montgomery were each determined to be the first into Messina, wrote Nicholson, "and Alexander . . . saw no reason to dampen their enthusiasm for such a prize.[75]" It was the Americans who "won", largely because they appear to have attached more importance to the result than did Montgomery. Brigadier J. C. Currie, commanding the lead tanks of the British 4th Armored Brigade arrived a few minutes after the U.S. 7th Army vanguard. "I congratulate you, sir," Currie said as he saluted "It was a jolly good race.[76]" One hates to use the word "mendacious" in connection with a highly esteemed Allied general, but Alexander's August 17 message to Churchill: "By 10 A.M. this morning, August 17, 1943, the last German soldier was flung out of Sicily and the whole island is now in our hands" represents a somewhat more high-spirited version of the facts than was presented later in his formal dispatch: "On the night of August 16th, the leading troops of the United States 3rd Division entered Messina. . . . Just before dawn on the 17th. . . . General Hube . . . . sailed from a beach north of Messina in the last boat to leave the island, Sicily had been conquered in thirty-eight days.⁷⁷" Had he lived, General Hube might have taken exception to having his orderly departure characterized as being "flung" off the island.

## Air Operations During the Sicily Campaign

Although USAAF and RAF activities proved very effective in creating initial air superiority over Sicily, all subsequent reports by ground and naval forces involved point to a marked reluctance on the part of the air forces to participate in the planning process, and a strong disinclination to accept orders or even suggestions from other services⁷⁸. Hewitt would later complain that the Air Command did not work with the navies; there was no unity of command, no air force that he or Patton could call on. They were all fighting the same war, he said, but the air forces were interested in long-distance bombing, and supporting a landing or the troops on shore was a bit of a side show. Immediate air support was there on paper, but nobody afloat at the scene of the action could call for air. You could ask for it; maybe if they could find the planes you might get it in the next hour or so or the next day⁷⁹.

The U.S. Army's official history is equally critical: "Primarily concerned with other matters . . . the Allied air commanders devoted little thought and attention to providing close air support to the ground forces during the campaign. . . . The cumbersome system of requesting missions, with attendant delays in transmission and identifying targets, proved almost unmanageable⁸⁰." It appears that the air forces were still working out their relations with the ground forces. Historian S. W. Pack would later write: "The air battle was separate and foreign, apparently unconcerned about the situation (at the beaches).⁸¹"

Some Air Force commanders were reluctant to give Army or Navy commanders' control over air units; when criticized for this they would argue that their assets could be more profitably employed against enemy airfields and supply lines, often invisible from the battle front. Others were more innovative and accommodating. One account of Husky singles out RAF Air Vice-Marshal Harry Broadhurst as being totally committed to direct air support of the ground forces, despite the reluctance of his superiors[82]. Moreover, ground commanders complained, the air forces would obliterate towns along the crucial German retreat routes, doing little to slow down the escape, but complicating the Allies' advance and creating a huge body of civilian killed and wounded[83]. On the other hand German sources indicate that battle hardened troops maintained their mobility even under prolonged air attack: "In no case did (the enemy) succeed in causing a prolonged blocking of the roads. Even after Randazzo had been attacked 21 times in one day by waves of twelve planes, it was possible to reopen this to through traffic after only four hours.[84]" 15th Panzer Grenadier Division reported that the campaign demonstrated that air power alone cannot force a decision in battle. After initial losses the troops adapted themselves to a degree that could never have been reached in training[85].

## Allied Intelligence Pointing Towards an Imminent German Evacuation[86]

Throughout the period of Hube's retreat, Allied intelligence provided its armies in Sicily with excellent service, but little action was taken as a result. Ultra[87] decrypts received by Alexander on August 1 noted that the Germans had started practice ferrying maneuvers in the Straits and established separate assembly points on the Sicily side for each Wermacht formation. Decrypts four days later noted requests for more barrage balloons for ferry vessels and equipment to improve night lighting at the docks. Intelligence authorities at Allied Force HQ ("AFHQ") in Algiers were unimpressed. Nevertheless, on August 3, presumably in response to the August 1 information,

Alexander sent messages to Tedder and Cunningham warning them that there were definite signs that the enemy was preparing to withdraw, and promising timely advice as to when they should take action. "We must," he wrote, "be in a position to take advantage using full weight of navy and air power. You have no doubt coordinated plans to meet this contingency[88]." It appears that the "timely advice" was never provided, or appropriate plans coordinated.

Although AFHQ appeared untroubled by the likelihood of Axis evacuation, 8th Army intelligence appeared to be more concerned, wondering on August 5 whether it was significant that, of three Siebel[89] ferries seen by that morning's photo reconnaissance, one was returning loaded to the mainland while two had arrived empty in Sicily. Bletchley[90] too was becoming concerned, signaling AFHQ in August 6 that two days earlier the Herman Goering Division had asked that assault boats and inflatable rafts, be sent to a point near Messina. Nevertheless, AFHQ remained skeptical: its intelligence summary for the week of August 7, issued on August 10, reported that there were "no adequate indications that the enemy intends an immediate evacuation of the Messina bridgehead," although it was recognized that the Germans had prepared advance plans for an eventual evacuation. Slowness in disseminating intelligence may have been the result of the tortuous long distance communications links between the various commands, and the large bureaucracies involved in receiving and interpreting information[91]. Also, the vagaries of local interpretation: despite the fact that armies on the spot could see what was happening, high level interpretations made back in Algiers gave more credence to intuition and theory. It was felt at AFHQ that for prestige and strategic reasons it would be to the Axis advantage to maintain resistance in Italy and thus, despite the strain of heavy defensive fighting and lack of air support, the enemy would continue to defend the northeastern tip of Sicily.

Decrypts on August 8, however, indicated that the Axis withdrawal to a shortened bridgehead had actually started on August 6, and was proceeding according to plan. Fuel deliveries had been stepped up in anticipation of heavy demands on the ferry system. The same evening the 8th Army intelligence summary stated that "the enemy has started his evacuation and in the best conditions any evacuation has had in this war.[92]"

At midnight on August 10 the German Navy was indicating that fourteen landing craft were on their way to the Straits of Messina for a special operation, with eight more coming down from the north as a reserve. The following day's army intelligence summary told of an evacuation in full swing using seventy-five ferry craft, all under the cover of fierce flak.

By August 14, however, it no longer mattered what Ultra was telling the Allied commands: decrypts that night indicated that the evacuation had proceeded well, the ferry service was more efficient than expected, and General Hube was staying behind with a small operations staff until all forces that could be saved had left the island[93].

## Allied Preparations to Prevent Axis Withdrawal

Alexander's August 3 signal to his subordinate commanders "You have no doubt coordinated plans . . . etc." appears to be remarkably casual, considering the available intelligence. Lacking intervention from Eisenhower, Cunningham and Tedder did nothing, and at the time Eisenhower's attention was focused on a forthcoming meeting with the Combined Chiefs of Staff. Montgomery's reaction seems appropriate: "I fear the truth of the matter is there is NO plan[94]." So, what then did Tedder and Cunningham do in response to what was beginning to look like an extraordinarily successful evacuation? There was still no pro-active coordinating authority and it appears that each was waiting for the other to do something[95]. Alexander's post war *Despatch* devotes about half a page to the actions east of Mount Etna, treating the evacuation as if almost pre-ordained, dictated mostly by the difficulties of the terrain.[96]

Cunningham wrote dismissively later that: he "gave the matter very careful thought," but decided there was "no effective method" of stopping the enemy, "either by air or by sea[97]." However, he did suggest that the air force should operate without restriction over the Straits so that once the coast batteries were mopped up surface forces could operate further in[98]. Air Vice Marshal Coningham (commanding Allied tactical air forces in the theater) suggested that "only a physical barrier such as the Navy can provide, would be effective.[99]" So, having followed the army to the Straits of Messina on the heels of the retreating Axis, we must examine the further role played by the air forces and the navies.

## The Air Forces

We have already noted inter-service difficulties relating to the air forces in the Sicily campaign, and their cooperation in preventing the German withdrawal proved no exception. On August 1 Coningham told Tedder that the intense flak made the Messina area prohibitive for all except heavy bombers. Broadhurst agreed, saying that "exceptional flak on both sides of the Straits of Messina will need, I think, the use of B-17's if we are to maintain continuous air action to defeat an attempt at evacuation.[100]"

Strategic Air Force insisted the B17's remained reserved for action against enemy supply lines. However, as the evacuation got under way, they were released to be available at twelve hours' notice, on request by Coningham, but at the discretion of their commander. Some use of the heavy bombers was made, but at no time, notes Roskill, did the three Allied Commanders in Chief tell the Supreme

Commander that an emergency had arisen justifying the diversion of all available air strength. Had that happened, the bomber strength of the North West African Air Force available in August 1943 was over 1,800 strategic and tactical bombers[101] enough, one might assume, to provide the "physical barrier" the air forces had been seeking.

## The Navies

During the evacuation small craft made nightly sorties into the Straits and did what they could, but no larger vessels were brought into the picture. The German Naval Commander in Sicily reported after the war that, following an abortive encounter between Allied and Axis small craft, "no attempts seem to have been made to get at the ferries in the Strait.[102]" Admiral Cunningham may have had good reason to keep any but his least valuable vessels out of the Straits, but he says little about it and one must look elsewhere for an explanation. Correlli Barnett, in his masterly history of the Royal Navy in World War II, suggest that Cunningham was remembering Admiral Sir John de Roebeck's "disastrous attempt to take a fleet up the Dardanelles in 1915 with the loss of three battleships.[103]" Oliver Warner, Cunningham's biographer makes the additional point that on charts the Straits of Messina look very much like the Dardanelles. This writer finds that hard to believe: the long narrow passage of the Dardanelles would likely prove far more hazardous to surface vessels than the short bottleneck between Messina and Calabria. Poor de Roebeck barely had room to turn his fleet around in the narrow channel without running into the skillfully laid Turkish minefields[104].

Although the Messina straits in 1943 were very well defended by coastal artillery, the narrow roads along which the Germans had to pass to get to their disembarkation points were less so. (The Battle Summary and Official History are silent on the subject of mines in the Straits). Arguably Cunningham's cruisers, or the available 15-inch monitors, could have steered a course parallel to the coast roads with relative safety and inflicted considerable damage to the retreating Germans. Why didn't he employ them so? One explanation could be that no one asked him to, and he was reluctant to order a unilateral expedition without co-ordination with his nominal superior[105]. And although there is no evidence in support, it is not unreasonable to question whether the Commander-in-Chief of Britain's Mediterranean Fleet (long a near-proconsular position) would ever consider either Alexander or least of all Montgomery, his superior.[106] On the other hand, if (Supreme Allied Commander) Eisenhower had ordered him into the Straits, Cunningham would almost certainly have gone. A couple of weeks later, Eisenhower wanted to send a British squadron with a division of soldiers into Taranto harbor, still heavily mined. According to an Eisenhower biographer, Cunningham responded: "Sir, His Majesty's Fleet is here to go wherever you may send it[107]". Supreme Commander Eisenhower had asked and Cunningham delivered. Throughout the campaign Montgomery only once requested naval support and, when he did, it was too late – the enemy had already passed by[108].

## The German Navy's Role in the Evacuation

Meeting on August 5, Hitler and his top aides agreed that the Straits of Messina should be a naval command despite the fact that little could be done to reinforce the German Navy presence in that part of the Mediterranean. The Navy would be responsible for supplying the German troops already on Sicily and Sardinia, and would evacuate them should such become necessary.[109]

Vice Admiral Friedrich Ruge, the senior German naval officer attached to the Italian naval forces would be in overall charge of the German Navy in Sicilian waters. Previous to that appointment he had commanded naval defenses along the northern and western coasts of France. He had, as Grand Admiral Doenitz described him, great experience in the protection of coastal waters and convoys[110].

By August 1, the OKW debate had become focused on whether to abandon Sicily or hold on as long as possible: Doenitz and Rommel were in favor of hanging on; Jodl and Kesselring wanted to retreat up Italy to more easily held positions. All felt that evacuating Sicily would not be a problem so long as Southern Italy was in German hands, but agreed that only night traffic would be possible.[111] Kesselring agreed with Doenitz' suggestion to create a German transport system across the Straits under the command of the Navy; the Italians would be required to take care of their own needs using different routes.[112]

A capable and experienced naval officer, Fregattenkapitan der Reserve Freiherr von Leibenstein was appointed Sea Transport Leader, Messina Straits. All marine transport equipment, regardless of which service it came from, was put under his command. Italians were given the right to use 25% of transport space. Equipment unification worked well: before it took effect movement of 100 tons of supplies, 100 vehicles and 100 men per day was about all that could be expected. After reorganization 1,000 tons of supplies, several hundred vehicles and several thousand men could be moved on peak days regardless of air attacks.[113]

High altitude attacks by B-17's were of the greatest concern to the Germans, whose response was two-fold: first keep the enemy air well above the crossings by creating a heavy concentration of flak batteries around the Straits, and second moving the ferry routes. Traditional Messina ferries ran between the ports of Messina and Reggio on opposite sides of the Straits. Von Liebenstein and Ruge agreed to create more landing places, well dispersed from the traditional routes. By the time the evacuation began there were fourteen in operation on the mainland and twelve on the island. Construction battalions created new jetties and, since the main roads ran parallel to the beaches but behind the railroad line, new beach approaches had to be constructed[114].

A final anxiety arose from the fact that only one good road ran along either bank of the Straits, which could have been put out of action for some time by constant bombardment. It was a great relief, wrote Ruge later, that Allied bomber command never pursued this idea tenaciously[115].

Heavy flak, reorganization of the ferry routes, and lack of tenacity by Allied heavy bombers significantly reduced the impact of high altitude bombing. On the other hand, the heavy flak batteries lacked the flexibility to deal with fighters and dive-bombers, and there was insufficient light AA available to protect all the landing places. Drawing on his successful experience in the English Channel, Ruge decided the best answer was to provide the ferry vessels with their own flak protection: 37 and 20mm cannon and heavy machine guns, protected by armored shields, although shortage of steel plate meant that reliance had to be placed on less effective concrete and sand bags. Barrage balloons towed by the ferries provided further affective defense[116].

Surface vessels appear not to have represented a serious threat to the defenders of the Straits and no bombardment was attempted. Nevertheless, Italian submarines were ready to intercept larger vessels north and south of the narrows, while 88mm flak batteries were deemed sufficient protection against smaller vessels. Heavier shore mounted guns ordered from Germany when invasion appeared imminent never made it south of the Alps[117].

Evacuation took place in three phases. First, as soon as the Allies invaded, all men and equipment for which there was no immediate use were shipped back to the mainland. The second phase was the evacuation of western Sicily in the face of Patton's rapid advance there, the speed of which so surprised the defenders that supplies were still arriving just ahead of the Americans. Of particular significance to the fuel-short Germans was the loss of over eight thousand tons of gasoline that had to be destroyed[118].

The last step was the evacuation of the northeast corner of the Island. Already, from July 15 to August 17, some 13,500 wounded men had been taken over to Calabria. About 60,000 men remained, together with 10,000 vehicles and the Navy was confident that all of this could be brought back in the space of a few days with the vessels available, even in the face of enemy air activity. The Army felt this could only happen at night; the Navy was confident it could be done by day as well, particularly during early morning and at lunch and teatime, taking into account Anglo-Saxon habits[119].

When the evacuation proper started on the evening of August 12, von Liebenstein concentrated the ferries onto six of the available routes, keeping the remainder in reserve. Enemy activity, particularly flares and bombs, was so intense that ferrying on the four routes over the narrowest part could not begin until 2:00 A.M. At dawn there were a lot of vehicles left on the Messina side but they, and significantly more that had been set aside for destruction, were safely carried over in the morning. On the following night attacks were still worse, so based on the prior night's experience, the greater part of the troops and vehicles were carried over by daylight[120].

This experience led to the only serious disagreement between Army and Navy. Von Liebenstein said later that he always had doubts about night crossings: all movements to and from the landing points, and all loading and unloading operations would be much more difficult in the dark; crews and engines would be overworked; enemy high altitude bombing had to be expected. However, even when day traffic turned out to be feasible, and despite the fact that there was close to a full moon during most nights of the evacuation, and the actual results of night crossings were disappointing when compared to the achievements by day, the army still tried to insist on crossing by night. Fortunately for the German troops waiting patiently for their embarkation, it was Von Liebenstein who had control of the ferries.

Air attacks did increase in intensity and proficiency on the third day, no longer conforming to a fixed timetable. Nevertheless, troops and vehicles that reached the embarkation points were ferried over, practically without loss. Night bombing was the greatest nuisance though, in Ruge's opinion, evacuation would have been impeded much more effectively had bombing been more concentrated, focused on the main roads on either bank, and carried out around the clock. The main roads were never blocked, not even by the repeated naval bombardments near Taormina[121].

He had also noted the almost clockwork regularity with which the low-level air force attacks took place: dive bombers arrived every two hours[122]. At this point it is worth noting that, during his previous appointment, Admiral Ruge was one of the two German admirals involved in the successful escape of the battle-cruisers *Scharnhorst* and *Gneisenau* and cruiser *Prinz Eugen* from Brest in February 1942 (see Chapter Three). The German navy believed that such an escape could only be made round the north of Scotland or, with great risk, at night through the Straits of Dover. Hitler over-ruled his admirals, his argument being his experience of what he thought to be British inflexibility.[123] It is not implausible to suggest that Ruge, prior experience in mind, had a role in von Liebenstein's decision to opt for daylight crossings. Successful experience in the English Channel may have encouraged the admiral in the decision to give the ferries their own flak defenses, as well as towed barrage balloons, that proved very effective against dive bombers[124]. But despite these tactical innovations, it was the heavy flak concentration in the Messina area, thought to be more intense than anything encountered over the Ruhr, which really troubled the Allied air forces.

Von Liebenstein's principal anxiety was the coastal roads leading to embarkation points. There was only one good road along either bank of the Straits which, he felt, could have been put out of action for a long time by steady bombing and/or shelling by night and by day. He was, greatly relieved that Allied bombers never pursued this idea with any vigor[125].

Discipline among the embarking German troops was enforced rigorously. Every German soldier had to be carrying his infantry weapon and ammunition. "These weapons," according to Herman Goering Division orders, "are tickets to the ferry." Soldiers without these would be "ruthlessly prevented from crossing." Italians getting in the way are to be "thrust aside.[126]"

## Analysis and Conclusion

The evacuation of the German and remaining Italian forces took place over a five day period starting August 14 and, when completed, 39,000 men as well as 5,000 wounded and some thousands of Italian troops, had been allowed to get away in good order, together with 10,000 vehicles, 94 guns, 47 tanks, 1,100 tons ammunition, 970 tons fuel, and 15,700 tons of gear and supplies[127]. That is a lot of troops and material to escape from an enemy that had overwhelming superiority in men and equipment, and it is not surprising that, as Morison noted after the war, "the episode has never received proper attention; partly because nobody on the Allied side has cared to dwell on it[128]." However, although the Allies did force the Axis to evacuate, I think it's worthwhile taking a careful look at who might be to blame for allowing them to do so with such success. The guilty parties, if you can call them that, are several:

First, the Anglo-American command and planning structure that served the allies so well as the war continued was, at the time of Husky, in its infancy and relatively untried. Although the invasion of Sicily provided an excellent educational experience, continuing the process begun with the earlier invasion of North Africa, serious flaws continued, some noted in this narrative. Such faults evidenced themselves in the deliberations of the Combined Chiefs who, by their unwillingness to allow the planners to look beyond Sicily, eliminated the possibility of a coherent local strategy directed towards any goal other than capturing land mass[129]. Then, in mid-July when things in Sicily appeared to be going well, the Combined Chiefs, Marshall now in full concurrence, decided to proceed with an invasion of Italy: both across the Straits and further north in Naples. This decision, although delighting Churchill, may have distracted local commanders, making them less attentive to the fate of the Germans in Sicily[130].

Second, Eisenhower, who did not provide the Allied forces with the kind of leadership he would later furnish in Europe. He was probably over conscious of his lack of battle experience and was reluctant to exercise his supreme power.[131] Busy elsewhere, he failed to delegate to his deputy and ensure that he was doing his job.

Leaving the land battle for a moment, we can turn to Cunningham and Tedder. Cunningham was a genuine war hero who had kept the Axis at bay in the Mediterranean through four long years of war. This may have been the only time he lacked his customary daring[132]. He does make it clear however, that he saw his role in situations such as Sicily as an agent of the army rather than an independent force. His seemingly passive behavior when involved in land operations has been noted earlier: "The Navy can only provide the means, and advise on the practicability . . . of the projected operation. It may be that, had I pressed my views more strongly, more could have been done." One wonders whether Cunningham was waiting to be asked, and Montgomery was too proud to do so. Nevertheless, given the circumstances and the personalities involved, it does appear that "frivolous" seems overly damning when applied to the Allied naval role in the Axis retreat during the last two weeks of the campaign

Tedder, and the air forces under him were, I suggest, too beholden to their institutional "growing but ultimately delusional conviction that airpower alone could single-handedly change the course of the war, if not end it entirely[133]". Both sides of the battle agree that bombing by B-17's could have slowed or stopped the withdrawal, but they were never reliably made available in quantity.

Eisenhower may have been deficient, but he did have a deputy, and I think the real blame for the failure to trap the Germans lies with Alexander more than any other commander, assuming throughout that Eisenhower would have delegated the necessary powers to him had such been requested. The reader must recall Brooke's interpretation of Alexander's appointment: " . . . to deal with the military situations and to restore the necessary drive and coordination which had been so seriously lacking." Alexander in Sicily, to this observer, exuded neither drive nor coordination.

- It was Alexander who failed to pull the other Commanders in Chief into one joint headquarters;

- It was Alexander who was unwilling or unable to properly control Montgomery from the planning stages until the end of the campaign;

- It was Alexander who failed to order Montgomery to emulate Patton, and employ the navy to leapfrog Catania;

- It was Alexander who permitted his two field commanders to embark on the sophomoric "race to Messina".[134] Sophomoric, except that it involved men's lives[135].

- It was Alexander who failed to follow up his August 3 message to his fellow Commanders in Chief with clear cut orders, plus an urgent request to Eisenhower to endorse them.

Who won in Sicily? That is a difficult question. Clearly if the Allied objective was to occupy the Island, they achieved it and thus should be considered the victors. On the other hand, the greatly outnumbered Germans left across the Straits of Messina in good order, with much of their equipment intact so, in the words of Carlo D'Este's title, for the Allies Sicily was indeed a *Bitter Victory*. The German soldiers who opposed the Allies in Sicily and all the way up the mountainous length of Italy were, if one may follow Churchill's alliteration, part of the grisly gang who worked Hitler's wicked will[136] and, appropriately, they finally lost, but in doing so they demonstrated a fighting toughness one commentator described as unsurpassed in human history[137]. Writing for the British Government in 1951, military historian Eric Linklater highlighted the extraordinary ability of the German generals and soldiers and "the most resolute endurance of noncommissioned officers and private soldiers." A German army in the field, he thought, "was a formidable and brilliant instrument that deserved, indeed demanded, an unfailing and often anxious respect… It was not easy to appreciate, and impossible to admire them. But now the swiftness, sagacity, and brave robustness of their fighting must be recognized . . . [138]"

Many of Hube's troops did go on to fight another day, putting up a stubborn resistance at Salerno and Monte Cassino and in the Apennines, killing thousands of Allied soldiers, and delaying the Allied advance so much that it took them more than 1½ years to reach the North Italian plain.[139] Hube, on the other hand returned to the Eastern Front, where he died in a plane crash and was given a hero's funeral.

MICHAEL H. COLES

# 5 THE DESTRUCTION OF THE *SCHARNHORST*
## THE BATTLE OF NORTH CAPE

North Cape, Europe's most northerly point, lies over 300 miles above the Arctic Circle, bounded by the inhospitable Barents Sea where normal winter weather consists of violent gales with freezing temperatures. On the day after Christmas 1943, Boxing Day to the British, North Cape lived up to its reputation: 35 to 40 knot winds, heavy seas, icy waters, all shrouded by the near perpetual darkness of the arctic winter. Early in the evening lookouts on the bridges of several Royal Navy destroyers peered anxiously through the flying spindrift, steadying themselves against the enormous waves eerily illuminated by star shells and searchlights, seeking survivors of the great ship they had just helped sink. Finally, after an hour's search, only 36 could be found from *Scharnhorst*'s original crew of 1,968. Further efforts were fruitless; no one could survive longer in the icy oil coated seas. As the destroyers headed east to Murmansk the scene they left marked the end of an era: the last duel between battleships in European waters. On the other side of the globe a new naval age was opening as the United States Navy's *Essex* class carriers began their inexorable drive across the Pacific. Britain's battleships, having ruled the waves for over two centuries, had enjoyed their last hurrah.

Germany entered World War II with four modern capital ships; two in service (*Scharnhorst* and her sister ship *Gneisenau*) and two due to be commissioned in late 1940 (*Bismarck* and *Tirpitz*). Naval expansion plans agreed in 1938 between Hitler and his Naval Commander in Chief, Admiral Erich Raeder, had contemplated the creation of a balanced blue water fleet consisting of six more large battleships, four aircraft carriers, over 200 U-boats and numerous supporting vessels. Hitler, after assuring Raeder that war with Britain was in no way imminent, approved the plan with a 1945 completion date. The outbreak of war in 1939 thus caught the Kriegsmarine ill prepared and out-numbered. Its two available capital ships faced nine of the Royal Navy's in European waters, it had no aircraft carriers compared with Britain's four, the British maintained substantial additional strength in the Mediterranean, and their new construction promised five more battleships and several heavily armored carriers. Throughout his tenure as C-in-C Raeder was aware of the inexorable pressure of arithmetic: the loss of only one of his big ships reduced his force by 25%; the same loss would have proportionally a much smaller impact on his enemy.

Aware that his small battle fleet, if exposed, faced the danger of being destroyed in detail, and afraid of Hitler's anger should any of the prestigious vessels be lost, Raeder exercised great operational caution that paradoxically may have contributed to their piecemeal annihilation. The official British account of the Battle of North Cape says in its Forward: "It is difficult to read the German staff records without reaching the conclusion that the German High Command really attached more importance throughout to preserving the *Scharnhorst* intact than to inflicting damage on the convoy, an attitude which reflected itself in what is known of (fleet commander) Admiral Bey's handling of the operation at sea, and which may account in some degree for the disaster which overtook him."

*Scharnhorst*

The British analysis may be true, but arguably places insufficient weight on the fact that, by the end of 1943, the Royal Navy possessed all of the necessities for victory in a surface engagement: overwhelming advantage in fire power; vastly superior technology; intelligence (Ultra) that, unknown to the enemy, provided accurate forecasts of his movements; and, arguably, much better trained ship's captains. On the other hand, from what can be learned about *Scharnhorst*'s final hours, her crew fought to the last with incredible bravery, pointing to the probability that, better led and equipped, they might have caused the British far more grief than they did.

Prior to her arrival in northern Norway, *Scharnhorst* had an eventful, but not overly productive war, much of it spent in company with her consort *Gneisenau*. Their most significant accomplishment occurred during the 1940 Norwegian campaign when the two ships attacked and sank the British aircraft carrier *Glorious* and her two escorting destroyers. Damage sustained in that encounter required their return to Germany for repairs. In January 1941 the sister ships were at sea again, conducting two months of convoy raiding in the Atlantic, during which they sank 22 ships with a total of 115,600 tons. The fleet commander's caution in the face of possibly superior British forces explains these mediocre results. For the following year they were based in Brest, constantly under observation and attack by the Royal Air Force and unable to put to sea without attracting the attention of Britain's powerful Home Fleet. Then, on February 11, 1942, *Scharnhorst, Gneisenau,* and the heavy cruiser *Prinz Eugen* made a dramatic escape from Brest, sailing unscathed up the English Channel, through the Straits of Dover, and into the safety of Wilhelmshaven (see Chapter Three). However, while off the Dutch coast, *Scharnhorst* suffered mine damage that took the rest of 1942 to repair. Then, shortly after her arrival, *Gneisenau* was attacked by British bombers, receiving substantial damage. Thereafter she played no significant part in the war. With *Bismarck* already sunk, Hitler's roster of capital ships was halved; only *Scharnhorst* and *Tirpitz* survived. Following the rout of superior German forces by a British convoy escort on New Year's Eve, 1942, a furious Hitler had insisted that the navy's heavy ships should be scrapped and their guns and crews better employed elsewhere. A few days later, however, he relented and grudgingly allowed Raeder to base the battleships in Norway.

Hitler's principal rationale for reprieving the battleships was his conviction that the Allies were preparing to attack Norway, and the requirement for adequate resources there to provide both deterrence and defense. But there were more compelling arguments: the German were facing stiff resistance on the Eastern Front, one of the reasons being the flow of supplies from Britain and America brought to Murmansk by the Arctic convoys. The Kriegsmarine had a duty to do what it could to assist the army by sinking the supplies before they landed. Doubtless its sense of duty was reinforced by Hitler's vituperative comparison between the sufferings of the troops on the

Eastern Front and the idle naval crews in Norway.

By 1943 the British had begun to doubt the need for the Russian convoys deemed so essential in 1942, believing that their cost in terms of air and naval support probably outweighed their utility to the Russians. In addition, successes in the Mediterranean had enhanced the Allies' ability to send supplies to Russia via the Persian Gulf. On the other hand, the powerful *Tirpitz* and *Scharnhorst*, still lurking in north Norway, continued to represent a threat to any naval operations in that area. Admiral Sir Bruce Fraser, who assumed command of Britain's Home Fleet in mid-1943, believed that the Arctic convoys could be justified in the long run only if they represented bait to lure the German vessels to their destruction.

The convoys had been suspended during the summer months owing to the enormous advantage provided the Luftwaffe by nearly twenty-four hours of daylight. However, by the end of September several factors had changed in favor of the British. Most importantly on September 21 an audacious attack by Royal Navy X-Craft (midget submarines – see Chapter Six) had significantly disabled the battleship *Tirpitz*. Subsequent intelligence indicated that it would be mid-March before she could be expected back in service. *Scharnhorst*, always known as a lucky ship, was away from her customary anchorage for gunnery practice, otherwise she too would have met the same fate. Now she remained the only serious surface threat. Moreover, the Luftwaffe squadrons in northern Norway had been significantly reduced to meet requirements in other theaters, particularly the Mediterranean. Winter weather and vanishing daylight rendered the remaining air units much less valuable. Bad weather also reduced the effectiveness of U-boat operations, although winter ice forced the convoys to pass within 250 miles of the German naval units based in Altenfjord, increasing the threat from both underwater and surface vessels.

Arctic convoys resumed in November of 1943 and, although the situation had shifted in the Royal Navy's favor, the passages remained highly risky. Admiral Fraser's plan of defense involved a strong force of destroyers and other small craft to provide close escort of the convoy, cruisers available nearby, and distant battleship cover during the period of maximum vulnerability while passing Bear Island. Running an eastbound and a westbound convoy simultaneously provided some economy of force, since the same cruisers and battle ships could provide protection to both convoys in the vicinity of Bear Island. Starting in November, four convoys, both east- and west-bound, arrived unmolested. Fraser concluded that the Germans, although biding their time, would be unable to ignore the opportunity offered by the next pair of sailings. His hunch was well supported by intelligence indicating that *Scharnhorst* and her escorts were at full war readiness and training with unusual intensity.

Meanwhile, in Germany the running debate between Hitler and his naval high command had been resolved in the latter's favor. Grand Admiral Raeder feeling that he had failed to convince Hitler of the need for a balanced fleet, and its proper use, resigned on January 30, 1943, to be succeeded by Doenitz. After a careful review of the situation the new Commander-in-Chief concluded that Raeder had in fact been right: while the battleships remained operational they represented a continuing threat to the Royal Navy that otherwise would be able to transfer significant resources from the Home Fleet to the Mediterranean or the Far East. In addition, if given full tactical freedom the battleships' chances of success were good, while the advantages of laying them up were minimal. On February 26 Doenitz recommended that the Northern Battle Group's cruisers be withdrawn to the Baltic, leaving *Tirpitz* and *Scharnhorst* and their destroyer escorts responsible for the defense of Norway and the destruction of the Arctic convoys. Hitler grudgingly assented, giving Doenitz six months to demonstrate the correctness of his proposal.

The key decision, in the eyes of local fleet commanders, was the reversal of Hitler's doctrine of total risk avoidance, something Raeder had fought for unsuccessfully since the beginning of the war. On December 20 Doenitz informed Hitler of his intention to use *Scharnhorst* against the next Arctic convoy. Four days later, however, he reduced the Northern Battle Group Commander's freedom of action, instructing him to: "Make bold and skillful use of the tactical situation. The fight is not to be half-finished. . . Use own judgment in breaking off action. Important to do this on encountering superior forces."

Ill-defined mission orders were not the only matter plaguing *Scharnhorst*'s operations. An inexperienced fleet commander, and technical deficiencies also reduced her effectiveness. Admiral Oskar Kummetz, commander of the Northern Battle Group, had returned to Germany for medical treatment in November. Possibly "medical leave" was a useful euphemism; Kummetz had already made clear his belief that *Scharnhorst* should not be employed during the winter, but rather held in reserve until the spring when completion of repairs to *Tirpitz* would permit their use as a squadron. Temporarily replacing Kummetz was Rear Admiral Erich Bey, a popular destroyer officer who had never commanded a big ship or directed a task force. His background was thus poor preparation for his new task, as evidenced by an appreciation he wrote shortly after moving his flag to *Tirpitz* (still Battle Group flagship) in which he argued that chance, or a major mistake on the part of the enemy, would be a necessary ingredient for success. As one historian noted, this was not the thinking of a cool and calculating strategist. Command inexperience was not confined to Bey: *Scharnhorst*'s new captain, Fritz Hintze had come aboard only two months earlier, and this would be his first (and last) operational sortie. Shortage of fuel oil meant that whatever crew training could be undertaken in the short time available largely took place while at anchor.

*Scharnhorst*'s development took place in 1934 while Germany, still notionally adhering to the warship limitations contained in the Versailles Treaty, was negotiating a bi-lateral naval agreement with Great Britain. Thus, although her size grossly overstepped Treaty limits, her main armament was restricted to the 11-inch called for under its terms; nine guns mounted in three turrets. Apparently Hitler believed that he could deceive his potential enemies on a matter of size, but that larger guns might prove too much of an open noncompliance. The new British battleships, on the other hand, each displaced over 40,000 tons and carried 14-inch guns. The difference is significant: an 11-inch shell weighed just over 700 lbs., a 14-inch projectile closer to 1,600 lbs. It was shells from one of these new ships, the *Duke of York*, that would sink the *Scharnhorst*.

*Scharnhorst*'s guns were not the only part of her equipment placing her at a disadvantage. Possibly of even more significance for a mid-winter action in the near permanent darkness of the Arctic was her lack of effective radars, both for surface search and for gunnery direction. The sets she did carry had poor range and performed unreliably. British ships, on the other hand, not only carried surface search radar effective out to 20 miles, or more, but also employed newly developed centimetric (short wave) gunnery control radar that finally enabled warships to fire effectively at long range in the appalling visibility conditions of northern waters. One account of *Scharnhorst*'s sinking indicates that neither Bey nor Hintze were aware of this development, probably because of the considerable lack of trust between the Luftwaffe, that had the information, and the Navy that needed it.

Eastbound convoy JW 55A sailed from Loch Ewe on December 12th; the second half, JW 55B followed a week later, with its own strong destroyer escort. [Eastbound convoys carried the prefix "JW," westbound "RA." Convoys generally sailed in two parts, "A" and

"B", the latter sailing about a week after the first.] Close cover of both convoys was provided by Vice Admiral Robert Burnett's Force 1, consisting of the heavy cruiser *Norfolk* and the light cruisers *Belfast* and *Sheffield*. Admiral Fraser's Force 2 maintained distant cover in the battleship *Duke of York*, supported by the light cruiser *Jamaica* and destroyers *Savage, Scorpion, Saumarez* and the Norwegian *Stord*. JW 55A's passage was uneventful; Force 1 remained in Kola, the Soviet naval base, until December 23 when it sailed to cover the initial passage of westbound RA 55A. Force 2 returned to Iceland to refuel.

On December 23rd JW 55B was sighted by a routine German meteorological aircraft. Convinced that this convoy was *Scharnhorst*'s intended prey, Fraser sailed from Iceland that evening with Force 2, heading northeast towards North Cape. For the next two days the British Admiral played a masterly game of naval chess; his board was the turbulent waters of the Barents Sea and the crucial pieces were the *Scharnhorst*, the convoy, *Duke of York*, and Burnett's cruisers. As one of his staff commented after the event "Force 2 was at sea for one purpose only – to sink the *Scharnhorst*," nevertheless Fraser never lost sight of the importance of the convoy to the Allied war effort. Every move he made was designed to create a trap: Force 2 to the southwest, Force 1 to the northeast, and JW 55B the tempting bait out to the northwest. Fraser anticipated that as *Scharnhorst* came north towards the convoy she would find herself caught between the cruisers on the right and *Duke of York* on the left. In a bold departure from normal practice he broke radio silence three times to pass his orders: the convoys were temporarily slowed down or re-routed, their escorts were detached or re-assigned. One risky but crucial decision was to switch the 36th Destroyer Division (*Musketeer, Matchless, Opportune* and *Virago*) from the convoy escort to support Force 1. At no time did the Admiral doubt the enemy was somewhere out there, his only worry was whether he could cover the distance in time to catch her.

With a full gale blowing from the southwest, *Duke of York*'s accompanying destroyers spent an unhappy Christmas; conditions on board were miserable and the helmsmen struggled to keep station. Even aboard the battleship things were very uncomfortable, and her crew enjoyed little sleep that night. Early the next morning, however, Fraser's preparations paid off: a signal from the Admiralty informed him that *Scharnhorst* had left Altenfjord the previous evening, accompanied by five destroyers. She was steering to the north, 200 miles to the east of Force 2.

*Scharnhorst*'s last sortie had not started auspiciously. Already alerted by air reconnaissance, a U-boat patrolling west of Bear Island had provided the precise location of the convoy and the composition of its escort. But on the 25th Admiral Schniewind, Commanding Naval Group North, based in Kiel, learning that the Luftwaffe had cancelled all flights for the following day, tried to persuade Berlin to postpone the operation, citing the lack of air reconnaissance and the deteriorating weather. Doenitz, conscious of the situation on the Eastern front, and determined to prove the Kriegsmarine's worth, insisted that the operation go ahead. Moreover, in direct contradiction of his earlier assurance of freedom of action for the commander on the spot, he changed Bey's operational plan, which called for the destroyers to attack while *Scharnhorst* provided long-range support, insisting that the battleship be the centerpiece of the offensive. Paradoxically, therefore, Doenitz sent Germany's only operational battleship to sea on what increasingly looked like a suicide mission in order to convince Hitler of its value.

Early on December 26, and in marked contrast to the reluctant Luftwaffe, volunteer naval pilots took off in six flying boats. Shortly after 10:00 A.M., one of them reported that his radar showed what appeared to be five ships northwest of North Cape, including what was probably a heavy one. However, the watch officer in Navy Group North deleted the reference to "a heavy one", arguing that the observer should report only what he had actually seen. Thus, when the signal reached Bey, it failed to carry the warning that a powerful warship might be nearby, the information he most needed. In addition, the Germans radio intercept service was picking up a large amount of radio traffic in the area, possibly indicating the presence of a British heavy force at sea. But they were unable to decipher it and did not pass their suspicions on to Bey.

Once in open water, Bey's fleet encountered the same terrible weather that had troubled Fraser's destroyers. However, the two forces' reaction to the storm reflected different traditions. The British escorts, displacing only 2,530 tons fully loaded, continued into the storm and remained on station with the fleet throughout the action. Bey, on the other hand, immediately became concerned whether his own escorts could operate effectively in the heavy seas. German destroyers were heavier and better armed than their British counterparts, but a higher center of gravity meant that they rolled severely in heavy seas. He communicated these concerns to Schniewind, again recommending that the mission be cancelled, but strangely without getting the opinion of the escort commander, presumably confident that his own experience gave him the answer he needed. Bey's message was passed to Doenitz who ordered that the operation should proceed, with *Scharnhorst* alone if the destroyers could not remain at sea; the final decision was Bey's. Shortly afterwards, in response to a belated question from the flagship, the escort commander reported difficult but not unmanageable conditions.

At 4:00 A.M. on the 26th Admiral Burnett's Force 1 was 150 miles to the east of the convoy, heading southwest at 18 knots. Fraser's Force 2, 350 miles southwest of Burnett, was forging east at 24 knots, the battleship's bows plunging under tons of freezing water, then shaking free "like a submarine breaking surface" as one of her officers described it, the destroyers in constant danger of losing control and broaching across the following sea. Anti-aircraft weapons on *Duke of York*'s focs'le broke away, leaving holes through which freezing water poured into the mess decks below. Admiral Fraser later reported: "The stage was well set, except that if *Scharnhorst* attacked at daylight and immediately retired, I was not yet sufficiently close to cut her off."

At 7:30 A.M., believing himself in the convoy's general area, Bey turned towards the southwest and placed his destroyers in search formation ten miles ahead. Half an hour later he reversed course, at which point all communications between the flagship and its escort was lost. Although German accounts indicate some further radio transmissions, it appears that throughout the subsequent battle the destroyers received little or nothing in the way of meaningful instructions, apart from an unsigned signal ordering them to return to Norway. Why Bey divested himself of his escort at a time when the tactical situation appeared all in his favor is incomprehensible. Since none of the officers on *Scharnhorst* survived to provide an explanation, the only conclusion to be drawn is that at some time Bey lost the ability to control his fleet and failed to regain it before he died. A further conclusion is that the commander of the destroyer flotilla showed very little initiative or fighting spirit; receiving little guidance from Bey, he proceeded on the last course ordered until told to go home, despite considerable evidence that *Scharnhorst* was under attack. Several commentators have questioned whether the German's lack of current sea training meant that the sailors were suffering badly from seasickness. Whatever the reason, as the British battle summary put it " . . . while the *Scharnhorst* was being gradually hounded to her doom, the German destroyers had played a singularly ineffective part".

At 8:40 A.M. Fraser's appreciation of the tactical situation finally paid off: radar on Burnett's flagship *Belfast* picked up the unmistakable echo of a large warship between it and the convoy, twenty miles to the northwest and closing rapidly. Forty minutes later came the signal all had been waiting for "Enemy in sight!" Sheffield's lookouts had spotted the enemy seven and a half miles southwest. *Belfast* immediately illuminated *Scharnhorst* with star shells and a few minutes later Burnett ordered Force 1 to open fire, turning towards the enemy as he did.

On board *Scharnhorst* the first evidence of enemy action came in the form of disconcertingly close shell splashes; it remained unclear for some time what kind of force was engaging them. *Scharnhorst* returned fire, but with nothing better to aim at than the muzzle flashes from the enemy guns, little damage was done. On the other hand, *Norfolk*, the most heavily gunned of the cruisers (8-inch), scored a hit that proved disastrous for *Scharnhorst*, putting her forward radar out of action. This was Bey's first indication that the British might be using radar-controlled gunnery. Poor as her own radars were, the loss of one of them meant that the great warship would be fighting in darkness with no ability to scan the waters ahead of her. Firing ceased at 9:40 A.M.

*Scharnhorst* possessed a considerable speed advantage over the Royal Navy cruisers and, as she managed to put more distance between herself and the British, she turned away to the south and then, ten minutes later, back to the northeast, apparently trying to work her way back to the convoy. Recognizing that a chase would be in vain, Admiral Burnett decided that he should place himself between the battleship and her prey. Sensible from a tactical point of view, Force 1's turn to the northwest had unfortunate operational consequences, for at 10:20 A.M., with the enemy now over twenty miles off to the northeast, Burnett lost radar contact.

This first engagement represented the time of greatest vulnerability for the British. Had Bey decided to take advantage of his speed and firepower and turn on Force 1 he could well have destroyed or severely damaged the much lighter cruisers, despite his disadvantage in terms of gunnery control. Burnett's movement towards the convoy did make sense in terms of its survival, and Force 1's position at 10:50 A.M., ten miles ahead of JW 55B, now augmented by the 36th Destroyer Division, provided the best available protection. But Fraser had a bigger problem: his primary goal was to destroy or contain *Scharnhorst*, and having lost contact with her, he had to take into account all of Bey's possible courses of action.

*Scharnhorst* could run for home, but appeared not to be doing so; she could try again to attack the convoy, which was why Force 1 was out in front of it, or, worst of all scenarios, she could try to make a break for the Atlantic. It was with this latter possibility in mind that the British had maintained a powerful fleet in north Scotland throughout the war, yet still the Germans had from time to time succeeded in getting through. In 1941 the results had not been too severe, but now in 1943 the build up of American troops in Britain for the invasion of Europe was in full flood. Fast Atlantic liners such as *Queen Mary* and *Queen Elizabeth*, sailing unescorted because of their speed, were each delivering complete divisions in a single voyage, and *Scharnhorst* was the only enemy vessel capable of catching and sinking them. By taking Force 2 to the east, Fraser was leaving the door open, and *Scharnhorst* could at that very moment be heading towards it. Only one thing was certain: at that time nobody on the British side knew where the enemy ship was, and unless Force 1 could regain contact soon there would be no chance of finding her. So, at 11:50 A.M. he made a truly heart-breaking decision, turning his ships back towards the west.

Fifteen minutes later, shortly after noon, the situation changed dramatically. Force 1, now nine miles northeast of the convoy, regained radar contact with *Scharnhorst* seventeen miles further out. Bey, having come sufficiently north, had turned back to a southwesterly heading so as to meet JW 55B head on. Shortly afterwards sharp eyed *Sheffield* was again the first to report "enemy in sight." Burnett immediately ordered the cruisers to begin firing and his four destroyers to attack with torpedoes, but *Scharnhorst*'s rapid turn away, and the high seas prevented the smaller vessels from getting into a firing position. *Scharnhorst* set off to the southeast at 28 knots, and a running gun duel continued for some twenty minutes. From *Sheffield* her shooting appeared good, several shells falling uncomfortably close. John Wilson, a seaman stationed in *Belfast*'s air defense position on top of the bridge superstructure, had a bird's eye view of the action. He described what happened next: "Suddenly I saw black smoke pouring from *Norfolk*'s 'X' turret aft, and realized that she had been hit. It occurred to me for the first time that *Scharnhorst*, now four or five miles off to the southward, had guns too and was firing at us." Now was Bey's opportunity. *Scharnhorst*'s gunfire, visually directed during the brief period of faint arctic daylight, had become quite accurate, hitting and badly damaging *Norfolk* and closely straddling *Sheffield*. He still was unaware of the presence of Fraser yet, instead of turning and engaging in a fight he had every possibility of winning, he chose to head for home and end up unwittingly in a battle he could not help but lose.

Immediately upon receiving Burnett's second sighting report, Fraser turned Force 2 back onto an easterly course. With *Scharnhorst* now gradually coming round to a southerly heading, the situation was almost ideal for *Duke of York*'s group to intercept. Realizing this, Burnett decided to shadow *Scharnhorst*, keeping her carefully on his radar, but just outside visual range, maintaining a constant bearing on the battleship at 28 knots, about his maximum speed. At one point *Norfolk* had to drop back to fight a fire that had broken out, and later *Sheffield* suffered mechanical damage that caused her speed to drop to 10 knots, with the result that she missed the battle her keen eyesight had been crucial in initiating. All afternoon pursuers and pursued headed south, while Force 2 forged steadily up from the west. For some reason Bey never added the extra knots he was capable of, thus escaping the net closing around him. Nor again did he turn and fight. For a while *Belfast* was alone and as her Captain noted later: "She'd only got to turn round for ten minutes and she could have blown us clean out of the water," an opinion that Doenitz, writing later, clearly agreed with; the three cruisers certainly did not represent the superior forces his ambivalent orders had cautioned against.

At 4:17 P.M. the trap was sprung: just over the 25 mile range marker on the north-easterly edge of *Duke of York*'s surface search radar appeared an unmistakable blip; it could only be *Scharnhorst*. Still unseen, Force 2 closed into a firing position, and the final action opened at 4:48 P.M. with four perfectly placed star shells from *Duke of York*'s 5.25-inch secondary armament. As the Admiral recalled to his biographer more than three decades later: "Four star-shells, and there she was, guns still fore-and-aft. It was terrific – I can still see that illumination now." Two minutes later – at 4:50 P.M. – *Duke of York* opened fire, hitting *Scharnhorst* with her first and third 14-inch salvoes. "When *Duke of York* opened fire at 12,000 yards, there was every indication that the *Scharnhorst* was completely unaware of her presence; her turrets were trained fore and aft, she did not immediately reply to the fire of Force 2, and when she did so her fire was erratic," the British reported later, a belief confirmed by German survivors. One of the hits put her most forward turret out of action, reducing her offensive power by one-third. The other landed near the after turret. Five minutes later Naval Group North's worst fears were realized when they received Bey's signal: "Am in action with a battleship." It was at this point that the absence of his escorting destroyers extracted a further price: the British gunnery radar had only one target to track and plot, instead of a confusing five had the escorts been there.

Bey's immediate reaction was to turn to the north, away from *Duke of York*. Then, realizing that he was now heading directly towards the shadowing Force 1 and its deadly torpedoes, he altered course back to the east. *Belfast* and *Norfolk* also turned east, paralleling *Scharnhorst* to prevent her breaking away to the west, and firing at her with their 6-inch and 8-inch main armament. For the next hour, though, the main action was a running fight between *Scharnhorst* and *Duke of York*. Bey's appreciation of the situation arrived at Naval Group North at 5:24 P.M.: "Am surrounded by heavy units." However, he had the advantage of greater speed, and as the chase continued the range increased.

One of the paradoxes of naval gunnery is that large caliber shells do more damage as the range increases; guns fire at higher trajectories and thus the shells come down on their target at a steeper angle, the steeper the angle at which shells hit armor, the more devastating the effect. *Duke of York*'s shooting was accurate, doing extensive damage to the enemy's upper works and disabling the second forward 11-inch turret, but did not slow her down. Moreover, *Scharnhorst*'s greater speed meant that, while she was entering a more dangerous portion of *Duke of York*'s field of fire, she was also rapidly approaching the maximum range of the British 14-inch guns. At 6:20 P.M. *Scharnhorst* was nearly twelve miles ahead of Fraser's flagship.

J.A.J.Dennis, *Savage*'s First Lieutenant, witnessed:

> " . . a spectacular duel in an extraordinary setting of darkness, wind and heavy seas. Both heavy ships were firing shells fitted with tracer, so that one could follow their leisurely flight, ending in a forest of splashes around the targets. The guns thundered, the wind howled, and great flashes marked the salvoes. All in all a splendid sight, especially as they weren't firing at us."

German battleship protection included a heavily armored deck intended to counter the effect of falling shot. However, it was placed low down in the ship, covering the engine and boiler room and ammunition storage, but providing scant security for living and operational spaces. Survivors insisted that none of the British shell fire penetrated this deck, but shells exploding on contact with it caused much interior damage and numerous casualties, as well as destroying four of *Scharnhorst*'s six 6-inch turrets, her principal defense against enemy cruisers and destroyers.

At 6:20 P.M. the likelihood of the Germans escaping complete destruction, already improving, increased dramatically: a fragment of one of *Scharnhorst*'s 11-inch shells struck *Duke of York*'s mainmast, cutting the electrical cable running down from her gun control radar aerial. The British guns, hitherto shooting with great accuracy, were now firing blind, further impeded by smoke shrouding the target. At 6:24 P.M. Fraser ordered cease-fire; it was, he acknowledged later, the lowest point in his career. Adding to his depression was his earlier order to *Duke of York*'s destroyer escort: "Take up advantageous positions for firing but do not attack until ordered." At the moment when *Duke of York* first illuminated the enemy the destroyers were indeed in an excellent position for launching torpedoes. The Royal Navy's official historian is critical of Fraser's decision to restrain them, calling it a lost opportunity, while the Admiral's biographer justifies it largely on the basis that the destroyers could well have been annihilated by an as yet undamaged *Scharnhorst*, which *Duke of York* could well take care of on her own. Nevertheless, at this stage of the battle, it was a decision he bitterly regretted.

Moments later, however, Fraser realized that the battle was in fact his; unknown to him at the time, just as *Scharnhorst* disabled *Duke of York*'s gunnery radar, a lucky British 14-inch shell penetrated one of the enemy's boiler rooms. The shock was such that many on board thought she had been torpedoed; steam spread throughout the ship and her speed fell off to 8 knots. Prompt and effective damage control repaired the worst of the damage, but even so superior speed, her main advantage, was lost. She could barely make 22 knots, and this gave the destroyers, previously struggling to get into attack positions, the chance for which they had been waiting. At 6:20 P.M. *Scorpion* and *Stord* were just under 6 miles on *Scharnhorst*'s starboard beam, while *Savage* and *Saumarez* were about the same distance astern; whichever way the enemy turned, one of the two pairs would be in a good firing position.

At 6:50 P.M. Commander M.D.G. Meyrick, in *Savage* began execution of what became an extraordinarily well-coordinated torpedo attack. While *Savage* and *Saumarez* were closing in from the northwest, undeterred by heavy fire from *Scharnhorst*'s remaining 11-inch and 6-inch guns, *Scorpion* and *Stord* were coming up on the enemy's starboard beam. On the enemy's bridge all eyes were on the two destroyers approaching from astern, apparently not noticing the two out to starboard. Star shells from *Savage* illuminated the battleship as she turned to the south, placing *Scorpion* and *Stord* in an ideal firing position, only a mile and a quarter away. Swinging to the right they each fired eight torpedoes, scoring one hit, while hitting the enemy several times with their own 4.7-inch guns. *Scharnhorst*'s return fire was described as heavy but ineffective: according to survivors an order to the crews of the lighter weapons to take cover when the action commenced had never been countermanded, and disagreements between gunnery officers resulted in confusing and often contradictory orders. *Stord*'s desire to cripple the German battleship was particularly intense; her Norwegian crew justifiably resented the way *Scharnhorst* swung arrogantly at anchor in their national waters.

As *Scharnhorst* continued her turn to the southwest, apparently to avoid the first torpedo salvo, she placed *Savage* and *Saumarez* in an even better position on her bow. *Savage* fired all eight of her torpedoes, three of which found their target; *Saumarez*, the most heavily engaged by the enemy, also fired eight but none hit home. As Lt. Dennis noted, with masterly understatement, it was "an exciting five minutes . . . the be-all and end-all of the destroyer man." The destroyers withdrew under a smokescreen, while *Duke of York* and *Jamaica* rejoined the battle from the southwest, opening fire at 7:01 P.M., at just under six miles. Force 1 remained to the north, outfielders ensuring that the enemy could at no time break in that direction to threaten the convoy. *Scharnhorst*'s fire appeared concentrated on the destroyers; part of what remained of her main armament fired at *Duke of York*, but only intermittently.

The second battleship engagement lasted about half an hour. After only five minutes a number of hits by *Duke of York*'s 14-inch batteries had reduced the enemy's speed to only 5 knots; numerous fires had broken out, and ammunition could be seen exploding. As one eye witness described it: "The tracer bands of her 14-inch shells enabled one to follow little circles of light thrown, like illuminated quoits, on to the glowing target now less than 3 miles away. As each salvo registered, flames and sparks flew up as high explosive disintegrated, piece by piece, the great structure that had been the *Scharnhorst*." In the two battleship engagements the British fired 77 14-inch broadsides, expending 443 shells and confirmed a total of thirteen hits.

With both forward batteries out of action, and the aft battery running out of ammunition, the crew of the *Scharnhorst* resorted to carrying shells from the now useless guns back to where Third Gunnery Officer Kapitanleutnant Fugner continued directing the only remaining 11-inch guns, doing so until the ship went down. Both *Norfolk* and *Belfast* joined the one-sided battle, but in the confusion *Norfolk* had difficulty finding her target and stopped after two salvos. Battered and smoke wreathed, fires breaking out all over, nearly dead in the water, *Scharnhorst* still refused to surrender or sink. Her last defiant signal had gone out during the torpedo attack "The *Scharnhorst* will go on fighting to the last shell. Long live the Fuehrer! Long live Germany!" After this message had been sent, and according to survivors, Admiral Bey and Captain Hintze both shot themselves.

HMS *Duke of York*

As the British official account comments acidly: "This does not seem a particularly helpful proceeding ..."

Throughout the battle *Jamaica* had loyally followed astern of *Duke of York*. As the cruiser's torpedo officer described it a few days later:

> "... we opened fire at the same time as her. However, our little 6-inch shells cannot have made much of an impression on *Scharnhorst*'s enormous armor. This gun action was most exciting and *Scharnhorst*'s shooting good. We were near missed several times. Of course, a single salvo of her heavy stuff would have put us out."

*Belfast* too was joining the action, as was the 36th Destroyer Division. Knowing the enemy was mortally wounded but, given the amount of punishment she was taking, uncertain how long it would take to finally sink her, Fraser's main concern became the danger of self-inflicted wounds as his fleet hungrily surrounded the dying enemy. As *Scharnhorst*'s last remaining heavy weapons stopped firing, he ordered *Belfast* and *Jamaica* to "Finish her off with torpedoes," while telling his remaining ships to stay clear.

It was 7:25 P.M. when *Jamaica* and *Belfast* closed the doomed ship from opposite sides. Each fired three torpedoes, none of which appeared to have hit. *Jamaica*, after turning to bring her remaining tubes to bear, was more successful. A few days later her torpedo officer recalled: "I got two torpedoes into her guts which exploded with the most glorious clashes. When the smoke cleared away she was lying on her side. She sank shortly afterwards."

It was not quite that simple; *Scharnhorst*, although stopped, still refused to die. The 36th Division, hungry for blood, came in one sub-division on either side, *Musketeer* and *Matchless* aiming for the enemy's port side, her starboard list making her horribly exposed. Three of *Musketeer*'s torpedoes slammed home while *Matchless*, momentarily disabled by an overpowering wave, was unable to fire. When *Belfast* finally obtained a firing position she could see nothing except dense smoke, flames and debris.

No British participant saw the enemy sink, although at 7:45 P.M. sonar picked up a heavy underwater explosion. However, Fraser was loath to claim victory until 9:00 P.M. when Burnett assured him that *Scharnhorst* was indeed destroyed. Only then did he send a two word signal to the Admiralty: "*Scharnhorst* sunk," the reply being "Grand, well done."

German survivors were sure that it was the British torpedoes that settled *Scharnhorst*'s fate, insisting that gunnery alone, however well directed, would never have sunk her. Although she was constructed to withstand multiple torpedo hits, it was the concentration on her exposed port side that overwhelmed her. Only a few minutes after *Jamaica*'s second salvo Captain Hintze ordered abandon ship. The exodus was orderly despite the fact that there appear to have been no formal practice drills. Moreover, life jackets were not routinely worn and many of the crew, unable to locate one, went over the side without them.

Struggling in the icy water, grasping on to any piece of wreckage that might keep them afloat, the survivors' last sight of their vessel was as she lay almost on her side, lit by star shells from overhead and the garish beams of probing searchlights. From across the water where a few men had gathered on a raft came the words of an old song: "On a sailor's tomb . . . no roses bloom . . ." The cold was not slow in penetrating the fuel oil that coated the men in the icy water. The howling wind, blowing sleet straight across the waves, added to their agony. The final blow, however, was when the sound of gunfire echoed across the water; the immediate thought on the rafts was that the British were firing on them. Then, as they were caught in the glare of starshells, they realized that the Royal Navy had detached two destroyers for rescue operations. With extraordinary skill one of the ships (later identified as *Scorpion*) drifted slowly downwind towards the survivors, climbing nets dangling over her side, sailors with ropes waiting anxiously to help them on board. There was little chance of survival, however; *Scorpion* picked up thirty men, *Matchless* only six, before it became apparent that further search was hopeless.

The British cared well for their prisoners; oil soaked German uniforms were exchanged for dry British ones, and the shivering men given hot drinks and warm food. The following day, after arrival in Murmansk, they were brought up on deck where, to their horror, they were loaded onto a Russian tugboat. Seeing their consternation, a German speaking British officer assured them that they were being transferred to *Duke of York* for passage to Britain, not given up to the Russians. Before leaving *Scorpion* the grateful Germans gave their rescuers three rousing cheers.

Blindfolded *Scharnhorst* survivors, in merchant seaman rescue kit, being landed at Scapa Flow after the sinking of the German warship on 26 December 1943.

On passage from Murmansk to Scapa Flow the survivors were ordered to parade in front of Admiral Fraser and his staff. Facing the Germans, the British came to attention and saluted for a full minute, honoring both the living and the dead. Later, as she passed close to the spot where *Scharnhorst* went down, a large wreath was dropped from the *Duke of York*.

Earlier the question was asked, "What went wrong?" More appropriately one might ask what went right? For the Germans, ineptly led and operating under impossible constraints, the answer would appear to be very little apart from extraordinary courage. The British, on the other hand, went after *Scharnhorst* with a commander who knew exactly what he had to do and how to do it, with equipment that was in nearly all respects better than the enemy's, and backed by intelligence that was vastly superior to that available on the other side. But one thing without which Bey might have escaped, and which was unproven until put to the test, was Vice Admiral Burnett's superb handling of his cruiser squadron. As Fraser's biographer noted "Their joint success in this battle was due very largely to the seamanship and tactical anticipation displayed throughout by Burnett. No commanding admiral in modern naval history was ever better served, or admitted as much so gracefully". But Fraser qualified this praise, writing: "There is no doubt that *Duke of York* was the principal factor in the battle. She fought the *Scharnhorst* at night and she won." From the distance of sixty years a detached observer might feel differently. In a gunnery duel with *Scharnhorst* the odds were clearly on *Duke of York*, but without the courageous and tenacious shadowing by Burnett's cruisers, there would have been no gunfight to bet on.

# 6 HITLER'S FLEET IN BEING
## *TIRPITZ* AND THE ARCTIC CONVOYS

(See "Fleet in Being" sidebar at the end)

This article was first published in *MHQ;*
*The Quarterly Journal of military History/ Winter 2000*

*Tirpitz*, the most powerful of Germany's World War II battleships, spent much of her life hidden among the Norwegian fiords well north of the Arctic Circle; only twice did she go to sea with aggressive intent; her main armament was used only once in a surface action, and then its target was a weather station. Yet seldom in the history of naval warfare has a single ship had such a far-reaching impact on enemy fleet dispositions or required such enormous resources to ensure her destruction.

Despite the U-boats' considerable success against Allied merchant vessels in WW I, Grand Admiral Erich Raeder, Adolf Hitler's prewar naval commander, favored surface ships for trade interdiction. As a result, naval construction under Germany's re-armament program in the 1930s included both battle cruisers (*Scharnhorst* and *Gneisenau*) and larger battleships (*Bismarck* and *Tirpitz*), the latter designed to be the finest of their kind ever built. Displacing forty-two thousand tons, capable of thirty-one knots, and carrying eight 15-inch guns, they would out-range, outpace, and outgun any equivalent ship then contemplated by the British. *Tirpitz*, launched on April 1, 1939, and commissioned in late 1941, demonstrably did more damage to the Allied cause than did her more famous sister ship *Bismarck*.

Geography had historically favored the British during any naval confrontation with Germany. In mid-1940, however, with the defeat of France and the occupation of Norway, the English Channel and North Sea choke points, which had for so long frustrated Germany's ability to wage war in the world's oceans, were unblocked. By giving his navy anchorages in the Norwegian fiords to the north and deepwater ports at Brest and St. Nazaire to the west, Hitler provided Germany with much-improved access to the Atlantic trade routes and inflicted a significant setback to Britain's position of dominance at sea.

Germany's invasion of the Soviet Union in June 1941 prompted British Prime Minister Winston Churchill to provide his new-found ally with all the aid his country could afford, and even some it clearly could not. Just six weeks after the invasion, the first Arctic convoy sailed for North Russia, carrying planes, trucks, and tanks. Eight more convoys followed before year's end, all arriving without loss. Given the restricted capacity of Persian Gulf ports and the poor inland communications, for most of the war the Arctic provided the best route for Allied supplies to reach the Soviet Union. In 1942, with America in the war, the safe passage of these supplies became a high priority for Anglo-American strategists.

In January 1942, influenced less by the flow of aid to the Soviets than by his fixation that the Allies would mount a major attack on his positions in Norway, Hitler decided to send all his available heavy naval units and related escort vessels to Trondheim and Narvik. "Every ship that is not in Norway is in the wrong place," he intoned, and so, in the middle of January, *Tirpitz* arrived in Aasfjord, a well-sheltered anchorage some fifteen miles east of Trondheim. Although a shortage of fuel oil and a lack of adequate escorts curtailed German offensive capabilities for much of *Tirpitz*'s time in northern waters, she and her consorts nevertheless remained at the forefront of the British Admiralty's concerns, influencing fleet dispositions from Murmansk to America.

Admiral Sir John Tovey, commander in chief of the Royal Navy's Home Fleet, faced a formidable array of German warships in northern Norway: *Tirpitz*, pocket battleships *Admiral Scheer* and *Lutzow*, and the heavy cruiser *Admiral Hipper*, as well as their escorts. In addition, Ultra de-crypts indicated that Luftwaffe strength in northern Norway was also being significantly expanded by the addition of torpedo bombers and long-range reconnaissance aircraft. As a result, Tovey greatly increased the number of warships committed to arctic convoy protection, regularly employing battleships and an aircraft carrier to provide distant cover, in addition to customary close escorts. This represented a major commitment on the part of a fleet already stretched thin and reinforced Tovey's determination to bring the German surface fleet to action and, by destroying it, relieve pressure on his scarce resources.

As the arctic winter gave way to a bleak spring, nature too appeared to be on the side of the Germans. The ice pack continued to move south, driving the convoy routes closer to Luftwaffe airfields in northern Norway, while lengthening days provided more hours of good visibility for German pilots and reduced the advantage enjoyed by the Royal Navy through its more advanced radar. As a result, when two important Allied convoys sailed in early March, Germany's enhanced naval power benefited from considerably more favorable hunting conditions.

Fifteen merchant ships left Iceland on March 1, while on the same day a similar number of vessels sailed westward from Murmansk. Tovey, alerted by Ultra intelligence that *Tirpitz* might venture out to sea, was covering the convoys with the battleships *King George V* and *Duke of York*, the battle cruiser *Renown*, the fleet carrier *Victorious*, a cruiser, and nine destroyers. Although the first German shadowing aircraft sighted the eastbound convoy when it was only four days out, it missed seeing Tovey's covering force some fifty miles to the south. Thus the Germans knew nothing of the presence of the Home Fleet when later the same day *Tirpitz*, escorted by three destroyers and flying the flag of Vice Adm. Otto Ciliax, sailed to attack the convoy. The Royal Air Force's regular patrols off Trondheim failed to spot this movement, and it was not until the evening of the sixth that a Royal Navy submarine sighted the battleship steaming north along the Norwegian coast.

Ciliax's intentions were the opposite of Tovey's. His primary task was to destroy the enemy convoy, at all costs avoiding action with superior forces and only confronting equal strength if it stood between him and the convoy. He had little faith in the ability of his own escort vessels to handle the fearsome arctic seas and recognized that the Royal Navy could summon significant support from close by. He did not, of course, realize quite how close it was that day.

During much of March 7 the convoys, Home Fleet, and German task force all played what the Royal Navy's official historian described as "a curious game of hide and seek," mostly within a hundred miles of each other. *Tirpitz* searched in vain for the convoy, the Home Fleet unsuccessfully looked for *Tirpitz*, while the convoys steamed along their assigned routes. Both sides' efforts that day were hampered by the weather, which was cold, misty, and just below freezing.

Ciliax eventually gave up the search and turned for home on the morning of the eighth. The Admiralty, aided by unusually rapid Ultra decryption, picked up Ciliax's signal reporting this decision and ordered Tovey to intercept *Tirpitz*. The destruction of *Bismarck* had provided the Royal Navy with valuable lessons. *Victorious*' reconnaissance planes would seek out the enemy battleship, then her torpedo planes would inflict damage sufficient to allow the battle fleet to catch her and administer the *coup de grace*. Up to that point all went according to plan. At 8 A.M. reconnaissance aircraft sighted *Tirpitz* eighty miles east of the fleet, and forty minutes later the striking force of twelve Albacore torpedo bombers was in contact. But then things started to go wrong. The Albacore, which entered fleet service in 1941, was a fixed undercarriage biplane with a normal cruising speed of ninety-five knots. On the day in question, *Tirpitz* was steaming away from the striking force at thirty knots, into a wind of similar strength. The closing speed was a mere thirty knots. In addition, despite the presence of more experienced, but lower-ranked aviators, Home Fleet doctrine required that the torpedo attack be led by the pilot with the most seniority, even though the pilot in question, Lt. Cmdr. W.J. Lucas, was new to the ship, and the air group and had not practiced torpedo bombing since 1937.

The attack was made with remarkable bravery in the face of *Tirpitz*'s massive primary and secondary armament, but it was launched prematurely and from a poor position. The Germans, maneuvering violently, were able to avoid all the British torpedoes. Two Albacores were lost, the remainder returning to *Victorious* to face recriminations, which many members of the aircrews believed were unjust.

Tovey was bitterly disappointed since the tactical situation prior to the attack had appeared quite favorable. By the time another strike could be attempted, however, the Home Fleet was within German land-based fighter range, precluding further daytime operations, and the weather made night carrier operations impossible. This abortive attack was the first and only time that the Royal Navy had an opportunity to tempt *Tirpitz* into action on the open sea. Its failure appears to have been due to poor equipment, command rigidity, and lack of training--certainly not any shortage of courage.

Tovey's report on the operation accurately summarized the real value of *Tirpitz* to the Axis cause. "By her existence," he wrote, "she contains very large British and United States forces and prevents their transfer to the Far East or the Mediterranean." So valuable was the battleship, he thought, that she would not be exposed to any unnecessary risk. He questioned his orders that listed convoy protection as his fleet's primary objective, asserting that *Tirpitz*'s destruction would contribute much more to the conduct of the war than would the delivery of supplies to Russia. The two differing objectives, the Home Fleet commander pointed out, required very dissimilar fleet disposition. There is no evidence of a formal Admiralty response, but internal documents demonstrate respect for *Tirpitz*'s destructive potential in light of the heavy damage inflicted by *Bismarck* prior to her sinking, and question whether a covering force of only two battleships was sufficient to counter the threat she posed to the Russian convoys.

The Kriegsmarine also believed that this sortie had provided important lessons, mostly mirror images of Tovey's assessment. Ciliax believed that his tactical situation in northern waters was fundamentally weak and that only sheer good fortune had saved *Tirpitz* from damage by Royal Navy air, surface, and submarine units. His lack of aircraft carriers and poor Luftwaffe cooperation meant that operating his surface ships within reach of the British fleet imposed unacceptable risks. If *Tirpitz*'s main task was to defend against a possible Allied invasion of Norway, then she should only be used elsewhere with enormous caution. And such became the rule; it would be three months before she sailed again. Ciliax and Tovey both faced conflicting strategic situations. Ciliax had a dual responsibility: defend against an invasion of Norway, which Hitler was convinced was imminent, and destroy the convoys to Russia. Although by his own admission ill-equipped to do either, he decided to split his forces, making *Tirpitz*'s primary mission the defense of Norway and using smaller vessels and U-boats as the principal naval weapons against the convoys. The British, on the other hand, had no serious intention of invading Norway, so Tovey's dilemma was deciphering whether his job was convoy protection or *Tirpitz*'s destruction. Lacking specific instructions from above, he continued to attempt both, with disastrous results.

One way of hobbling *Tirpitz* was to prevent her from obtaining needed re-fits. Outside Germany there was only one dry dock capable of taking the giant battleship: at St. Nazaire on the French Atlantic coast, which might be reached with less risk than a return through the North Sea to Germany. The British determined to eliminate this option and, on the night of March 28, mounted a daring combined operation against the French port. HMS *Campbeltown*, one of the elderly U.S. Navy destroyers transferred in 1940 to the Royal Navy, tricked the German defenders into believing that she was friendly and was able to approach within twenty-five hundred yards of her objective before meeting any serious opposition. Heavy and accurate fire came too late to prevent *Campbeltown* from reaching the lock gates and ramming them squarely in the center. More than two hundred commandos swarmed ashore and began destroying machinery essential to the dock's operation. They met determined German resistance and took many casualties, but the dry dock remained unusable until the end of the war.

By this time *Tirpitz* was at anchorage in Fottenfjord, a branch of the larger Trondheim Fiord, where she would remain for the next three months. Safe from surface attack and, so he thought, subsurface attack, and largely protected against bombing by excellent camouflage and the steep cliffs only a few hundred yards on either side of his ship, Captain Karl Topp's main preoccupation was the morale of his crew.

HMS *Campbeltown*, laden with explosives, beached at St. Nazaire on 28 March 1942. Funnel arrangements were altered to resemble German destroyer.

But life on board *Tirpitz* was not totally tranquil. While Royal Navy submarines kept watch at the entrance of Trondheim Fiord and the Home Fleet provided distant cover against a break-out, the Royal Air Force began the first of many attempts to sink the enemy battleship. During March and April several heavy bomber attacks were mounted, with little success. Bad weather prevented many of the aircraft from finding the target. Spherical mines filled with high explosives and set to go off underwater augmented conventional bombs. Neither weapon did any serious damage. Topp was right: the natural defenses of the fiord, heavy anti-aircraft fire, and dense smoke screens, which could be released when attack appeared imminent, all made *Tirpitz* a very difficult target. The RAF lost twelve bombers during these failed raids.

Meanwhile, the arctic convoys continued. Although the Germans now had a powerful squadron of U-boats available, lack of fuel restricted the boats' ability to interfere with Allied convoys. On the other hand, bad weather, which forced the convoys to scatter, and increased aggressiveness by the Luftwaffe, resulted in quite significant Allied losses. Realizing the vulnerability of the convoys during the long daylight hours, the Germans forcefully augmented their air and submarine resources in the area. Greater Luftwaffe cooperation was ordered by Hitler, and, for the first time, dive bombers were augmented with torpedo planes. By mid-summer the Luftwaffe had a formidable and balanced force of 264 aircraft available at North Cape. In addition, there were twenty U-boats assigned to the arctic convoy routes.

Although the British countered these moves by increasing the close escort for the convoys, ice and the enemy continued to take an increasing toll, and they wondered if the risks entailed in forcing the convoys through during the summer were justified by the rewards. Tovey concurred with the recommendation of his escort commander that unless the Luftwaffe could be neutralized, the convoys should be halted until the shorter days of autumn. If for political reasons they were to continue, there would be very heavy losses. First Sea Lord Admiral Dudley Pound agreed, writing to Admiral Ernest J. King, U.S. chief of naval operations, "the whole thing is a most unsound operation, with the dice loaded against us in every direction." However, political pressure from President Franklin Roosevelt and Josef Stalin—the former concerned about a Soviet military and political collapse, the latter preoccupied with building the force that would eventually prevail at Stalingrad--outweighed the judgment of Churchill's naval advisers and, far from being eliminated, the convoys were enlarged. An eastbound convoy in the latter half of May bore out Tovey's fears. Consisting of thirty-five ships, it was the largest yet to sail. Heavy air attacks resulted in seven ships lost and one damaged, with commensurate destruction of valuable cargo.

Even while at anchor in Fottenfjord, *Tirpitz* continued to exercise her baleful influence over Allied naval dispositions worldwide. Fearing that a Japanese occupation of Madagascar would deny access to the eastern Mediterranean, the British decided to get there first. Naval forces to cover the expedition, however, could only be provided by calling on units vitally needed elsewhere, so Churchill asked Roosevelt if he could supply United States Navy reinforcements in the Arctic. Admiral King saw the logic of this and in early summer agreed to lend ships badly needed in the Pacific to the Home Fleet. The battleship *Washington*, the heavy cruisers *Wichita* and *Tuscaloosa*, and Destroyer Squadron Eight (Task Force Ninety-nine) were placed under Tovey's command. Together with *King George V*, *Victorious*, a light cruiser, and five British destroyers, these ships provided distant protection for the next several Russian convoys. This was the first time in World War II that United States naval forces had been placed under British command. The heavy commitment of Allied resources was based principally on the continuing fear that *Tirpitz* would either break out into the Atlantic or, taking advantage of Luftwaffe air cover, go north to decimate a Russian convoy. And it was the latter concern that dominated British tactical thinking when planning the next convoy.

Code-named PQ 17, this convoy suffered the worst fate of any during World War II. As he prepared for it in June, Tovey was alarmed by the enemy's many advantages, which he believed could only be mitigated by reducing the size of the convoy and by tempting the German heavy ships toward his battle fleet. The Admiralty, on the other hand, insisted that he run one large convoy, strengthening his close-escort group with cruisers. War materiel for the Soviet Union was piling up in American and British ports and had to be delivered during the summer campaigning season. If heavy enemy forces were encountered, the convoy should scatter. Tovey, who disliked the idea of sending his precious cruisers eastward into the Barents Sea, was appalled at the idea of scattering the convoy; it would become easy prey for enemy aircraft and submarines.

The German naval command too was preparing for PQ 17. Their fuel situation in Norway had improved sufficiently to permit operation of heavy ships, and on June 1 Hitler reluctantly approved their use, subject to the condition that they could only sail if the Royal Navy's aircraft carrier had been located and could be attacked by the Luftwaffe. Recognizing that this would so hamper the operation of his ships as to render them useless, Admiral Raeder ordered that, once the convoy had been sighted, *Tirpitz* and her consorts should move north to Altenfjord, awaiting Hitler's permission to sortie.

PQ 17 sailed from Iceland on June 27. German aircraft first sighted the thirty-five-ship convoy on July 1. By the morning of the fourth the convoy was 130 miles northeast of Bear Island. It had survived intense air attacks in good condition. Station-keeping was excellent, and a number of enemy aircraft had been destroyed by anti-aircraft fire. In the words of Commodore John Broome, the convoy's senior officer, "provided the ammunition lasted, PQ 17 could get anywhere."

A Luftwaffe reconnaissance plane had finally sighted the distant covering force, including the carrier *Victorious*, early the previous day, but the ships had not been seen since then. Admiral Raeder, conscious of Hitler's respect for the Royal Navy's carriers, refused to sanction any further movement. In London, however, nothing was known beyond the fact that Germany's heavy units had sailed. When Pound and his staff met during the evening of July 4, the enemy ships had vanished. If they were on their way to attack the convoy, they could be in the vicinity of PQ 17 any time after 2 o'clock the following morning. Required to provide cover for a simultaneous westbound convoy as well as PQ 17, Tovey's battleships in addition had to remain concerned about a possible *Tirpitz* breakout into the Atlantic. These factors, combined with continued respect for the Luftwaffe's capabilities, caused him to position his covering force some 230 miles west of the convoy, too far away to intercept before both the convoy and its cruiser escort could be destroyed. The Admiralty gave the order for the convoy to scatter and for its escorts to withdraw to the west. The commander of the cruiser escort, assuming that *Tirpitz* and her consorts were in the immediate vicinity, prepared to do battle with vastly superior forces. But to the dispersing merchant vessels, the majority of them American, it appeared as if their escort was running away.

In fact, the Admiralty knew no more about the German heavy units than did the local commanders. Indeed, the British officer responsible for intelligence about the German battleship believed that she had not sailed, but he could not convince Pound of this. The certainty of sustained air and U-boat attacks on the scattered and thus defenseless convoy was weighed against the possibility of it encountering German battleships, and a choice was made that--with benefit of hindsight--was calamitous. During the next week German air and subsurface forces destroyed twenty-one out of the thirty-five merchant ships that had sailed on June 27, compared with only three sunk while the convoy remained intact. Fourteen of the vessels lost were American. Although *Tirpitz* did in fact sail, she was recalled once it was realized that her presence was unnecessary. She had served her purpose simply by making the convoy easy prey for submarines and aircraft and thus, without firing a shot, had inflicted major damage on supplies badly needed by the Soviets.

For six weeks following the destruction of the convoy, *Tirpitz* lay at anchor in Narvik Fiord, doing little but still effectively tying down the British Home Fleet. The occasional exercise with other units of the fleet and the Luftwaffe, together with recreation ashore, did little to relieve the boredom. One account tells how a frustrated German sailor deserted but was captured, brought back on board, and interrogated. Was he trying to get to Sweden, he was asked? "No," he replied, "I wanted to get to Britain or the United States and serve in one of their navies. Something happens with them, nothing does here." He was taken to the quarterdeck and shot.

The German battleship *Tirpitz* in Bogen Bay in Ofotfjord, near Narvik, Norway, during World War II.

Naval and air dispositions during the summer and fall of 1942 reflected significant operations in other parts of the world. During July and August the United States Navy's Task Force Ninety-nine was gradually withdrawn to reinforce the Pacific Fleet as America went on the offensive at Guadalcanal. The survival of strategically vital Malta called for desperate measures to force the passage of convoys essential for relief of the island, which in turn required Tovey to provide major units, including his one precious carrier, for Mediterranean escort work. By the time the survivors rejoined him as the end of August, two of his cruisers had been damaged and one sunk.

On the other hand, the Allied invasion of North Africa later in 1942, deemed at the time by U.S. Army Chief of Staff General George C.

Marshall to be an unnecessary distraction from a cross-Channel invasion, had an unforeseen but beneficial impact on the Russian convoys. The Luftwaffe, drawn south to counter the Allied landing, would never again reach its past strength in Norway. U-boats now represented the main danger to the convoys, and these would be subjected to a war of attrition by escort carriers and reinforced escort groups.

Largely as a result of the PQ 17 disaster, Russian convoy traffic was halted until September. Admiral Raeder's plans to use *Tirpitz* to attack the next convoy found little support from Hitler and were canceled. Shortage of fuel oil also continued to be an important constraint on operations by the surface ships. In addition, *Tirpitz* was badly in need of a homeport refit but, at Hitler's insistence, she returned to Trondheim where workers sent from Germany performed miracles of improvisation. Nevertheless, fears of the damage she could do if loose on the high seas continued to dominate the Royal Navy's strategic thinking.

Clearly the *Tirpitz* had to be destroyed, but how? She refused to come out from under the protection of the Luftwaffe, and the Royal Navy, its battleships bloodied by Japanese aircraft off Malaya, prudently declined to go in after her. No British submarine had been able to get within shooting range, and, although a Soviet sub claimed to have scored two torpedo hits, there is no mention of such in *Tirpitz*'s war diary. Royal Air Force attacks on her anchorages in the Norwegian fiords had proved fruitless.

The Royal Navy decided to try a new approach that was probably inspired by the Italian navy's audacious human torpedo attack on the battleships *Queen Elizabeth* and *Valiant* in Alexandria Harbor six months earlier (see Chapter Two *Decima Flottiglia Mas* herein). One of the weapons was captured and copied. Codenamed "Chariot" by the British, the tiny vessels carried two men in diving suits sitting astride an electrically powered torpedo. A six-hundred-pound warhead could be detached and fixed to the target, a timed fuse permitting the crew to escape.

On October 26, 1942, a fishing boat commanded by Norwegian resistance fighter Leif Larsen sailed from the Shetland Islands bound for Trondheim with two Chariots on board. Operation Title, as the venture was called, appears to have been doomed to failure. Mechanical breakdowns, watchful enemy aircraft, and bad weather blighted the venture from the beginning. Larsen, however, had managed to come almost within sight of *Tirpitz* when the Chariots were lost overboard in a sudden squall. Title was abandoned, the fishing boat scuttled, and nine of the ten men on board walked sixty miles across enemy-held Norway to safety in neutral Sweden. The tenth man was captured by the Gestapo, interrogated, and shot. Although Title was an operational failure, its near success nonetheless encouraged the British to attempt a better-conceived and equipped infiltration of *Tirpitz*'s anchorage. Operation Source, which was already in preparation at the time of Title, would not take place for nearly a year, but would be much more successful.

*Tirpitz*'s refit, meanwhile, took three months. Seasonal leave in Germany was given to those not needed on board, while routine onboard maintenance and recreation ashore occupied the others. But on New Year's Eve, as Captain Topp was making an inspirational speech to his men, a battle was raging several hundred miles to the north that would have significant effect on German naval policies.

Spurred by the *Wehrmacht's* pleas for help on the Eastern Front, the Kriegsmarine determined to destroy an eastbound Russian convoy consisting of fourteen merchant ships. To do this they deployed the pocket battleship *Lutzow* (six 11-inch guns), the cruiser *Admiral Hipper* (eight 8-inch guns), and six destroyers against the much weaker British force of six destroyers and five smaller vessels. Rear Admiral

Oskar Kummetz in *Lutzow* was surprised when the outgunned and outnumbered British destroyers aggressively counterattacked the pocket battleship, the cruiser, and their attendant escorts—and kept them away from the convoy until Royal Navy cruisers could come up. A broadside from *Admiral Hipper* devastated the destroyer leader *Onslow*, killing forty men and leaving her skipper, Robert St. Vincent Sherbrooke, horribly wounded, his left eye dangling on his cheek. Sherbrooke refused medical attention until he had passed command to another captain—courage that earned him a Victoria Cross for his role in what became known as the Battle of Barents Sea. When the supporting British cruisers appeared on the scene, Kummetz withdrew. *Admiral Hipper* was sufficiently damaged to cause her removal from the war, and the convoy escaped unscathed.

Kummetz had been operating under orders to use caution even against an enemy of equal strength and not to take any great risks—orders that one German naval historian has described as remarkably inhibiting for an admiral engaged in an offensive sweep with many unknown hazards. The British official historian, commenting on this and other actions, pointed out that the German naval staff, probably reflecting Hitler's own opinions, "seems to have shown a remarkable aptitude for depriving its seagoing commanders of all initiative."

The following morning Hitler reacted violently when his naval aide brought him the news. The heavy ships were useless and should be scrapped, he said. Their guns could be used in defense of Europe and their crews employed to better purpose elsewhere. Unlike the British, the German navy retreated rather than fighting to the bitter end. The air force would do what the ships could not.

A few days later, when Raeder was ordered to decommission the heavy ships, he submitted a letter of resignation that set forth the basic elements of sea power, pointing out the deterrent value of *Tirpitz* and the other big ships that were tying down large elements of the Royal Navy that would otherwise be available in the Mediterranean or Far East. Hitler, unimpressed, selected U-boat commander Admiral Karl Donitz as Raeder's successor. His first decision on taking command concerned the disposition of the capital ships.

Donitz initially agreed with Hitler that, provided adequate Luftwaffe support could be guaranteed, resources presently devoted to the capital ships would be better employed in repairing and manning U-boats. Two weeks later, however, he surprised the Fuhrer by recommending a partial reversal of the decision. Arguing that the capital ships' greatest strategic value was their mere existence, he suggested that, while some of the German cruisers should be decommissioned and the remainder withdrawn to the Baltic, *Tirpitz*, the battle cruiser *Scharnhorst*, and appropriate escorts should remain in Norway for local defense and Russian convoy interdiction. After acrimonious debate, Hitler grudgingly agreed.

*Tirpitz* and *Scharnhorst* remained in Altenfjord during the spring and summer of 1943. Promoted to rear admiral, Topp had been succeeded in command of *Tirpitz* by Captain Hans Meyer. Shortage of fuel meant that the big ships could only put to sea briefly for gunnery practices. But they were now out of range of British bombers and thus relatively safe from hostile action and continued to represent a powerful challenge to the Royal Navy.

On June 1, Admiral Sir Bruce Fraser succeeded Tovey as commander in chief, Home Fleet. It was Fraser's judgment that the Russian convoys could only be justified if they were essential to winning the war, or if they served as bait to tempt the German heavy units into action. He believed that the arctic route was no longer vital to the Soviet Union, and shared Tovey's view that the German fleet was unlikely to put to sea unless the Home Fleet was in some way incapacitated. In the late summer Fraser's command was indeed considerably weakened. He was already chronically short of destroyers and lacked an aircraft carrier, since *Victorious* had been sent to the Pacific at Admiral King's request. He had received in return two American cruisers and the carrier USS *Ranger* but still lacked battleships after *King George V* and *Howe* were transferred to the Mediterranean in preparation for the invasion of Sicily. On September 6, 1943, presumably taking advantage of this weakness, *Tirpitz* and *Scharnhorst* sailed with their escorts north to Spitzbergen, where they used their massive guns to bombard a weather station after landing a party of soldiers and taking the British garrison captive. It was the only time *Tirpitz*'s main armament was ever used against a surface target.

The only sure way to eliminate the threat of the German surface fleet was to attack it within its well-protected Norwegian anchorages. Fortunately, three years earlier the Royal Navy had begun development of midget submarines, eventually known as X-craft, with *Tirpitz* as their intended target. Orders for six of these boats had been placed in mid-1942. They were to have a surface speed of six knots, a submerged speed of five knots, and a range of eighty miles at two knots. Each craft would carry two four-ton magnetic charges attached one on each side of the boat. The first boat, X-5, was laid down in September, and the last, X-10, was delivered in January 1943.

Although all six X-craft were supposed to take part in Operation Source, only four of them survived the towed passage to the Norwegian coast. X-9 parted her line and was never seen again while a badly leaking X-8 had to be scuttled. The evening of September 20, 1943 after aerial reconnaissance confirmed that *Tirpitz* and *Scharnhorst* had returned from their raid on Spitzbergen, the four remaining craft slipped away from their towing submarines and headed toward the minefields guarding the approaches to Altenfjord. Plagued with mechanical difficulties, X-10 was unable to undertake her planned attack on *Scharnhorst*. There was no official confirmation of X-5's fate after she and X-7 crossed the minefields together.

British Midget Submarine X-7

The following day X-6, listing badly and partially blinded by a leaking periscope, crossed the minefields safely and proceeded submerged up Altenfjord. Unable to navigate the protective nets across Kaafjord by periscope, her skipper, Lieutenant Donald Cameron, boldly surfaced and followed a ferryboat as she passed through. Diving again, he felt his way up the fiord, running aground once and later fouling a mooring cable. Barely able to make out *Tirpitz*'s protective netting, he threaded his way through it. Then, at 7 A.M., he sighted a large, gray mass through his clouded periscope just before his sub grounded on a nearby rock.

On board *Tirpitz* a petty officer had seen an object on the surface that he took to be a dummy. Captain Meyer's insistence on frequent exercises using simulated frogmen may have been overdone; the crew was jumpy, and false alarms were frequent. Then, realizing it was a submarine, the petty officer alerted the officer of the watch. By the time Captain Meyer had been informed and action station sounded, precious minutes had passed, and Cameron, machine-gun fire now raking his sub's hull, had come alongside *Tirpitz* and released his charges under one of the ships turrets. The lieutenant and his crew abandoned X-6 just before she sank, surrendering to German sailors in a nearby motorboat.

Lt. Godfrey Place

Lieutenant Godfrey Place, in X-7, had set off a little earlier than X-6 and remained submerged while he followed a minesweeper through the Kaafjord nets. Inadvertently running into *Lutzow*'s now empty nets, he took some time to escape and then, finding *Tirpitz*'s own nets impenetrable, surfaced to find his sub only one hundred yards from his objective. Submerging again, he slowly closed on the battleship until he hit her side, at which point he slid underneath the massive hull to lay his charges, one under "B" turret, the other between the engine room and "C" turret. The protective nets again forced him to go to the surface on the way out, and he was compelled to surrender.

Suspecting that the submarines had laid mines under his ship, Meyer tried to shift her using the anchor cables, but the movement was limited and too late. Some ninety minutes after the first X-craft sighting, Captain Meyer saw an immense column of water off his starboard bow while his ship rocked underfoot. Within the ship, lights went out while steam hissed through broken pipes. *Tirpitz* remained afloat, however, with only a modest list and oil spreading on the surface of the fiord as evidence of the attack.

Although her hull was relatively unaffected, other damage to *Tirpitz* was extensive. There was considerable destruction within the machinery spaces, shafts were distorted so that propellers could not be turned, and the port rudder was inoperable. Each of the four massive fifteen-inch gun turrets had been jarred off its track, and all of the optical range finders were unusable. One seaman had been killed and forty wounded. Details of the damage were soon available to the British through Ultra decrypts, amplified by reports from the local resistance and Soviet intelligence. Ultra also revealed that, since protection for a return passage to Germany was impossible, repairs would be carried out locally. The German naval staff believed that she could not be made operational before April 1944, at the earliest. Lieutenants Place and Cameron received Victoria Crosses for their roles in Operation Source.

Place spent the rest of the war in a German camp. On return to England when released, he was offered a low level appointment in submarines, reflecting all the time he had spent on land while a prisoner. Turning his back on submarines, he became a naval aviator, serving in the carrier HMS *Glory* as a squadron commander during the Korean War.

Despite the fact that *Scharnhorst* was still at large, the injury done to *Tirpitz* by the X-craft significantly altered the strategic situation in arctic waters. A new series of Russian convoys started immediately, and Fraser abandoned the Home Fleet's waiting game and began boldly attacking Axis merchant shipping off the Norwegian coast. In the words of the official historian, these decisions underline "the influence exerted by the single powerful enemy battleship throughout the twenty-one months which had passed since she first arrived in Norway."

The strategic situation changed even more in the Royal Navy's favor on Christmas Day 1943. Admiral Fraser--relying on Ultra intelligence and superior radar, skillfully deploying numerous widely dispersed forces, including an aggressively handled cruiser squadron under Rear Adm. Robert Burnett--sank *Scharnhorst*, Germany's only remaining operational capital ship (see Chapter Five: Destruction of the *Scharnhorst*). Donitz had earlier persuaded Hitler to give him tactical discretion as to the use of *Scharnhorst* against the convoys, and the results probably indicated that the Fuhrer, although a self-described "land animal," had a better instinctive feel for the balance of naval power than did his naval chief of staff. *Scharnhorst*, like *Tirpitz*, exacted a greater price from the Allies in harbor than she ever did at sea.

Thus *Tirpitz* lay in her berth throughout the winter of 1943-44, like an angry hibernating bear, liable on the first days of spring to hurl herself against her enemies. Forces that were badly needed to create the British Pacific Fleet and join in the fight against Japan were still held in readiness at their Scapa Flow anchorage in case she put to sea. Although it had damaged her badly, the Royal Navy could not rest until she was destroyed.

On the other hand, the balance of sea power as it related to the arctic convoys had changed even further in the Allies' favor. Luftwaffe air power in the area continued to be increasingly diluted because of demands in other regions. Although U-boat strength in the far north was now maintained at as many as twenty-five to thirty vessels, these were more than offset by vastly more powerful anti-submarine forces, including the invaluable escort carriers whose patrol planes represented a new and lethal threat to enemy submarines. A February convoy, consisting of forty-two merchant ships and escorted by three cruisers, an escort carrier, and seventeen destroyers, arrived in northern Russia with no losses. Weather conditions, appalling even by arctic standards and including a series of unusually severe storms, also tended to favor the defenders rather than the attackers.

The German navy indicated the importance it attached to *Tirpitz* by sending seven hundred skilled workers to Norway to repair her. They were successful, and by mid-March she was able to work up to twenty-seven knots during sea trials. She was still out of range of Royal Air Force bombers, so Fraser, aware of her imminent return to operational service, accelerated a planned strike by carrier-based dive bombers.

Operation Tungsten was the first of several Fleet Air Arm attacks on the battleship during the spring and summer of 1944. The striking force consisted of fleet carriers *Victorious* and *Furious* and escort carriers *Emperor*, *Searcher*, and *Pursuer* together with battleship *Anson*, flying the flag of Vice Adm. Sir Henry Moore. Their crews had benefited from intensive rehearsals among the Scottish lochs, and on April 3, forty-two bombers and eighty fighters were launched in two waves, commencing at 4:15 A.M. In the process of weighing anchor for sea trials when the attacking aircraft arrived, *Tirpitz* was taken completely by surprise. Her crew had no time to make smoke or close watertight doors, and the ship's very effective anti-aircraft armament, already caught unprepared, was further confused by well-coordinated attacks from either side. The bombers' principal weapons were sixteen-hundred-pound semi-armor-piercing bombs, but the mix also including five-hundred-pound semi-armor-piercing and high-explosive and anti-submarine bombs designed to maximize damage from near misses.

While none of the bombs penetrated *Tirpitz*'s main armor, they caused widespread damage. The ship was armored so heavily as to be virtually unsinkable, but she did have one serious design flaw: The main horizontal protection was built at the waterline, protecting magazines and machinery spaces effectively, but leaving essential areas above, except for the fifteen-inch turrets, extremely vulnerable to the kind of weapons used in Tungsten. Luftwaffe cooperation in *Tirpitz*'s defense, as usual, was abysmal. The British fighter escort thus encountered no air opposition and used its ammunition on *Tirpitz*'s decks, providing valuable flak suppression. German casualties were substantial: 438 men wounded, including Captain Meyer, and 122 killed. However, Admiral Moore's conclusion that *Tirpitz* was now useless as a warship proved overly optimistic. Although fifteen of the bombs had hit the ship, her engines and main armament remained undamaged, and she was ready for sea again in three months, by then under the command of her former executive officer, Captain Wolf Junge.

The Fleet Air Arm mounted four more attacks in July and August, losing a total of sixteen aircraft in the process, but it was apparent that British carrier-based aircraft could not haul bombs of sufficient weight to penetrate *Tirpitz*'s vitals. Something heavier was called for. In addition, *Tirpitz*'s defenses were improved, watchers on nearby mountains provided early warning of attack, smoke screens had been made denser, and the ship's fifteen-inch guns were used to provide additional anti-aircraft barrages.

Barnes Wallis, a gifted British aircraft designer, had shifted his attention during the war to the development of more effective bombs. After intensive study he had developed the special weapons used to attack the dams feeding Germany's Ruhr industrial complex. This was followed by the remarkable "Tallboy"--a ballistically perfect, high-terminal-velocity, twelve-thousand pound armor-piercing bomb--exactly what was needed to penetrate *Tirpitz*'s horizontal armor. To be fully effective, however, the Tallboys had to be dropped from as great a height as possible.

In September 1944 Commander General Dwight D. Eisenhower, who at the time controlled most of the RAF's bomber resources, released two squadrons of Lancaster bombers, thirty-nine planes in total, to attack *Tirpitz*. Surprisingly, the Soviets, previously reluctant cooperators in dealing with threats to the arctic convoys, agreed to permit the RAF to use their air base at Yagodnik, only six hundred miles from Altenfjord. The Royal Air Force apparently was not overeager to divert resources from its night bombing of Germany to attack *Tirpitz*. One account describes how Churchill had earlier told Air Marshal Sir Arthur Harris of Pound's concerns about the continued survival of *Tirpitz*. "Tell the First Sea Lord he need not worry," said Harris blithely, "I'll sink it when I have a spare moment."

The squadron selected to eliminate *Tirpitz* once and for all was the legendary 617 Squadron, the "Dambusters," which had, by use of advanced bomb-aiming devices and painstaking practice, achieved the hitherto unheard of ability to release bombs from twenty thousand feet and place them within a ninety-yard radius. The squadron was now under the command of Wing Commander Willie Tait, a highly decorated twenty-six-year-old Welshman. For the *Tirpitz* attacks he would be reinforced by Nine Squadron, which, although less well-equipped than 617, had a reputation for extraordinary bombing accuracy.

The first attempt took place on September 15 but was frustrated by the German smoke screen. Tait, leading twenty-eight Lancasters, dropped one Tallboy using a brief glimpse of *Tirpitz*'s mast as his aiming point. A few aircraft bombed through the smoke by dead reckoning, while the remainder did not drop any bombs. All but one of the planes returned to Scotland.

Subsequent air reconnaissance showed that *Tirpitz* had left Altenfjord, causing great alarm among the naval staff until Norwegian resistance reported her in Tromso with a large hole in her bow indicating that Tait's bomb had actually scored a hit. The news was thus doubly good since Tromso was two hundred miles closer to Scotland and hence within range of British-based bombers. Moreover, unknown to the British, *Tirpitz*'s damage was more than a visible hole: Two near misses had caused severe destruction amidships, and the main engines were incapable of sustained power. Captain Junge had recommended to Donitz that the vessel be written off, but the grand admiral refused. *Tirpitz* therefore limped south to a berth selected not only for ease of repair but also in the hope that, if damaged further, she would settle on the bottom and be able to use her fifteen-inch guns for local defense.

It was not until October 28 that the weather forecast for northern Norway again indicated good enough bombing conditions. Tait took off at 1 o'clock in the morning, leading thirty-six heavily loaded Lancasters, but he was frustrated by unexpected cloud cover over the target. There now followed a race against time since after the end of November the twenty-four-hour arctic night would settle over Tromso, making precision bombing impossible. The Germans, probably recognizing that the next week or so could seal *Tirpitz*'s fate, had reinforced their northern defenses with an additional two dozen aircraft based only thirty miles from the battleship's anchorage.

On November 12 Tait tried again, despite the possibility of icing conditions, which could cripple his badly overloaded aircraft. The sun was just rising as they reached the coast of Norway. Flying at fourteen thousand feet, the thirty-two Lancasters were an easy target for radar, and the German air defenses were immediately alerted. As the bombers came over the last mountain range before Tromso, however, there was no sign of enemy fighters and, more important, no smoke. The smoke pots had been moved from Altenfjord with the battleship but had not yet been connected.

Aboard *Tirpitz* morale was at rock bottom. There was a general feeling that the ship was doomed, despite reassuring declarations from Captain Robert Weber, who had relieved Captain Junge a few days earlier. *Tirpitz*'s guns were effective as ever, he said, and she now enjoyed the added protection of nearby Luftwaffe squadrons. There was, however, no sign of fighter cover at 9:38 A.M. that Sunday as *Tirpitz*'s fifteen-inch guns opened fire on the unwavering Lancaster formation while Weber frantically called the Luftwaffe base at Bardufoss.

At 9:41 A.M. Tait began the bombing run. Of eighteen Tallboys dropped, sixteen fell near the ship, mostly on the port side, two scoring hits and penetrating the main armored deck. Taking water from the damaged side, the great ship immediately developed a list, firing ceased, electrical generators stopped, and telephones fell silent. As the list increased and the water level rose, spaces between decks became untenable, and Weber ordered those who could to evacuate. There was still no sign of the Luftwaffe. Explanations for the absence of fighter cover differ, but one thing is clear: The German air force had never provided *Tirpitz* the air defense appropriate for a valuable capital ship. Between January 1941 and November 1944, she was attacked thirteen times from the air by a total of some six hundred British aircraft, but the only one of these to be countered by a German plane was an elderly Albacore bi-plane that skirmished with one of *Tirpitz*'s own floatplanes in March 1942.

At 9:50 A.M. an explosion lifted C Turret with its two fifteen-inch guns--seventeen hundred tons in total--out of its mountings and over the side. By 10 o'clock the ship was almost upside down, and Weber ordered those remaining to abandon ship. Many of the fifteen hundred men then on board *Tirpitz* were trapped inside her, although rescue operations during the next several days managed to extract eighty-seven of these through holes cut in the bottom. Seven hundred crew members perished, but only 165 bodies were recovered for burial in Tromso.

Fleet Air Arm attack the German battleship *Tirpitz* as she was about to move off from her anchorage at Alten Fjord, Norway, on the morning of 3 April 1944. The wake of a fast moving motor boat as she hurries away from the battered Tirpitz can be seen as a huge cloud rises from an early bomb hit on the German battleship.

All Tait's planes returned safely to Scotland, but with hindsight it was an empty victory. *Tirpitz* had already ceased to be a threat and, as Bomber Command historian Max Hastings comments, "Many of the greatest feats of precision bombing such as the sinking of the *Tirpitz*--which would have been a vital strategic achievement in 1941, 1942, even 1943--had become no more than marvelous circus tricks by the time they were achieved in 1944 and 1945."

A local salvage company bought *Tirpitz*'s remains from the Norwegian government, but by that time her task was completed. One by one, during the fall and winter of 1944, the carriers and battleships of the Home Fleet, previously held captive at Scapa Flow by the threatening presence of the last German battleship, sailed off to the Pacific. They were, however, too late. Badly needed there in 1942 and 1943, it is hard to argue they made any appreciable difference to victory in 1944 and 1945.

## "FLEET IN BEING" DEFINED:

The concept of maintaining a "fleet in being" was first developed in the seventeenth century, in the aftermath of the Battle of Beachy Head. In June 1690 the British strategic situation was grim. The exiled King James II had, with French support, gathered a large army in Ireland. To counter this threat King William III had taken the greater part of his regular forces across the Irish Sea, leaving a sparsely defended England under the regency of Queen Mary. The British fleet, dispersed between the Channel and the coast of Spain, was ill equipped and lethargically led.

On May 30 Admiral Lord Torrington took command of the Channel Fleet with 50 men of war and 20 fireships. Only three weeks later, at anchor off the Isle of Wight, he was surprised to learn that the French were just the other side of the island, also at anchor, but with 80 men of war and 30 fireships. Writing that day to Secretary of State Lord Nottingham he said, "My Lord, I know my business and I will do my best with what I have, but pray remember it is not my fault that the fleet is no stronger."

Torrington's preferred course of action was to take up a defensive position among the shoals at the mouth of the Thames where, difficult to attack but able to come out at any time, he could hold the French in check. However, goaded by ill-informed instructions from London, he reluctantly gave battle although, realizing he had no hope of winning, he took great care not to be beaten. British losses off Beachy Head were high, the enemy's minimal. The French landed in Devon and burned a small village, creating great fears of imminent invasion. Then, beaten off by the local militia, they retired to Brest. Meanwhile King William, victorious at the Battle of the Boyne, had driven James and the French out of Ireland, securing the Union for over two centuries.

Torrington, whose unaggressive tactics were deemed to have lost the Battle of Beachy Head, was the subject of a politically motivated court-martial, but received a naval-inspired honorable acquittal. In his defense he argued: ". . . most men were afraid that the French would invade, but I was always of another opinion; for I always said that, whilst we had a fleet in being, they would not dare to make an attempt . . . whilst we observe the French, they can make no attempt either on sea or on shore, but with great disadvantages; and if we are beaten, all is exposed to their mercy."

Two and a half centuries later, on the day following the sinking of the *Tirpitz*, the *Times of London* wrote: "The importance of this great ship as a threat has been all out of proportion to her actual achievement; but as a threat, her strategic value was that of a fleet in being, and capital ships had always to be kept ready to fight her if she should make a sortie."

# 7 ERNEST KING AND THE BRITISH PACIFIC FLEET

## THE CONFERENCE AT QUEBEC, 1944 ("OCTAGON")

*[This article originated largely because of my suspicion that Fleet Admiral Ernest King, USN, must have had better reasons than simple Anglophobia (something he was often accused of) when during 1944 he strongly resisted the addition of the British Pacific Fleet to the already enormous naval forces that the United States was assembling in the Pacific in preparation for the final defeat of Japan. The following analysis is based on nearly three years of research. It was published in the (peer reviewed) Journal of Military History in 2001 and awarded the Society of Military History's Moncado Prize the following year.]*

Britain's Pacific Fleet represented the largest aggregation of naval power the country had assembled during World War II. However, it arrived in U.S. Fleet Admiral Chester W. Nimitz's theater at a time when his own command was at the apogee of its strength, so vastly superior to its ally that the Royal Navy (RN) was barely noticed in the roster of available forces. Thus, in most accounts of the naval war against Japan, the British contribution remains a minor footnote or, as one writer comments, "an embarrassing endpiece to the story of more heroic endeavors made elsewhere."[1] Indeed, the Royal Navy encountered considerable difficulties in taking what it deemed to be its appropriate role in the war against Japan, a matter that many of the more comprehensive accounts, most of them British, tend rather simplistically to blame on the prejudices of Fleet Admiral Ernest J. King, Chief of Naval Operations (CNO) and Commander in Chief, U.S. Navy. One narrative, for example, refers to the "Anglophobic Admiral Ernest King's . . . determination to keep the Limeys out of the picture so that the US Navy should have the sole honor and glory of . . . avenging Pearl Harbor." The biographer of British Pacific Fleet commander Admiral Bruce Fraser noted that "Fraser needed no reminding that the formidable Anglophobe Fleet Admiral 'Ernie' King, US Chief of Naval Operations, would do everything he could to 'keep the Limeys from muscling in' on the defeat of Japan."[2] Another historian maintained that Admiral King disliked the British, observing however that the reason for his Anglophobia was obscure. More recently, an American writer submits that "Admiral King, a notorious Anglophobe, had not wanted Britain to interfere at all in his war and did everything to prevent it."[3]

King's British contemporaries, it should be noted, do not seem to have subscribed to the simple theory that his prejudices dictated Allied Pacific War dispositions. Field Marshal Sir John Dill's biographer, for example, wrote of King that "There was substance to the unabashed Anglophobia of his public image, but it was not the whole truth. Dill confessed to a 'sneaking regard' for him. . . . Yet Dill also identified the quality which, being undisguised, so infuriated the British. 'He does not trust us a yard.'" Prime Minister Winston S. Churchill's military chief of staff, General Hastings L. "Pug" Ismay, suggested that King, although "intolerant and suspicious of all things British, particularly the Royal Navy, . . . was almost equally intolerant and suspicious of the American army."[4] A more recent British writer concedes that while King was the chief opponent of any British contribution to the Pacific War, and his Anglophobia was widely recognized, "There was indeed a certain validity to King's view of the RN's inexperience, and an understandable reluctance to allow a foreign navy to share, however modestly, in the credit for victory over the Japanese." American historians have naturally been less concerned with Britain's quite small contribution to the naval defeat of Japan, and more understanding of King's position. Samuel Eliot Morison adopts a reasoned perspective: "It was not that King was anti-British, or that he disliked sharing the anticipated spoils of a Pacific victory. The root of his objections, purely and simply, was logistics."[5]

Ernest King

There was a tongue-in-cheek remark about King, made by one of his daughters, repeated by Naval personnel at the time that "he is the most even-tempered person in the United States Navy. He is always in a rage." Roosevelt once described King as a man who "shaves every morning with a blow torch."

None of the relevant histories suggest that King was a lovable man. According to his mythology, he shaved with a blowtorch. His principal biographer describes him as unyielding, intellectually arrogant, stubborn, and egotistical. Indeed, it was King himself who reportedly claimed that it was only "when they get in trouble they send for the sons-a-bitches."[6] It is clear that he had little time for those he deemed inefficient, and less for those who, in his opinion, were not totally dedicated to prosecuting the war against Japan. Nevertheless, although the British did from time to time fail to meet both these tests, it remains difficult to believe that President Franklin D. Roosevelt's "shrewdest of strategists"[7] would have fought to keep the Royal Navy out of the Central Pacific if personal prejudice was his only motive. It is indeed possible that King was Anglophobic, although it is hard to reconcile such a general antipathy with his British ancestry, the pleasure he took in his visits to England, and the respectful and often warm relations he developed with many of his wartime British colleagues.[8] More likely he was, as one contemporary commented, pro-American rather than anti-British.[9] He also had very clear ideas regarding how the war against Japan should be fought. He resented the use of American resources for any purpose other than the destruction of the Japanese, and strongly resisted any strategy that would slow progress towards that end.[10] However, as this article argues, there were significant reasons--political, economic, and operational--behind King's worry that a British fleet in the Pacific might be more hindrance than help. Historical tensions, only partially submerged during the war, may also have fueled King's concerns. These factors, although poorly articulated at the time, influenced much of the debate in September 1944 when President Roosevelt, Prime Minister Churchill, and their staffs assembled in Quebec for Octagon, the last of the great Anglo-American military strategy conferences during World War II.[11]

## The Quebec Conference, September 1944

The participation of the British Pacific Fleet in the final phase of the war against Japan--a question that had been simmering for well over a year--was a key item on the Octagon agenda. Although the conference participants expected Germany to collapse at any moment, Japan's surrender was not anticipated until the spring of 1946 at the earliest. The battles for the Philippines, Iwo Jima, and Okinawa were all in the future, as were American incendiary air raids on Japan and Japanese Kamikaze attacks on the Allied navies. While the Allies had no doubts about ultimate victory, the U.S. Joint Chiefs of Staff (JCS), who bore the principal responsibility for the war against Japan, anticipated continued tough resistance.[12]

Octagon Conference, Sep 1944; sitting: Marshall, Leahy, Roosevelt, Churchill, Brooke, Dill; standing: Hollis, Ismay, King, Portal, Arnold, Cunningham

The British delegation came to Octagon with an agreed position regarding its country's role in the Pacific War. A sizeable Royal Navy carrier task force could be made available in the Pacific by mid-1945. The British government wanted to see it employed under American command in the main operations against Japan, clearly implying those being conducted by Admiral Nimitz in the Central Pacific. Should the Americans be unwilling to place a British fleet under Nimitz, the distant second choice would be Empire land, sea, and air forces, which would operate in the Southwest Pacific Area under U.S. General Douglas MacArthur. [13]

For the British, reaching agreement had not been easy. The debate between Churchill, who favored operations whereby British Empire forces would liberate the Southeast Asia colonies (referred to contemptuously by First Sea Lord Sir Andrew Cunningham as recapturing their own rubber trees), and the Foreign Office and the Chiefs of Staff, who wanted to see their forces engaged in the Central Pacific, lasted for most of 1944 prior to Octagon.[14] The primary issue in London was political rather than military. Once Roosevelt had made it clear to Churchill that he saw no need for Allied support in the Pacific, at least until mid-1945, the Prime Minister's advisers appear to have given greater priority to laying the ground for fruitful postwar Anglo-American financial negotiations, than they did to the defeat of Japan.[15] Nevertheless, it was only on the eve of Octagon that Churchill finally gave in to his Chiefs of Staff who, believing a Central Pacific presence would use scarce military resources more economically and with greater public visibility, threatened resignation if they did not get their way.[16]

American staff analyses of the British proposal clearly favored an Empire task force operating under MacArthur's command, despite the fact that both the General and Australian Prime Minister John Curtin feared that this would unsettle the former's well-established command arrangements. More significantly, the staff focused attention on the considerable American support that would be needed for the contemplated British activities. The Admiralty had furnished little information regarding the logistical backing it intended to provide, and the Americans were concerned that the Royal Navy did not recognize the serious difficulties involved in keeping a major naval force supplied at sea thousands of miles from its main bases.[17]

Admiral William D. Leahy, Roosevelt's personal military chief of staff and the senior officer on the JCS, recognized the validity of the American concerns, but thought it would be unwise to express anxiety about the Royal Navy's capabilities. He felt the British should be informed immediately that the Joint Chiefs would be pleased to have the assistance of any force their ally could send to the Pacific. They should not dwell too much on details. The committee agreed with this diplomatic approach, approving a memorandum to be presented to the Anglo-American Combined Chiefs of Staff, welcoming a British naval task force in the main operations against Japan. Its initial use would be on the western flank of the Southwest Pacific advance. It would have to be balanced and self-supporting. Noteworthy is the fact that there is no record of Admiral King contributing to any of these discussions; indeed, there was no opportunity for the Combined Chiefs to discuss their differences before the first plenary meeting of the conference convened, and events overtook all the earlier careful thinking.[18]

In his opening remarks, the Prime Minister emphasized that the British Empire was eager to play the greatest possible part in the defeat of Japan and offered a fleet to take part in the main operations under American command. It would be a powerful and well-balanced force whose fleet train, of "ample proportions," would render it independent of shore-based support for a considerable period of time. He asked the President how it would be employed.[19]

The President replied that it would be used in any way possible, but King interjected that the matter should be studied by the Combined Chiefs. The Prime Minister insisted: the offer had been made, was it accepted? The President agreed that it was. General Ismay recalled that Roosevelt's acceptance was a surprise to all in view of King's well-known opposition.[20]

When the Combined Chiefs met the following morning, matters appeared a little less clear. British Chief of the Imperial General Staff Sir Alan Brooke asked the Joint Chiefs to redefine their earlier position in light of the proposal made by the Prime Minister and accepted by the President. It was essential for political reasons that the British fleet participate in the main operations against Japan.[21] The ensuing, often rancorous, discussion centered on what, if anything, had actually been agreed the day before and what was really meant by "main operations against Japan." All this was complicated by reluctance on King's part to accept the presence of a fleet he was convinced he could neither employ nor support. King suggested that the matter be referred to the President, at which point Leahy rather brusquely told him that if he felt that way he should take it up with his Commander in Chief himself. Although there is no reference in the official minutes, Admiral Cunningham remembered stronger words:

> King was finally called to order by Admiral Leahy, the President's Chief of Staff, with the remark: "I don't think we should wash our dirty linen in public." King, and the other American Chiefs of Staff against him, eventually gave way, but with very bad grace.[22]

The Combined Chiefs of Staff thus agreed that a British fleet would participate in the main operations against Japan, its precise employment to be decided in accordance with prevailing circumstances.[23]

Whether or not Cunningham correctly recalled Leahy's admonition to King not to wash dirty linen in public, the official record of the Octagon meetings does raise the question of why the CNO remained so silent during the Joint Chiefs' earlier private conversations on the role of the British Pacific Fleet. King thereby failed to rally his colleagues' support for his position during subsequent meetings with the British. There is, of course, always the possibility that he was so outspoken that little of what he said found its way into the record. King was a logical man, however, with a fine grasp of the technical aspects of operating large carrier fleets, something his British counterpart lacked. He may have felt that the factual arguments for his position were so obvious and compelling that they would require little further support from him. He thus could have been taken aback when the final decision came to the senior political level before the Combined Chiefs had had a chance to discuss it. Then, given Churchill's claims regarding the capabilities of his fleet's supply train, he was faced with an impossible choice: either suggest that the Prime Minister was lying (which arguably was the case)[24] or retreat into a petulant and poorly expressed rear guard action, which he did.

The British felt that the Octagon Conference had opened and closed in a "blaze of friendship."[25] Although that may have been the prevailing sentiment, a more rigorous assessment must consider whether sending a major portion of its navy into the Central Pacific was the best way of achieving London's primary goal: impressing American public opinion so greatly that economic aid would continue well after the war's end. After five years of war, the Royal Navy suffered from shortcomings that appeared more obvious to Washington than they did to the naval leadership in London, at least at the highest levels. King's practice of rotating his staff between the Navy Department and the various theaters of war gave him excellent understanding of his own and the Allied navies' operational capabilities.[26] In contrast, there seems to have been a notable reluctance within the Admiralty to acknowledge any serious weaknesses, although among the working staff some did appear to recognize their existence. Had the Prime Minister's military advisers been more realistic about their nation's naval capabilities compared with those of their much more powerful ally, they might have realized, as historian Correlli Barnett points out, that their Central Pacific strategy unnecessarily exposed "Britain's shrunken relative stature as a power."[27]

## **Political concerns**

Although Octagon was, in fact, one of the less significant of the Churchill-Roosevelt conferences, its conclusions appear to have made all except Admiral King happy. Yet, while the two national leaders were negotiating the high politics of Britain's role in a postwar world and how to sustain it economically, difficult issues remained unresolved which would complicate the alliance during the remainder of the Pacific War. For example, there still remained a considerable ambivalence in American opinion regarding Britain's proper role in the drive against Japan's Home Islands or, indeed, whether such a role existed at all. On one side, there were those in Washington who looked beyond hostilities to the postwar world and agreed with Roosevelt that the British had to play a major part in the defeat of Japan. Immediately prior to the Octagon conference, U.S. Ambassador to Britain John G. Winant had written to presidential adviser Harry L. Hopkins asserting that failure to permit British participation in the main war against Japan would "make for schisms in the postwar years that will defeat everything that men died for in this war." Roosevelt received similar advice from Secretary of State Cordell Hull, who also wanted to bring the British into war operations in the Far East to the greatest possible extent. Failure to do so, he argued, would create a hostile popular reaction, while expansion of British exports as a result of reversion to a peace economy would be much resented by the business community.

Postwar Anglo-American relations would suffer accordingly.[28]

Realists, in contrast, saw matters in more complex terms: historian Robert Sherwood later commented that, whereas in Europe the British and Americans had a clear and agreed objective—Berlin--"In South East Asia, on the other hand, the British and Americans were fighting two wars for different purposes." The British, he implied, were more concerned with restoring their own empire than defeating Japan's. Hull pointed out to Roosevelt, prior to Octagon, that "All reports indicate that the military operations of SEAC are aimed primarily at the resurgence of British political and economic ascendancy in South East Asia and the restoration of British prestige."[29] Americans in Admiral Louis Mountbatten's South East Asia Command put it more succinctly: SEAC, they said, stood for "Save England's Asian Colonies."

Uninformed of the President's anxiety about the world order after victory, and unswayed by considerations of putative national interests, the majority of Americans remained strongly opposed to colonialism in all its forms. A 1944 *Washington Post* article described Churchill's memorable declaration that he had no intention of presiding over the liquidation of the British Empire as "a horrible example of the British government's intransigence on matters of empire." Two years earlier, *Life* magazine had written an open letter to the British people, urging them to quit fighting a war to hold the Empire together since such was certainly not among most Americans' war aims.[30] Indeed, to some British observers, the paramount American war aim at times seemed to be the dismantling of their empire. Moreover, as historian John Charmley points out: "The very speed with which the Japanese overran the British Empire in the Far East convinced many Americans that the British were not only imperialists, but bungling imperialists."[31] During a global war against what was seen to be a far worse tyranny, Americans were prepared to associate themselves with imperial systems they deemed distasteful, be they Soviet or British, but that did not mean they liked them any the more. Although King reputedly disdained public opinion, undoubtedly he was acutely conscious of the likely negative popular reaction if American losses were incurred in restoring colonial rule.

American reluctance to become involved in the recovery of imperial possessions did, however, have a certain disingenuousness to it. The principal problem was that, despite major successes against the Imperial Japanese Navy, the Americans had barely touched the enemy's ground forces which, according to an intelligence estimate prepared for the Octagon conference, remained large, fairly well equipped, and very well trained, and as strong or stronger than in 1941.[32] As late as April 1944, the Japanese Army was able to mount Operation Ichi-Go which, over a twelve-month period, cut a broad path through Central and South China. This eliminated the American air bases there and established direct land communications between Manchuria and Indo-China. Outside China, the Japanese Army occupied Burma, Malaya, Hong Kong, Borneo, the Netherlands East Indies, and numerous other Pacific islands. In Burma the Japanese faced a large Allied (mostly British Empire) army in an area whose terrain and internal communications favored the occupier, but whose liberation was deemed by Washington to be essential for supplying the beleaguered Chinese.[33] In the Netherlands East Indies, the intelligence estimate stated, the enemy would maintain strong ground forces despite loss of sea communications in order to continue to deny the Allies access to vital oil and other raw materials.

Although the conviction was not necessarily shared by the naval leadership, a strong body of American opinion felt that Japan would not surrender while her army was still intact. In order to defeat the Imperial Army, it would probably have to be met on the ground, and much of the ground it occupied was part of the British, French, or Dutch empires. These colonial territories could be recaptured either by the Americans or by the British, but the British could not do so without American aid--certainly material, and probably human. Thus Washington was left with a conundrum: how to defeat the Japanese without involving American treasure or manpower in wars of colonial reconquest. It was a puzzle never properly solved, but Washington, recognizing that London's political objectives in the war against Japan differed from its own, remained constantly watchful lest its ally direct its efforts other than towards the immediate defeat of the enemy.

While there were good strategic arguments why a Royal Navy presence in the Southwest Pacific might be encouraged, there were serious countervailing political considerations. Although King thought the British could help the Australians recapture the vital Borneo and Sumatra oil fields, he worried that once they became involved in the East Indies they would attempt to colonize the former Dutch territories for themselves. King, influenced by the writings of Alfred Thayer Mahan, had a clear understanding of the relationship between naval strength and commercial vitality.[34] Southeast Asia contained vital raw materials, hitherto under the control of the colonial powers. American rather than European hegemony would advance Washington's security interests in the area, and important American export markets could be developed.[35] The United States would be better served if the rich resources of Southeast Asia were liberated by American forces and, correspondingly, hurt to the extent the Royal Navy established a meaningful presence there.

Another area of politics, considerably more complex than reflexive anti-imperialism, also bedeviled decisions regarding Britain's role in the war against Japan: The tensions between the U.S. Navy, intent on developing its Central Pacific strategy, and MacArthur, who felt that progress could be made more efficiently, and honor more rapidly restored, if the advance to Japan focused on a New Guinea-Philippines axis and his Southwest Pacific Area. MacArthur's problem was that he needed a fleet to carry out his plans, and major U.S. Navy units remained firmly under the thumb of Admiral Nimitz, available to MacArthur only as the Joint Chiefs (where on naval matters Ernest King held sway) allowed.

MacArthur wanted a fleet and, in late 1943, in the absence of help from the U.S. Navy, would have welcomed significant British units. In January 1944 strategists meeting at Pearl Harbor supported the shifting of additional naval resources to MacArthur's theater, but King successfully opposed the idea when it reached the Joint Chiefs. For a time, however, the general wrongly believed he had received a mandate to undertake the main thrust against Japan, and requested that all Allied naval forces (including a British Pacific Fleet) be placed under his control, with U.S. Admiral William F. Halsey as their commander. Urging Halsey to assume this command he promised: "How about you, Bill. If you come with me, I'll make you a greater man than Nelson ever dreamed of being." Later, British visitors to MacArthur's headquarters came back saying how much the general would welcome a Royal Navy squadron under his command.[36] At all times, however, emphasis was on the fact that any British fleet would be under the general's control and that existing command arrangements, along functional rather than national lines, would remain unchanged.

Ever sensitive when he felt his prerogatives threatened, MacArthur's suspicions were fully aroused by a 21 July 1944 letter from Admiral King. In it he summarized conversations a month earlier in London regarding British participation in the war against Japan. King warned the general that: "the British may propose certain extensions in the Southeast Asia Theater to include most of the Dutch East Indies . . . after the Southwest Pacific forces have become established in the Philippines."[37]

The general's reaction, predictably, was one of outrage and thenceforth his attitude towards prospective British naval support changed.[38] Instead of welcoming a powerful new addition to his command, he became fixated with concerns that the unscrupulous British were going to take away much of his strength and most of his territory. He thanked King for disclosing "the British plans for taking over a large portion of the Southwest Pacific Area" and indicated his strong opposition, which he felt would be seconded by the Dutch and Australians. The British, he said, had contributed nothing to his campaign, and now wanted to reap the benefits of his successes. They would provide little other than a command structure, would look to him for necessary manpower, and would expect the United States to support them logistically. MacArthur added that the presence of British forces in the Southwest Pacific Area would be most welcome and that strenuous efforts had already been made to secure their assistance. His concern was the proposed change in command arrangements which, he felt, were based entirely upon their anticipated political and economic benefits.

Despite assurances from Washington that any British fleet in the Southwest Pacific would come under his control, seeds of suspicion had been sowed in MacArthur's fertile mind. He feared that this apparent change of heart was merely a subterfuge, enabling London to achieve its more ambitious objectives later. Although he would still welcome an Allied fleet in his area, he was even more determined that it should not arrive until lines of authority had been firmly established in his favor.[39]

King's motives for sending this letter are unclear (although the Joint Chiefs' concern that a British presence in the Pacific would provide London with arguments for combined strategic planning does provide a plausible rationale). Combined planning for the defeat of Japan, similar to that employed in the European theater, was something the Americans wanted to avoid at all costs.[40] Perhaps King raised the possibility of change in the Southwest Pacific command structure as a straw man; he knew that MacArthur would reject it, and this might eliminate them for the whole Pacific, not just MacArthur's theater. Whatever the reason, the letter certainly complicated the issue. Before King sent his message, it could be argued that the general would have welcomed a British fleet; after the letter (even assuming London's willingness to accept the assignment) the fleet's arrival would have been controversial.

The Royal Navy also became an involuntary participant another American political dispute: The struggle over wartime resource allocation. At various times, the army, the Congress, and the budget bureau all claimed that the navy was capturing a disproportionate share of national production capacity. In his account of the politics of American World War II naval expansion, historian Joel Davidson asserts that, before the Pearl Harbor attack, United States naval construction was predicated on the assumption that, should Britain and France be defeated, the United States would find itself in a two-ocean naval war against the combined Axis fleets, possibly augmented by captured units of the Allied navies.[41] In 1944, the situation had changed and the Allies enjoyed a two to one advantage over the remaining Axis surface fleets. However, King continued to argue that every ship American yards could build would be needed to support amphibious operations in the Pacific, especially since losses were expected to mount as the war moved closer to Japan. Although the U.S. Navy's high command largely managed to convince its civilian superiors of this, powerful voices including the Office of War Mobilization and Army Chief of Staff George C. Marshall were beginning to question the continued production of new warships in the face of changing conditions.[42]

The British entered the picture in 1944 when it appeared that they would be able to make substantial naval forces available in the Pacific. Once a potential threat should it fall into the hands of the enemy, by early 1944 the Royal Navy represented a handy alternative to the continued high pace of American naval construction.

Informed Washington opinion suggested that the substantial shipbuilding program could be significantly curtailed. Nevertheless, throughout 1944, the U.S. Navy continued to ignore possible British help when forecasting warship requirements. The British offer at Octagon to furnish a powerful fleet for service in the Pacific must therefore have embarrassed King by providing timely ammunition to those who were urging serious cutbacks in American warship production. Much current American construction would not be available for two years or more, and here apparently was an immediately available force of modern aircraft carriers with all appropriate escorts.[43] Thus, in order to justify continued new construction, King would have to provide the administration and his fellow chiefs with compelling reasons, in addition to those already advanced, why the Royal Navy would not represent a significant enhancement of Allied power in the war against Japan.[44] The arguments were at hand, both economic and operational. King's inability or unwillingness to articulate them at Octagon meant that an important British role in the Central Pacific became enshrined in a Presidential-Prime Ministerial communiqué and would continue until Japan surrendered.

## Economic Considerations

The second main concern of London's delegation to the Quebec conference was Britain's parlous economic situation, and its bleak outlook should American Lend-Lease aid be discontinued. Indeed, from the British Treasury's point of view, this was probably the principal purpose of the meeting. Only the British, with Empire support, had fought the Germans from first to last, and in 1944 they were approaching the limit of their endurance. Once there was peace in Europe they would rightfully seek some improvement in their lot. Moreover, if their country was to be able to pay its way in the postwar world, there must be some reversion to civilian production and some attention devoted to the export trade.⁴⁵ American opinion on this matter was divided. Lend-Lease authorities wanted to restrict aid to Britain to material needed for the war in the Pacific. Indeed, many in the U.S. military felt that assistance should be discontinued, since they doubted that their ally's help was necessary to defeat Japan. The President and his political aides, on the other hand, saw things differently: They wanted Britain to perform a leading role in postwar Europe, something it would be unable to do without American economic help. The Royal Navy's vigorous participation in the Pacific War would provide the Roosevelt administration with a persuasive argument when it asked Congress to continue much needed peacetime assistance.⁴⁶

Fortunately for the British, the matter was laid to rest early in the conference when the President accepted the Prime Minister's offer of a Royal Navy fleet in the Pacific. Lend-Lease would continue, providing military supplies sufficient to permit Britain to play her sought-after role against Japan, and civilian supplies designed to allow a reasonable pace of conversion to a non-war economy. Yet Octagon provided further evidence (if such was needed) that Britain no longer had the power to play a global military role without American support. Indeed, a cynic might have questioned how the British were suddenly able to promise a major presence in the Pacific when only a few months earlier they had been forced to seek the loan of an American carrier and a French battleship in order to counter Japanese threats in the Indian Ocean.⁴⁷

King's opposition to the Octagon agreement was clearly justified in hard economic terms: Lend-Lease credits to Britain, while discussed only in the broadest financial outline at Quebec, would, in due course, translate into the provision of specific weapons and supplies. The Chief of Naval Operations' job was to take the resources made available to him by the enormously productive American economy, and put them to work to bring the war against Japan to a rapid close.

From a purely military point of view, he and his fellow Chiefs had to determine whether assets diverted from their own services for use by their ally would help or hinder this objective. For example, the British were relying greatly on American-supplied escort carriers (CVEs) and naval aircraft, both of which were in short supply as the tempo of Pacific operations increased. However, severe manpower shortages and modification to British standards had caused considerable delays in bringing Lend-Lease CVEs into action. At the end of 1943, out of thirty-three CVEs delivered, only two were in active service.[48] Naval historian Morison noted that the British failed to make good use of American-built CVEs which, he argued, spent too long in dockyards between operations and, during the time they were at sea, operated inefficiently compared to American counterparts. Admiral Max Horton, the Royal Navy's Commander in Chief, Western Approaches, agreed, urging the Admiralty to use fewer CVEs rather than man them inadequately.[49]

The Royal Navy also insisted on modifying its Lend-Lease aircraft; pilots' oxygen and radio systems, for example, were "Anglicized" to permit the use of British helmets and oxygen masks, while F4U "Corsairs" destined for British use required a modified wing-fold arrangement in order to fit into British hangars. This meant that airplanes intended for use by the Royal Navy in the Pacific could not be delivered directly from U.S. Navy local reserves but rather had to wend their way along a lengthy route via the North Atlantic, the Mediterranean, and the Indian Ocean.[50] Furthermore, front-line deficiencies could not normally be filled by a simple local transfer. King, who had already questioned why the British could not use material his own navy found perfectly acceptable, may well have wondered whether supplying equipment for the Royal Navy's future employment in the Pacific represented the most effective use of American industrial capacity.[51]

## **Operational factors**

Even if the American economy could find enough material surplus to the needs of its own navy to supply British requirements, the question still remained whether these resources would be employed productively in operations against the enemy. This first became an issue in Allied planning in 1943 when, following the surrender of the Italian fleet, Churchill offered to send a large and powerful naval force to the Bay of Bengal via the Pacific. That August, during one of King's periodic conferences with Nimitz, the CNO's chief of staff, Rear Admiral Charles M. "Savvy" Cooke, explained the British plan to advance from Singapore up the coast of China. They had apparently given no thought of the requirements for supplies and air support. If the British were to be employed usefully anywhere in the Pacific their fleet must be balanced and they must arrange their own logistics. King saw, and would continue to see, serious difficulties in meeting either of these requirements. [52]

King worried not only that the Royal Navy was ignoring the enormous problems of supplying a fleet in the Pacific, but also that British requirements would strain American local resources. Although to British eyes, the Americans equipped their navy in a manner which seemed almost luxurious in its lavishness, the system had in fact been carefully designed to fit the needs of the U.S. Pacific Fleet. There was, as one British admiral admitted, nothing to spare.[53]

The joint staff study noted earlier pointed out that America's shipping capabilities were barely sufficient to support the planned deployment of its own forces, while shortages of advanced base facilities and training airfields, and lack of land masses and harbors all precluded logistic support from combined Allied sources. The American advanced base procurement program had never contemplated the addition of British units. Shore facilities in rear areas were already being "rolled up" for movement forward and could not be made available to the Royal Navy.

The Royal Navy would have to provide its own ammunition and ammunition supply ships, while substantial additional tanker and refrigerated cargo capacity would be required to meet its fuel and food requirements. Existing dry dock facilities were fully utilized on a twenty-four-hour-a-day basis, while yards at Pearl Harbor and on the West Coast were operating at capacity. The study noted caustically that British ships coming to American yards for repairs and alterations required more work than did their American equivalents. This was due to the amount of obsolete material in Royal Navy ships, as well as to the fact that their crews did less of their own repair work than did the Americans. [54]

Unfortunately, Pacific Ocean logistics represented a totally new development for a Royal Navy whose short-range, cold-climate fleet had seldom operated far from its established bases, and had limited experience in replenishment at sea. Moreover, the country had lost much of it prewar merchant tonnage, while greatly increased emphasis on warship construction meant that other building had fallen far short of replacement needs. Britain thus lacked the resources needed to assemble an adequate supply train. The U.S. Navy, on the other hand, had put together an extremely efficient logistical force, well designed to work closely with the new fast carriers.[55]

What support shipping the British could provide was largely worn out. Tankers were too few in number, slow, and inadequate for the task, while oiling gear, hoses, and fittings were poorly designed. Royal Navy ships refueled at sea mostly by picking up a hose trailed astern of the tanker, an awkward, unseamanlike business compared with the American method of refueling alongside.[56] Lack of proper equipment and insufficient practice often meant burst hoses or excessive time at risk to submarine attack while holding a constant course during fueling.

Realizing that a major Pacific effort was incompatible with other demands on sea transport, Churchill commanded that merchant shipping must have priority, and the British Pacific Fleet must tailor its size to what was left over to support it.[57] As one historian notes, the Prime Minister's statement at the 1944 Quebec conference that the Royal Navy would have a fleet train capable of supporting Pacific operations for a considerable time was "at best misleading and at worst a mischievous travesty of the truth." As the British official history recognized, the most obvious impact of adding a British fleet to Nimitz's command would be to increase supply difficulties rather than adding to its striking power.[58]

Apart from the vexatious question of logistics, which on its own provided ample basis for the Americans' reluctance to have the Royal Navy alongside them in the Pacific, Admiral King and his staff had serious doubts as to whether the British had any real understanding of the kind of war that was being fought there. The Central Pacific strategy adopted by the Joint Chiefs of Staff in mid-1943 represented an innovative development in the war against Japan, based on the mobility afforded by the U.S. Navy's new fast carriers. King's solution to the dilemma posed by a still strong Japanese army was effectively to ignore it, using swift bold naval strikes to cut off the homeland from its forward positions and vital supplies. King must have wondered whether a navy which had never operated for long periods of time away from its permanent bases, and which had little practice in replenishing at sea could operate alongside his better equipped and more experienced task forces. Moreover, the Royal Navy had seldom handled carriers in large numbers, a problem King had studied carefully as far back as 1938.[59]

Senior British naval officers present in the Pacific recognized the validity of King's concerns. The official British history of the Pacific

War acknowledges how little the Royal Navy knew about carrier warfare as practiced by the Americans; they had to fight alongside the exponents of the new naval warfare since, as Admiral Bruce Fraser admitted: "In no other way could we have learned the technical lessons which this type of warfare taught."[60]

Admiral Sir Philip Vian, Britain's carrier commander in the Pacific, wrote after the war:

> *There was, however, another and better reason why Admiral King was opposed to the Royal Navy joining in the Pacific War. While the Royal Navy had been operating in, and trained and equipped for the relatively short-range warfare of the Mediterranean, Home Waters and the Atlantic, an entirely new form of campaigning had been evolved in the vast spaces of the Pacific.*
>
> *Before joining the Americans we needed to be adept at using a great many more aircraft at a time, and for long periods.*[61]

To British observers, American carriers appeared much better equipped and more highly trained in operating aircraft than the Royal Navy's.[62] In early 1944, anxious to draw Japanese surface and air units away from Nimitz's Central Pacific operations, King agreed to lend USS *Saratoga* to the Royal Navy's Eastern Fleet, where she would operate under the command of Admiral Sir James F. Somerville, together with his then only carrier, HMS *Illustrious*. One account of this episode described the American ship's efficient flight deck operations as "something of an eye opener for British personnel accustomed to a more leisurely approach to carrier operations."[63] Her take-offs and landings were much speedier and her air groups took less time to rendezvous, an important factor when managing strikes of thirty to forty aircraft. The Americans benefited from decks which were bigger, uncluttered by guns and, being wooden, provided a better surface for taxiing, while deck-edge lifts and faster moving barriers also helped. In addition, American pilots profited from a standardized landing-on drill, something the Royal Navy's Fleet Air Arm appeared to lack.[64]

As the *New York Times*' military correspondent, Hanson Baldwin, wrote immediately after the Octagon Conference, the type of combat the Americans were undertaking in the Central Pacific was very different from the Royal Navy's experience. The British would need training, and while that was being done they would be more of a hindrance than a help.[65] Recognizing this, Somerville had asked the Americans to spend some time with his people to ensure that they understood the latest techniques for operating carriers in this new environment.

*Saratoga*'s air officers were surprised to find that, unlike their own navy, the Royal Navy had few aviators at senior levels. In 1944 only one British flag officer was qualified as a pilot, and none of the four fleet carriers designated for the Pacific Fleet would be commanded by an aviator.[66] The Fleet's carrier admiral would be Vian, an heroic but temperamental cruiser commander. Thus, it was not surprising that Somerville and his senior officers had some difficulty understanding the tactics *Saratoga*'s aviators were trying to teach their flyers.[67]

Americans operating with the British noted the marked difference in carrier design adopted by the two navies. American flight decks were wooden superstructures mounted on a partially armored hull. The British, on the other hand, concerned at the threat of shore-based enemy air in the North and Mediterranean Seas, had adopted armored hangars, believing that the ship's aircraft would be better off stowed below during air attacks. The armored hangar, however, imposed severe operational costs in terms of numbers of aircraft carried and the pace of their operations. British air groups numbered about half as many planes as were carried by comparable American ships, which meant that there were insufficient aircraft to mount effective combat air patrols while simultaneously saturating a target area.[68]

Thus, apart from the vexatious question of logistics, Admiral King and his staff had serious doubts as to whether in 1944 the British had any real understanding of the kind of war that was being conducted in the Pacific, or had the right equipment to fight it. The Americans questioned the value of a navy that had never operated for long periods of time away from its permanent bases, had insufficient training in replenishment at sea, and whose non-aviator flag officers had little experience of administering carriers in large numbers.[69] The need for considerable training of air group and flight deck complements to bring them up to American standards, the major refits required for Pacific service, and the lack of operational capacity, meant that a British fleet, even supposing it was, as Churchill promised, fully self-supporting, would likely require so much in the way of U.S. Navy facilities that it would be counterproductive alongside the Americans' battle-hardened task forces. With these factors in mind, King's desire to employ only American ships in the Central Pacific becomes more understandable.

## **Historical tensions**

None of this is meant to imply that King's resistance to a British presence in the Pacific was entirely objective. Anglo-American naval relations were burdened with considerable history, much of it adversarial, going back to the War of 1812 and beyond. There was, within the U.S. Navy officer corps, a long held institutional jealousy of the Royal Navy, and King was very much a product of that institution.

Ernest King had a front-row seat for much of the U.S. Navy's uneven twentieth-century relationship with its British counterpart. As a junior staff officer during World War I, he listened while his superiors accused the Royal Navy of failure in several key areas, including a poorly executed blockade, an inconclusive result at Jutland, inadequate preparations for antisubmarine warfare, and an unwillingness to adopt a convoy system. In addition, the Admiralty's apparent lack of a strategic plan provided early evidence of a preference for opportunism which would frequently irritate the methodical King during the next war.[70]

Strategic and commercial conflict provided ample grounds for friction between the two navies during the interwar period. A series of naval limitation treaties failed to mollify either of the powers. Despite the diplomats' general satisfaction with the arrangements, their naval advisers were less happy, each believing that the agreements had carried a high price in terms of security. The last of these treaties was agreed upon during the 1930 London conference, but by then Anglo-American naval rivalry had been firmly reestablished. Only two years later Ernest King discussed the likelihood of war with Britain or Japan in his Naval War College thesis. In it he argued dispassionately that the United States should be prepared for either since both were possible.[71]

British attitudes towards their ally during World War II did not always endear them to Americans. King's biographer wrote, "They ...came as seasoned warriors, ready to counsel and advise the inexperienced Americans." The British, with scant justification, continued to patronize their American colleagues, who in turn remained resentful of their ally, though with little reason.[72] Alan G. Kirk, who spent a considerable amount of the war working with the British, recalled that Royal Navy commanders "were so convinced-- and with reason from long historical background--of having exercised complete command of the sea, that they could not understand how anyone could question or doubt that their methods were not perfect." It was Ernest King, whose "outspoken bluntness went to extremes,"[73] who said directly what many of his colleagues had long been thinking in private. As early as 1942, while Admiral Cunningham headed the British Admiralty delegation in Washington, King felt obliged to point out that, although the British had been managing world affairs for some three hundred years, the U.S. Navy now had something to say about the war at sea, and that fact should be faced, whether palatable or not. Later, at the January 1943 "Symbol" conference, King determined to raise his colleagues' consciousness, saying: "The United States now has the principal power; therefore we should take the lead." However, the Royal Navy, long accustomed to command at sea, remained unwilling to acknowledge that it might have to operate subordinate to the world's most powerful navy.[74]

\* \* \* \* \* \*

So, as the war continued, and the balance of maritime power tilted more and more in favor of the Americans, Ernest King found himself in the position of having to embarrass what had been for long the world's dominant navy by implying that not only was its help unwanted, but that it might actually prove a liability. Nevertheless, he had a war to win in the Pacific, and his ally's sensibilities were low on his list of priorities. The evidence shows that his position was not unreasonable. Explaining it away as based largely on personal prejudice unjustly diminishes a great naval leader.

But the question whether King's position in September 1944 made sense must also be considered in the broader context of alliance warfare, and particularly the problems faced when the relative strength of the members was changing significantly. Both London and Washington had one overriding goal in the Far East: the complete defeat of Japan. Beneath apparent unity of military purpose, however, there were, as already noted, considerable differences with regards to desired political outcomes. With benefit of hindsight, therefore, one must ask whether the presence of the British Pacific Fleet helped or hindered attainment of the military goal. More importantly, given the fact that both sides realized that the Royal Navy's principal purpose in those final months was political rather than military; did its presence in the Pacific help or hinder the achievement of the respective nations' policy objectives?

The story of the British Pacific Fleet has been well dealt with elsewhere.[75] Most of the histories, however, to the extent they consider the question of net contribution at all, do so in isolation from the overall Allied naval effort against Japan. They focus more on the gallantry and determination with which the Royal Navy fought on the left flank of the vast armada arrayed against the Japanese on Okinawa, and less on its weaknesses. It is largely the records of the British participants which disclose the full extent to which their fleet had to rely on supplies obtained from local American sources in the closing weeks of the war, in direct contravention of the understanding reached at Octagon that the fleet would be self-supporting. Moreover, during the considerable absences from the battle, caused by its replenishment requirements, the British Pacific Fleet was quite effectively replaced by escort carriers from the U.S. Navy's Task Group 52.1. The ships of the very type that, in King's opinion, the British employed uneconomically elsewhere.[76] There is thus considerable evidence to support the argument that the vast resources deployed by the Royal Navy in the Pacific might have been provided directly and on a more cost-effective basis by the Americans.

Of greater significance, however, is the question whether the British Pacific Fleet could have survived beyond the fall of 1945 had an invasion of Japan proved necessary. At least one authoritative source thinks not. Writing on 26 August 1945, the Royal Navy liaison officer on board USS *Shangri La* submitted that: "TF 37 [the British Pacific Fleet] . . . would have been unable to continue operations because of lack of logistic support." H. P. Willmott's extensive study of these events also concludes that: "had the invasion of Kyushu gone ahead the British Pacific Fleet would have been seen to falter in full view of Britain's allies and commonwealth."[77] King was nothing if not a realist, and his planning for operations in late 1945 presumably took this possibility into account. Looked on in this light the British Pacific Fleet may well have been, as Hanson Baldwin suggested, a liability rather than an asset. Dennis Showalter described this situation aptly in his comparison of Anglo-American relations at the end of World War II with the Austro-German relationship in World War I, when the stronger power found itself "expending resources to sustain an ally that stubbornly refused to trim its behavior and pretensions to its diminishing capacities."[78]

Britain's political goals were closely related: national recovery, possible only with assistance from Washington, and retention of its empire as a political and economic unit. American aims were to some extent antithetical: a stable economic order which precluded imperial trading blocs and urged the elimination of colonialism. Examining the political outcome, one must assume that, if the British delegation to Octagon was correct in its belief that a willing and capable ally in the Pacific would receive commensurate postwar financial aid, the reverse might have been true and, without the timely intervention of the atomic bombs, the British could have found themselves playing high stakes economic poker with a losing hand. As it was, there is little evidence to show that events in the summer of 1945 had much influence either way on postwar American financial assistance to Britain, which appears to have been predicated more on current economic concerns than on appreciation for past services. As Dean Acheson succinctly described the 1946 American loan to Britain: "it is not a reward for an ally . . . it is an investment in the future."[79]

The defeat of Japan found Britain with its Asian Empire largely restored, apparently thus achieving its second political objective, although it is questionable what role its Pacific Fleet played in this result. Nevertheless, despite the fact that Churchill did not preside over the liquidation of the British Empire, his successors as Prime Minister did, and he himself lived to see much of it. In the long run therefore, despite the vast investment incurred, the British Pacific Fleet must, in the imperial context, be judged the expensive instrument of a failed policy.

Britain's role as a mid-twentieth-century world power rested on its empire, which in turn was largely a product of its navy. The fleet assembled in the Pacific in 1945 represented an illusionary halt in the steady decline in Britain's influence in Asia, starting off the coast of Malaya in December 1941, and ending ingloriously at Suez in 1956. Ernest King appears to have recognized this better than most. One wonders whether posterity might have dealt with him more favorably had he been less outspoken on the subject.

# 8 FAILED DETERRENCE
# KOREA, 1950-1953

*[This paper was originally submitted as part of the requirements for the Master of Arts Degree (History) at Columbia University, 1990]*

*******************

". . . no rational Japanese could believe that an attack on us could result in anything but disaster for his country."(Assistant Secretary of State Dean Acheson, August 1941, after having initiated an embargo on exports of oil to Japan, arguing that such action could not possibly provoke Tokyo into war.[1])

"ACHESON DOUBTS KOREAN WAR ENTRY . .
... it would be 'sheer madness' for the Chinese Communist Government to enter the Korean War." (Press report of televised speech by Secretary of State Dean Acheson, September 11, 1950, shortly after he had recommended to the President that United Nations troops be permitted to advance north of the 38th parallel. [2]

"To lose one parent . . . may be regarded as a misfortune; to lose both looks like carelessness."(Oscar Wilde[3])

*******************

## (I) INTRODUCTION

If much of the raw material of political science consists of historical evidence, it follows that flawed or misused evidence will cast doubts on any related scientific conclusions. This rather simplistic observation is prompted by reading Stephen Van Evera's article *Why Cooperation Failed in 1914*. Van Evera argues that states have an incentive to conceal their grievances because complaints may alert an enemy to the fact that tension is serious and conflict possible, thus prompting a preemptive strike. Not a startling conclusion, yet one poorly supported by the evidence provided:

> "In 1950, for example, the United States failed to recognize that China would attack if American armies approached the Yalu, partly because China failed to warn the U .S. with an ultimatum -- presumably because this would have deprived the Chinese armies of the surprise they would need if the Americans ignored their warning."[4]

This paper will demonstrate that Van Evera misused or misread the evidence, which shows in fact that China's warnings were clear, unequivocal and multi-faceted; and that tactical surprise was deliberately sacrificed in order to reinforce verbal messages with military demonstration. The history of the crucial summer and fall of 1950 shows that Peking's attempts to deter the United Nations from invading North Korea failed for two related reasons. First, although the message itself was clear, it was perceived by the recipients as irrational and thus disregarded. Second, even if the threats had been accorded some degree of plausibility, Washington policy makers would have been unimpressed: the immediate cost of acquiescing in Peking's deterrence was greater than the future cost of a conflict which the first line of reasoning had already made seem unlikely. In no way could the United Nations' move north of the 38th Parallel be considered a "preemptive strike."

Alexander George describes the Chinese-American military confrontation in Korea as "one which neither side wanted and both tried to avoid....a double failure of deterrence."[5] This implies symmetry of action and reaction which too is not quite born out by the facts. If the situation prevailing in the Fall of 1950 is looked at from the *Chinese* point of view, one can see a situation in which an acceptable status quo (friendly North Korea, unfriendly but unthreatening South Korea), already changed to Peking's disadvantage by Truman's interposition of the United states 7th Fleet between Taiwan and the mainland, was about to be further and radically altered. [Taiwan, the Chinese name for the island is used throughout the text, although Formosa, the Japanese name, may appear from time to time in quotations.]

A threatening and expansionist superpower was poised to thrust itself into the Peoples' Republic's most sensitive and vulnerable frontier area. Peking's diplomacy, designed to prevent this happening, was frustrated mainly because the Truman administration at no time understood how menacing its own actions appeared in Peking.

## (II) BACKGROUND

### (1) UNITED NATIONS INTERVENTION

Following a long series of military clashes across the 38th parallel, major hostilities broke out in Korea on June 25, 1950. Over the next several days President Truman introduced American ground, naval and air forces into the conflict under the flag of the United Nations, and ordered the Seventh Fleet to patrol the Taiwan straits in order to prevent any invasion of the island by communist China, or an invasion of the mainland by the non-communist Chinese now isolated on Taiwan. In making these decisions the President acted on the unanimous recommendation of his civilian and military advisers, although it is clear from the record that the State Department was very much in the lead in urging intervention and in determining how it should be done.[6]

United Nations forces withdraw from Pyongyang, the North Korean capital. They recrossed the 38th parallel in 1950.

From Washington's perspective North Korea's assault represented an invasion across a national boundary, the kind of aggression which, if unchecked, would lead to World War III as surely as the appeasement offered at Munich lead to World War II.[7] Moreover, since the prevailing view at the time was that all Communist actions were centrally controlled from Moscow, the Soviets rather than the Chinese, were seen as the driving force behind Pyongyang. Subsequent analysis bears out the view that, although Peking may have been informed of Kim Il Sung's intentions, it was initially very much a bystander. [Alan Whiting writes (China Crosses the Yalu, 1960): "It is possible that Stalin did not even inform Mao of the forthcoming attack ...although this is extremely unlikely." It was not until August 13, 1950 that Peking's first ambassador arrived in Pyongyang.]

Moscow, denying any complicity, claimed the war was a civil one in which the United Nations had no business.[8] Peking's main concern was the Seventh Fleet, which it saw as an intolerable intrusion into an internal conflict from which Washington had professedly withdrawn only a few months earlier.[9]

## (2) A CHANGE IN WAR AIMS[10]

In late September, 1950, following several weeks of debate, Washington decided on a radical shift in its war aims: to abandon the idea of returning Korea to the status quo ante, i.e. divided along the 38th Parallel, and to adopt instead the goal of reuniting the country by force. The decision to shift from a strategy of containment to one of roll-back was made by the President on the advice of a National Security Council strongly influenced by the Secretary of State. Although many factors entered into the decision to allow MacArthur to proceed north, arguably the most important was that it made political sense in the context of the time. On October 7 Washington's new strategy was adopted by a complaisant[11] United Nations in the form of an "Eight Power Resolution" implicitly sanctioning MacArthur's move across the 38th parallel. The same day patrols of the United States 1st Cavalry Division probed north of that line.

The decision to go north resulted in an immediate reaction from the Communist government in Peking, which claimed that the presence of American troops in North Korea was a threat to its vital interests. Notwithstanding the vehemence of the Chinese protests, which would continue for the next several weeks, and the logic of their case, American policy makers determined, and continued to believe, that Peking was bluffing. October 7, in this writer's judgment, was the date on which over-ambition caused a quick, clean, and effective demonstration of collective security at its best to become a long, dirty, and generally unsatisfactory war of attrition.

# (III) CHINA'S INTEREST IN THE KOREAN WAR

## (1) CHINA'S FOREIGN POLICY IN 1950[12]

Apart from the introduction of a new ideological bias, Communist China's foreign policy in the early 1950's was little changed from that of predecessor regimes: paramount goals were the protection of the Middle Kingdom and the recapture of lost adjacent territories. The new government's world was strictly bi-polar: its most immediate goal had been modification of the 1945 Sino-Soviet friendship treaty, originally designed to thwart a threatening Japan, so as to include the United States as a possible foe.

Recent experience supported China's suspicions. The West's refusal to provide serious resistance to Japan in the years prior to World War II, in contrast to Soviet support during the same period, demonstrated the wisdom of a "lean to one side" policy. Post-war United States' support of the Kuomintang added to misgivings about Washington's intentions, motivating virulently anti-American behavior which so aroused Congressional and public opinion that recognition of the new regime by Washington became impossible. Recognition withheld further enraged Peking, thus leading to an intensifying atmosphere of mutual distrust and recrimination. Of more immediate importance, non-recognition meant that there could be no diplomatic intercourse between Washington and Peking. All communications had either to be made publicly, or passed via third parties. As we shall see, this cumbersome arrangement contributed greatly to the Administration's failure to hear what its prospective enemy was so clearly saying.

## (2) CHINA'S INTERESTS IN KOREA

China had both economic and security interests in Korea, each inextricably entwined with the recent Japanese occupation. Forcibly seizing Manchuria in 1931, Tokyo proceeded to make massive infusions of capital in its new colony, which largely accounted for the fact that the province's industrial production under Japanese occupation outstripped that of all the rest of China. Although rich in raw materials, Manchuria produced insufficient electrical power, and had to rely substantially on supplies from Korea. Electricity generated from major Japanese built power complexes on the Yalu supplied the entire province, including its strategic cities Mukden, Port Arthur, and Darien. The fact that the generating plants were located on the Korean side of the Yalu, while the distribution lines lay mostly to the north, enhanced the system's vulnerability.[13]

Manchuria also represented two major security concerns for Peking. First, assuming that if the United States meant what it said and would cause General MacArthur to stop at the Yalu, China would be confronted with a hostile power in permanent possession of a long and hard to defend frontier, and would have its key industrial region in a hostage situation. Paradoxically, as development proceeded, the hostage would become more valuable and the Peoples' Republic thus more subject to coercion.[14] [Peking's concerns regarding the security of Manchuria would have been heightened had a late July memorandum from the Pentagon (*Foreign Relations of the United States*, 1950, Volume 7, 502-510) become public. Forcible reunification made sense, it was argued because, inter alia, "Manchuria....would lose its captive status...a free and strong Korea could provide an outlet for Manchuria's resources and could also provide non-communist contact with the people there and in North China."]

Probably of greater concern was the expectation that Washington's protestations of innocence really were covering aggressive intentions. Influential people in Washington had been calling for preventative war and General MacArthur's various public statements demonstrated little propensity for restraint.[15] Allowing the United Nations to proceed unimpeded up to the Yalu to test its sincerity represented a difficult task for an insecure Government conditioned to believe in the West's malign intentions.

Memories of the Japanese occupation were still fresh in the minds of Peking's new leaders, who recalled that a Japanese controlled Korea had been the launching point of the 1931 invasion:

> "The armed forces of the U.S. imperialists directly threaten the northeastern border of China. Just as with the Japanese imperialists in the past, the main objective of U.S. aggression in Korea is not Korea itself but China. History shows us that the existence of the Korean People's Republic …and the security of China are closely intertwined."[16]

An independent Korea, free from domination by any foreign power, had always been of paramount interest to China's governments, regardless of their political persuasion.[17]

## (IV) PEKING'S GROWING INTEREST IN THE KOREAN WAR.

By late August announcements from Peking began to demonstrate a growing interest in events on the Korean peninsula. When, following MacArthur's mid-September success at Inchon, it became apparent that the United Nations would likely authorize its forces to advance north of the 38th parallel, the Chinese made it increasingly clear that the price of such an advance would be intervention by the People's Liberation Army.

Peking's interest in the outcome of the Korean conflict developed through three distinct stages plus a fourth, which would become apparent by the end of October.

## (1) RELATIVE INDIFFERENCE

The first stage, during the period when the United Nations forces were on the defensive, was one of relative indifference toward events in Korea. As has already been noted, the presence of the U.S. Seventh fleet in the Taiwan straits was of far more concern to China's new leadership than were the misfortunes of the wretched Koreans. "There is no doubt," Peking Radio broadcast on July 17, "that the Korean people have sufficient strength to defeat imperialist aggression."[18] However, as the war developed, China's primary strategic concern shifted: bringing the civil war to a triumphant conclusion by "liberating" Taiwan became less pressing, while the security of the country's principal industrial base became paramount.

## (2) INCREASING INTEREST

Shortly after MacArthur's success at Inchon, when it became apparent that the North Koreans not only might not win, but conceivably could be defeated, Peking's security interest in the outcome of the war in Korea became increasingly manifest. Readily available contemporary evidence for this was three-fold: public announcements, diplomatic communications, and increased troop movements.

i. Public Announcements

Although the public announcements did not clearly communicate intent, they certainly demonstrated an interest. In mid-July Peking launched an intensive propaganda campaign against United States aggression in Taiwan and Korea[19]. Insisting that the North Koreans would prove victorious and that Taiwan would be liberated, various Chinese media participated in a rising chorus of attacks on the United States. A month later Peking radio announced that it was "impossible to solve the Korean Problem without participation of its close neighbor, China....the Chinese people cannot allow such aggressive acts of American imperialism in Korea."[20] China would not get involved in the Korean War, or fight in any area outside China, unless it was attacked. However, should the North Koreans be pushed back to the Manchurian border, China would fight the enemy outside rather than wait for him to come in.[21] A leading Peking newspaper proclaimed: "North Korea's friends are our friends. North Korea's enemy is our enemy. North Korea's defense is our defense. North Korea's victory is our victory".[22]

In late September Peking made its first official admission that North Korean troops had been released from Manchuria to participate in the war. "It is the proper right and sacred duty of Koreans in China to return to their fatherland to help in its defense and reconstruction. We shall ever stand on the side of the Korean people."[23] *The New York Times'* Henry Lieberman* believed these statements were advance propaganda regarding a possible United Nations drive beyond the 38th Parallel. The acknowledgement that Manchurian Koreans were already participating in the war appeared designed to point up the threat that People's Liberation Army troops could enter Korea too if the United nations forces drew too close to the Manchurian border.[24]

[*Henry Lieberman's reports from Hong Kong during this period are noteworthy for their prescience, which may owe something to the fact that, having been head of the Office of War Intelligence in China during World War II, he was possibly as well or better informed than official intelligence agents.]


ii. Diplomatic communications

Foreign Minister Chou En-Lai's concurrent messages to the United Nations also made it clear that Peking now considered itself a party at interest in the war. Parallel Soviet diplomacy was oriented towards trying to achieve some kind of a settlement before the United Nations move northward became inexorable. On August 20 Chou sent telegrams to United Nations' Secretary General Trygve Lie and Soviet delegate Jacob Malik calling for an end of the fighting in Korea and withdrawal of United Nations forces there as the first steps in a settlement. Communist China, Chou said, was firmly of the view that it should be represented in the United Nations Security Council for the Korean discussions.[25]

Chou En-Lai's message was the opening salvo in what was to prove an intensifying diplomatic offensive. On August 24 a further protest to the United Nations called on the Security Council to condemn what Chou described as America's "direct armed aggression" against Chinese territory and to order the withdrawal of the Seventh Fleet from the Formosa Straits. Two days later he again maintained that China's United Nations' seat rightfully belonged to the Communists: he insisted that his government's representatives be seated, and announced the appointment of a delegation to the September meeting of the General Assembly[26].

iii. Military Movements

Internal military movements during July and August provided Peking with desirable tactical flexibility should deterrence fail. Observers in Hong Kong noted in early July movement of between a quarter and a half million People's Liberation Army soldiers towards the eastern border of Manchuria, adjacent to North Korea[27]. Further reports identified these troops as being four armies belonging to General Lin Piao's crack Fourth Field Army, hitherto stationed in southeast China[28], but by then located in the Mukden Antung area, close to the North Korean border[29]. Troop movements, designed to create a capability for intervention even before the intention was made explicit, while not publicized, were certainly not a closely guarded secret. In late September India's Ambassador to Peking K.M. Panikkar found all Peking under curfew, with troop formations and trucks heading for the railroad station. Panikkar surmised that this was part of the general troop movement towards Manchuria already noted by others.[30]

## (3) PEKING'S INTENTION TO INTERVENE MADE CLEAR

The third stage, plain warnings from Peking of its intention to intervene if American troops crossed the 38th parallel, began only when it became apparent that Washington really intended to permit MacArthur to move north, and would seek approval from an acquiescent United Nations to do so. These warnings took the form of further public announcements, supported by private communications via India, which Chou estimated correctly, would shortly become public.

At the end of September General Nieh Yen-Jung, the Military Governor of Peking, told Panikkar that China did not intend to "sit back with folded hands and let the Americans come up to their border." The South Koreans did not matter, but an American incursion into North Korea would meet with Chinese resistance. Panikkar asked Nieh whether he realized the full implications of intervention, and was told:

> "....we know what we are in for, but at all costs American aggression has to be stopped. The Americans can bomb us, they can destroy our industries, but they cannot defeat us on land."[31]

Panikkar tried in vain to impress Nieh with the destructiveness of war with the United States, which would set China's economy back by fifty years. Nieh replied that all that had been taken into account, even the atom bomb: they might kill a few million people, but for a nation which mostly lived on farms the impact of nuclear weapons would be minimal.[32] Panikkar reported that there was now no doubt in his mind that China had decided on a more aggressive policy in North Korea. [Panikkar would send his reports directly to Nehru who forwarded them to London where they were retransmitted to Washington. The opportunities for delays and misunderstandings were thus legion.]

By the end of September an almost totally destroyed Seoul had been "liberated"; United Nations Commander MacArthur was calling upon the North Koreans to surrender unconditionally; and U.S. Ambassador to the United Nations Warren Austin was warning the General Assembly that North Korean troops must not be allowed to retire behind the 38th Parallel and continue to pose a threat to world peace. The Parallel, he said, was an imaginary line that had no basis in law or logic.

It was thus not by chance that Peking's level of anxiety moved significantly higher on the last day of September. In a major speech delivered on the eve of his country's first anniversary as a state, Chou En-Lai publicly denounced the United States as his country's most dangerous enemy: "Since the establishment of the People's Republic of China, the hostile attitude of the American Government toward the Chinese people has become intensified." Citing a long list of unfriendly acts by the United States, he said:

> "The United States Government, because of its frenzied and ruthless imperialistic aggression has been proved the most dangerous enemy of the People's Republic of China. The Chinese people will not be afraid to fight aggression in defense of peace. They will not tolerate foreign aggression, nor will they supinely tolerate seeing their neighbors being savagely invaded by imperialists."[33]

These appear to be the most open threats yet voiced by a Chinese official with respect to his country's intentions in the event the United Nations crossed the 38th Parallel.[34] Yet even as Chou spoke, the first South Korean troops advanced across the dividing line. The following day the Soviet Union unveiled its peace plan for Korea, which called for the withdrawal of all foreign troops, followed by nationwide elections.[35] The plan was decisively rejected a few days later as the General Assembly voted in favor of the Eight Power resolution which provided *de facto* authorization for United Nations forces to advance into North Korea.[36]

Chou En-Lai, meeting on October 3 with Ambassador Panikkar re-emphasized the fact that China would be forced to intervene if American troops crossed the 38th parallel. A *casus belli* was thus clearly defined. Reporting the meeting to New Delhi, Panikkar said he was convinced the Chinese decision was final[37] and that any movement across the parallel by U.S. forces would mean an extension of the Korean conflict.[38] Nehru forwarded Panikkar's message to London, saying that he felt Chou's words must be taken at their face value. Unless MacArthur's advance across the parallel was halted, there was no alternative but to assume that China would act at once.[39]

On October 12 the Foreign Office in Peking released a statement clearly designed to reinforce Chou En-Lai's earlier warnings. China was firmly opposed to an extension of the Korean War by America and its allies; it would prefer a peaceful environment to carry out much needed rehabilitation, but the United States should not mistake this for weakness.

> "Now that the American forces are attempting to cross the 38th Parallel on a large scale, the Chinese people cannot stand by idly with regard to such a serious situation as is created by the invasion of Korea....and with regard to the dangerous trend towards extending the war."[40]

The first ten days of October thus marked the end of one phase of Sino-Soviet strategy and the beginning of another. The General Assembly's overwhelming rejection of Moscow's attempt to negotiate a peace, and its *de facto* permission for MacArthur to march north, meant that Peking's attempts at deterrence by diplomacy had almost certainly failed, and that armed intervention represented the only alternative to secure its vital frontier against what it perceived to be an increasingly adventurous foe.

## (V) WASHINGTON IGNORES PEKING'S WARNINGS

There appear to be four basic reasons why, during the crucial month of October, 1950, Washington chose to ignore such clear deterrent signals from the government of a country with whom, officially at least, America had no intention of going to war. It didn't believe the message; it didn't trust the messenger; stopping the advance would involve a high price in terms of domestic politics, while the enemy's perceived capabilities promised that the likely cost of continuing north would be manageable. As Thomas Schelling writes, deterrence requires credibility on the part of the deterrer, and rationality on the part of the deterred. "If he cannot hear you, or cannot understand you, or cannot control himself, the threat cannot work..."[41]

Substantial evidence demonstrates that a number of well informed organizations and individuals, including the Central Intelligence Agency, George Kennan, Foster Dulles, Policy Planning chief Paul Nitze, and several press commentators, believed that any significant movement of United Nations troops north of the 38th Parallel would create a real possibility of a hostile reaction by Peking.[42] It is therefore worth examining carefully each of the reasons why key Administration policy makers, despite notable lack of unanimity at home, chose to disregard the unequivocal warnings coming out of China .

## (1) CREDIBILITY OF THE MESSAGE

Not believing the message was certainly the most commonly articulated argument for ignoring it. And several reasons can be advanced why, given the circumstances of the Fall of 1950, such disbelief may have seemed justified. The two cited most frequently are: first, that the Chinese, having no real intention of intervening, were bluffing in order to prevent the United Nations from destroying the North Korean Army; and second, that intervention would represent an irrational act.

The United States intelligence community generally was agreed that the Chinese were bluffing, probably in a last ditch attempt to intimidate Washington.[43] Majority opinion in the State Department seemed to concur, as did the British. Secretary Acheson commented that if the Chinese wanted to take part in the "poker game" they would have to put more on the table.[44]

Although there was near universal agreement that intervention would be an irrational act on the part of the Chinese, the definition of what was rational was based almost entirely on American perceptions, paramount among which was the certainty that, while America had no aggressive intentions towards China, centrally directed communism had become militantly aggressive on a global scale. There were thus two arguments supporting the belief that intervention would be irrational: that Peking had little to gain and much to lose politically, and that the time had long past when it could make any impact militarily.

Politically, it was felt, Peking would be foolish to intervene at a time when its application to join the United Nations was under consideration. Why, it was asked, should the Chinese imperil their entire reconstruction program, risk widespread bombing attacks, and throw away any chance they might have for admission into the United Nations?[45] Such views ignored the fact that the United Nations had, on September 20, overwhelmingly rejected Indian and Soviet proposals to admit Peking to membership. The vote, thirty-three to sixteen, held out little promise for rapid reversal. Unrecognized too was the view of the new government that China's United Nations seat was its by right, not by virtue of good behavior.[46]

Military arguments that intervention would be an irrational act by Peking were based entirely on the premise that any southward movement by the People's Liberation Army could have only aggressive intentions. The opportune time for intervention has passed: "Had they intervened in the first or second months," MacArthur told the President at Wake Island, "it would have been decisive."[47] Missing from these appreciations was an understanding of the dilemma facing the Chinese in terms of defensive strategy: if they had to fight the United States they preferred to do so on Korean soil rather than in Manchuria,[48] yet the further they advanced into

Korea, the more vulnerable were their lines of communication to American air attack. Correctly calculating that an aggressively intentioned Peking would have had the greatest success when the United Nations had its back to the wall at Pusan, Washington's strategists failed to realize that Manchuria could best be defended in the mountains just south of the Yalu, and in winter when frozen rivers would facilitate rather than deny movement and bad weather would inhibit air attacks.

## (2) CREDIBILITY OF THE MESSENGER

K.M. Panikkar was distrusted in London and Washington, thus impairing the credibility of his messages. Truman wrote later:

> "However, the problem that arose in connection with these reports was that Mr. Panikkar had in the past played the game of the Chinese Communists fairly regularly, so that his statement could not be taken as that of an impartial observer."[49]

Sadar Panikkar      Dean Acheson

According to British sources, he was indeed an admirer of the Communist regime in China, believing its access to power to have been inevitable. A strong believer that Asians should settle Asian problems, he found America's China policies incomprehensible. British distrust appears to be based mainly on the fact that he was a goateed intellectual. [This is not intended to be flippant. The conclusion is supported by the evidence, and appears a reasonable interpretation given the thinking of the British Foreign Office in the 1950s, which appears considerably more conservative than the Government it served.] It ignored the fact that he had served as Nehru's valued representative to both the Nationalist and the Communist governments in China.[50] A careful study of his writings and other contemporary evidence indicates little reason to doubt his capacity as an honest reporter, and much to indicate that Chou had made a sensible choice of intermediary.

Further impairing the credibility of Panikkar's messages was Acheson's poor relationship with Nehru, and his low opinion of Indians in general who, he half facetiously observed, must spend most of their time standing on their heads.[51] There was little love lost between two proud statesmen, probably exacerbated in the case of Acheson by a streak of racism that lay quite close to the surface. He was, recalls Dean Rusk, clearly a North Atlantic man. "He did not care about little brown, yellow or black people."[52]

India's role as a go-between was further compromised when, on November 2, China invaded Tibet. Although Chinese hegemony over that isolated kingdom was long acknowledged by India, it had been hoped that it would not be exercised in the form of military force. Now those who argued that Nehru and his ambassador were poor interpreters of Peking's intentions had been given further ammunition. Moreover, nearly a month had elapsed since Chou En-Lai's formal warning to Panikkar, and nothing had happened. Nehru, it was felt, had been doubly deceived, not only on Tibet, but also by Peking's failure to follow up its threat and move into Korea.[53]

## (3) THE PRICE OF STOPPING

Initial fairly unanimous support of Truman's actions with respect to Korea and Taiwan soon broke down once it appeared that foreign affairs would be a dominant election issue in 1950.[54] The bi-partisan approach to international concerns, which had largely prevailed since 1941, was eroding: Republicans who felt that the war was a result of Administration incompetence joined forces with those who desired it more vigorously prosecuted, placing Truman and his foreign policy advisers on the defensive where they would remain for the rest of their time in office.[55]

General MacArthur was the darling of those who believed that America's true interests lay in Asia rather than Europe, and that Chiang Kai-shek represented a stalwart ally in a vital region. Those who felt differently were responsible for the "loss" of China.[56] What the Democrats needed was a smashing pre-election victory in Korea and, as a recent biographer put it, "Douglas MacArthur, whatever his defects, was adroit at producing victories."[57]

By late September it was apparent that the Kim Il Sung's forces had been largely obliterated, leaving North Korea open to the United Nations armies.[58] The West thus saw its first opportunity to "rollback" communism, and popular opinion was eager to seize it. Secretary Acheson, who sided with the hawks over the doves in the State Department, had plenty of incentive to do so. Harried by the Republican right for being "soft" on Communism, for adopting incompetent or even traitorous policies in the Far East, and for "inviting" North Korea's attack on the south, he needed forceful action to refurbish his reputation. To have caused the United Nations, flush with victory, to stop at the 38th parallel just because of threatening noises coming out of Peking via India, would have provided fresh ammunition to his enemies. Ignoring the threats and giving MacArthur leeway to proceed was further demonstration that he could be as tough an anti-Communist as anyone in Washington.

## (4) THE COST OF GOING ON

Arguments advanced by the "doves" (principally George Kennan and Paul Nitze) against forcible reunification of Korea had placed considerable weight on the possibility of Soviet or Chinese intervention.[59] The CIA too believed that a United Nations move north of the 38th parallel involved a risk of general war.[60] Even John Foster Dulles was concerned enough to minute Paul Nitze:

> "In my opinion there is every reason to go beyond the 38th parallel except possibly one, and that is our incapacity to do so and the fact that the attempt might involve us much more deeply in a struggle on the Asian mainland with Soviet and Chinese Communist manpower because of the strategic bearing that the northern part of Korea has toward Port Arthur and Vladivostock."[61]

The possibility of the threat was thus apparent in Washington long prior to its expression from Peking. The decision to move north therefore was made less on the basis that the threat did not exist (although, as argued earlier, there were some reasons to discount it), but rather that it did not matter. The Soviet Union, on the other hand, was a different question. Policy papers[62] prepared during the summer distinguished between action to be taken in the event of Soviet intervention (minimize the commitment to Korea, prepare to execute war plans), and action to be taken if United Nations forces encountered the Chinese (continue fighting as long as success seemed attainable, while taking appropriate action outside Korea against Communist China). MacArthur's instructions from the Joint Chiefs of Staff, while requiring approval from above for any action outside Korea, preserved this dichotomous thinking.[63] As the war progressed and it became apparent that Moscow had no desire to come directly to the help of its allies in Pyongyang, the linkage between China and Russia via the Sino-Soviet treaty appeared of lessening concern to the West.

Although considerable lip service was paid in Washington to the undesirability of war with China, the policy makers who most influenced Acheson seemed positively to relish the idea. John Allison, Director of the State Department's Office of Northeast Asian Affairs and strong proponent of forceful reunification, admitted that it might mean "war on a global scale," but argued "when all legal and moral right is on our side why should we hesitate?"[64] But the most significant evidence that restraining MacArthur was low on the Administration's list of priorities before mid-November (when, it will be recalled, the elections were over) comes from two sources:

First, Defense Secretary Marshall's private instructions to the General: "We want you to feel unhampered tactically and strategically to proceed north of the parallel."[65] Much has been written about this, mostly designed to preserve Marshall's reputation.[66] However, it is hard not to argue that, at the time, MacArthur was entitled to believe that his civilian superior meant what he said.

Secondly, President Truman's meeting with MacArthur at Wake Island during which the President asked about the likelihood of Chinese intervention. MacArthur replied "Very little....we are no longer fearful of their intervention....The Chinese have 300,000 men in Manchuria. Of these probably not more than 100/125,000 are distributed along the Yalu River. Only 50/60,000 could be gotten across the Yalu River. They have no air force. Now that we have bases for our Air Force in Korea, if the Chinese tried to get down to Pyongyang there would be the greatest slaughter."[67]

Although most accounts of the meeting focus on the General's incorrect judgment regarding intervention, it in fact differed little from the views of other key advisers.⁶⁸ What is seldom noted is that most of what MacArthur had to say concerned what he would do if Peking did decide to intervene. None of the many experts present bothered to enquire exactly how the slaughter would be inflicted, although it was common knowledge in Tokyo that the General planned to bomb most of North China should he confront the People's Liberation Army.⁶⁹ None of the many experts present questioned whether MacArthur was not putting too much trust in airpower, although at least one of them (Omar Bradley) was outspoken in his criticisms of the inadequacy of tactical air.⁷⁰ A careful reading of contemporary accounts leaves only one impression: Chinese intervention mattered little, and indeed could provide an opportunity, as Acheson put it, for American air power to teach the "Asian hordes" a good lesson.⁷¹ "At the root of American action," writes military historian Max Hastings, "lay a contempt....for the capabilities of (China's) armed forces."⁷²

## (VI) PEKING'S FINAL WARNING, MACARTHUR'S REACTION: CHINA GOES TO WAR

It was noted earlier that Peking chose a fourth method of communicating its intentions. Deliberately sacrificing tactical surprise, the People's Liberation Army in early November entered the battle, demonstrated their presence and capability, and then withdrew. Several recent accounts of these events believe that this bizarre incident was a carefully designed final warning.⁷³ Tragically, it was interpreted in both Tokyo and Washington as a sign of weakness: the Chinese had intervened as threatened, felt the full weight of American firepower, and prudently withdrawn.⁷⁴

The final United Nations advance began on November 24: the "home by Christmas" offensive. General Ridgeway describes what happened:

> "....it was late November, the bitter Korean winter had already moved in. On November 26 the Chinese Communist forces fell upon the Eighth Army with full power and ferocity. Attacking first on the right....they practically destroyed Walker's flank, sweeping aside the remnants of the ROK forces in a matter of hours... then struck the U.S. 2nd Division which lost over 4,000 men....the situation was close to desperate. This was not a counterattack ....but a major offensive ...it would be necessary for UN forces to pull in their necks."[75]

## (VII) SOME CONCLUSIONS

The Introduction pointed out how an already precarious status quo in China's sensitive northeastern frontier appeared subject to further major change as the United Nations moved north. Peking's attempts to deter such a move were disregarded in Washington for several reasons: United Nations power in the area was deemed sufficient to permit the move north with little danger; the prospective defeat of North Korea represented an opportunity to demonstrate Western resolve to deter aggression everywhere; the domestic and international climates were dangerous enough to warrant the risks entailed; and most importantly, the cost of inaction, payable in the harsh coin of domestic politics, was deemed unbearable. [See Jervis, Robert, *The Meaning of the Nuclear Revolution: Statecraft and the Prospect of Armageddon*, 1989, 33, for arguments why deterrence can fail in circumstances where "political leaders have staked their domestic fortunes on forcing the other side to accommodate to their desires."]

Arguably, what was going on as winter encroached into the cruel mountains of North Korea, was a game of "Chicken."[76] Chicken works if both players share the same basic rationality: it is bad to be chicken but worse to be dead. One would therefore be adverse to playing chicken with, say, the Moslem driver of a dynamite laden truck who believed death was merely the shortest road to paradise. Similarly, Washington's perception of Peking's rationality was far off the mark: Truman's advisers believed war with the West would entail sacrifices too great for Peking to bear. Chou En-Lai and his associates, on the other hand, deemed no sacrifice unbearable if it forestalled a repetition of 1931. Peking went to war because it had much to lose but, until the blow fell, Washington doubted it would happen because it thought its opponents had so little to gain.

Steps taken by Peking to improve its security position in North Korea predictably did cause Washington to assume aggressive intentions. However, one must be careful in concluding that this is evidence of a classic security dilemma. Arguably, in the early 1950's almost any international action taken by the Soviet Union or one of its allies would be identified in Washington as aggressive. There was no room in America's ideology of that time for any different assumption.[77] What is noteworthy is that nothing Peking did caused any change of direction in the United Nations command until it was too late. China's actions neither stimulated nor deterred its enemy's aggressive movements, because such actions caused little or no alarm in Tokyo. Moreover, nothing China did to enhance its security could conceivably be deemed to have reduced that of the United States.

China's leaders acted sensibly in that when receiving mixed signals they chose to believe the one that could do them the most damage. Washington was sending assurances of innocence and restraint at the same time its armies in the field were demonstrating aggression and intemperance. ["It ought not to be necessary for the United States

Secretary of State to reiterate, again and again, that this country has no hostility towards the Chinese people, and no aggressive intentions in the far east....the Peiping regime knows the intent of this country is peaceful and that no American government could be guilty of an encroachment upon China and still face the American public." *The New York Times*, September 1, 1950.

"The Air force confirmed today that a United States F-51 fighter plane....strafed a Manchurian air base on August 27. The airstrip is at Antung, just five miles from the North Korean frontier. The Communists said that two F-51's had been involved and that three persons had been killed and nineteen wounded." *Ibid.*, September 2, 1950.]

The Administration was denying any desire to go to war with China, while its opponents were arguing that since war was inevitable, now was as good a time as any. A new and insecure regime can hardly be faulted for assuming the worst while waiting for events to demonstrate which voice should be heeded.

Finally, the most important lesson of the events of the Fall of 1950 is the need for a state to be realistic about how its actions must look to an opponent. Many observers, looking back, have asked how Americans would feel if a hostile army was advancing north towards the Rio Grande, all the time protesting the innocent intentions, while every now and then "accidentally" strafing El Paso.[78] Surprisingly, no one at the time seemed to see it that way.

# 9 BEDCHECK CHARLIE
## A SMALL AND MOSTLY UNKNOWN NAVAL OPERATION DURING THE KOREAN WAR

I would argue that the Korean war could never have been fought without either (a) full scale war with China, or (b) complete command of the trade routes leading to Japan and Korea, and the ability of the United Nations naval forces to operate almost without opposition in the Yellow Sea and adjacent waters. The world is fortunate that (b) proved to be the case. The navies operating in support of the UN ground troops (mostly American, but with consistent support from British and Australian allies) provided an important addition to the air forces arraigned against the Chinese and North Korean ground forces. And, as happens in most wars, there were small but important side shows. One of these was the night operations north of the front lines which attempted to eliminate the threat caused by old World War II bi-planes (mostly Polish built) that were used tactically against some important UN ground facilities.

"Bedcheck Charlies" (code named by an imaginative US Air Force intelligence officer) were elementary but very effective night intruders. During the course of the Korean War they frustrated all attempts on the part of the United States Air Force to intercept them and caused considerable damage. Most "Bedcheck Charlies" were

PO2's, wooden-framed, fabric-covered, open cockpit Soviet training aircraft. Their advantages in the night war over Korea were several: their ability to fly at low level down Korea's narrow valleys made detection difficult, a problem compounded by the poor radar-reflecting properties of the plane's rudimentary construction; their 80 knot speed made interception by high performance jet aircraft difficult if not impossible; and even if interception did take place, their slow speed and narrow turning circle facilitated escape.

Over a two-week period in early 1953 several different targets were attacked, causing minor material damage but considerable frustration to the defense. One PO2 was destroyed, but at the cost of the F-94 jet fighter, which had throttled down close to stalling speed in order to make the kill and subsequently crashed. PO2's continued to strew their small bombs pretty much at will around the Seoul and Inchon areas. Indeed, the pace if anything increased, raids coming in almost every night in June, 1953. On the night of June 9th, nine PO2's came close to hitting the Presidential mansion and slightly injured a *Life* magazine photographer sheltering in the Seoul press center. Another F-94, attempting to intercept one of these planes, closed at too great a speed and flew into its target. A Marine Corps AD Skyraider was luckier, downing one PO2 and breaking up the attack. The following night PO2's, aided by Russian built LA-11 and Yak-18 propeller planes, started several fires in Seoul and a blaze that destroyed five million gallons of fuel in the tank farm at Inchon. During this attack, radar, guns and aircraft were swamped with contradictory reports, causing the only interceptor that actually got airborne to be fired at from all directions by its own troops.

Given a lull before the next full moon, Fifth Air Force took two steps to find a solution to "Bedcheck Charlie." First, the Kimpo (Seoul) tactical air director was given authority to control all ground fire and air interception; systems were introduced to prevent overload of the information flow, and to provide focus only on those aircraft which failed to answer newly installed electronic interrogation (IFF). Second, the Air Force admitted failure in the interceptor role and turned it over to more task appropriate (i.e. slower) piston-engined aircraft. The aircraft selected, in addition to the already deployed Marine Corps AD's, were four Corsair F4U-5N single seat fighters from USS *Princeton* and three Firefly two-seat attack planes from Britain's HMS *Ocean*, the aircraft carrier I was serving on at the time, that was assigned to provide close air support for the British Commonwealth Division on the west of Korea. All these planes were radar equipped, the plan being to establish an all-night patrol along the Seoul-Inchon line which would lie in wait for any intruders from the north and be in a good position to intercept before they came too far south.

So that was the background to the events that brought three of *Ocean's* Fireflies and their crews ashore to the U.S. Marine Corps air base at Pyongtaek-ni (code named K-6). Everyone wanted to be involved in this task: it promised time ashore away from the sometimes rather monotonous shipboard life; it meant working closely with our American allies and, as I noted at the time, at least it would be a change from strafing ox-carts! Also, there had been an unfortunate fatal accident on board *Ocean*, and it seemed to be a good time to be away. I was fortunate enough to be one of the pilots selected. We were commanded by Lt. Cdr. "Pants" Bloomer, who seemed to share our enthusiasm about the prospect of a short absence from our shipboard home.

Our night fighter group was attached to the 12th Marine Air Group that operated from K-6, a vast base carved out of the Korean countryside near the little village of Pyongtaek-ni, some thirty miles south of Seoul. Most of its seemingly unending array of AD's and F4U's were engaged in close air support of the US Marines; pretty much what we had been doing for the Commonwealth Brigade. There were, however, four United States Navy F4U night fighters and a detachment of USMC night fighter AD's also employed, as we were, looking for Bedcheck Charlie.

A Fairey Firefly Mark IV FR flying a reconnaissance mission from HMS *OCEAN* along the eastern seaboard of Korea.

K-6's single 8,000 ft. runway seemed to stretch for eternity to those of us more accustomed to a 600 ft. deck. But to a carrier pilot used to returning to the reasonable amenities of his ship, which included a comfortable bunk, quite good food, and for the British, a well stocked bar, K-6 was barren indeed. The runway had been bulldozed out of red earth and laid with steel matting. Dust from the bare soil was everywhere, including the tents that provided our messing and sleeping accommodation.

We were shown the tents in which we would be living, and commented on the lack of furnishings. The marine showing us around suggested we talk to the supply sergeant. The supply sergeant shrugged his shoulders and suggested we make our own and pointed to some broken up packing cases. We asked about nails and tools and he shrugged again. Clearly whatever we arranged would be very much up to us: the Marines must have been missing from parade when the much-vaunted American hospitality was being issued.

Pants said nothing. We piled back into our jeep and went back to the field where he gave me my marching orders and a signed letter for the chief wardroom steward on *Ocean*. Half an hour later I was landing on our ship, and twenty minutes after that being catapulted off again, my precious crate firmly strapped into the back seat. Back at K-6, I was met by Pants and the jeep and we returned to the supply sergeant's office. Quietly placing a bottle of Scotch on his desk, Pants said, "And there's another one waiting if we have something to sleep on tonight."

A few minutes later a truck pulled up to our tent and the better part of a Marine platoon jumped out. They proceeded to unload a vast amount of lumber and what appeared to be an entire barrel of nails together with appropriate tools. Soon, as if by magic, we had beds with mosquito netting, chairs, tables, and, if not all the luxuries of life, at least a set of furniture that compared well with what our hosts enjoyed. The second bottle handed over, the team disappeared and we looked with some awe around our new quarters. America, it seemed, was a country where you could get anything you wanted as long as you had the right currency. In Korea, right then, Scotch was an excellent currency.

I should say right away that our time at K-6 was a truly welcome and valuable experience. It was for most of us our first close look at America at war, and although there were some quirks, most of what we saw was very impressive. The particular quirk was the Marine Corps, which seemed to us sailors to be determined to make life as miserable and uncomfortable for themselves as possible. Our US

Navy fellow pilots agreed with this. Indeed, to the extent there were lines drawn at all it was the Navy (US and RN) on one side and the Marines on the other, rather than Americans versus the Brits. The Marines seemed to want to create a physical challenge out of the most mundane day-to-day functions, while the navy men wanted just to make things as easy as possible. The Marines seemed to relish dirt and the huge boots to deal with it. The Navy hankered after their clean ships, decent showers, and relatively private heads.

Initial operations were confused by the inevitable problems associated with our respective misuse of the common language. We found it hard enough to get a frequency to use, and when we did were plagued with ground controllers who either could not, or would not, understand our English version of the English language. Considering it our own tongue, we did get rather testy with others who tried to bend it in their own direction.

I kept a diary:

> "July 22: It is pouring with rain when Reg Simmonds (my radar operator and a very good friend) and I get out of the jeep down on the line and, by the time we have buttoned on our Mae Wests and adjusted our helmets, we are wet through. It is ten minutes past midnight when I start up: following the traffic jeep is difficult and there is a slight delay on the end of the runway because an AD has just landed in the wrong direction. It is twenty-five past when, feeling as though I am casting myself off a high diving board, I open up the throttle and start to roll. Almost right away I am in cloud on instruments climbing to the north. My legs are shaking and I have a tremendous feeling of vertigo. It is a real struggle to rely on the instruments and not follow my instincts. We level out at 3,000 feet and try to contact the ground controller, but he is one of those who

make a great play of not being able to understand our accents. They give us an east-west patrol line, ten miles long above what appears, through breaks in the cloud, to be the Han River. We get the occasional radar contact, but they turn out to be mountaintops. Down below a battle erupts: red stars moving slowly along searchlight beams, flashes illuminating the far shore of the river. We ask for a fix and find we are right over the bomb line, so decide to head north. More contacts prove abortive.

We have been airborne for over two hours and have about another hour's fuel remaining so we're relieved when ordered to head for home. We are told that a number of planes are being diverted to K-6 and we must hold. We go into a port orbit and the controller tells us with some agitation that there is an airplane heading towards us from the north at an unknown height. Reg sees it on the radar and then, as I break away, he actually sees the other flash by. The cloud is now very dense and other fellow – whoever he was - must have been extraordinarily close. Our fuel is getting low, but after a further spell of orbiting we are given a Ground Controlled Approach into K-6 where they are reporting a 600 ft. base with heavy rain. They talk us right down to the runway.

I suddenly felt so tired that I followed the taxi jeep back in a daze: three hours night flying--two of them on rather primitive instruments (no GPS back then), hard IFR and the Firefly boasted no such luxury as an auto-pilot. I can hardly stand and after de-briefing drop into bed like a log."

That account reflects most of our patrols where the main variable was the weather. With moonlight and no rain the job was pure pleasure. A night like the one I have described was much less fun.

The other important inconsistency was the ground controllers. Some were really quite friendly and we worked well together. Others, often those who appeared to have a poor ear for the English language, had an annoying habit of putting two airplanes on a collision course and then leaving them to it. We later found out that the US Air Force, having a surplus of pilots at the time, had arbitrarily converted some of them to ground controllers with minimal training. They thus had little inclination to do the job, and less to do it well. Controller problems, and a very painful ache in my rear end after two or more hours sitting on lumpy dinghies, were on most patrols our worst problems.

Here are some thoughts following another patrol:

> "Up there on a clear night you could see for miles. To the north Suwon, where the North Korean Army once had its headquarters, was now a vast American air base. The walled town was built in seventeen hundred odd and these were just the last in a long series of Chinese, Japanese, Russians, communists and Chinese again who had overrun the country and treated the inhabitants in the way anyone would those who lived in a piece of land that was worthless except as the stepping off place for the next campaign.
>
> To the north of that was Seoul, you could just make out the lights. Between Suwon and Seoul the hills began, but a number of parallel valleys ran north and south down which you could fly at tree top level during the day. Seoul was on the Han River and at night you could see the starlight reflected on the twisting shallow flood. To the west of it was Inchon and the lights of the hospital ships, each with its red cross picked out in red lights, shining off the water in long rows. They were all full of wounded. What happened to the South Koreans who formed the majority of

casualties: no one ever seemed to know, but supposedly someone looked after them. We had seen them, hundreds of them, sitting up at the airhead at Seoul waiting for a freight plane to come and take them somewhere. I wondered if anyone ever bothered to tell them where they were going. If I was sitting on a hard bench with a clean white American bandage where my hand used to be, I would like to know where I was going."

Although we were busy at night, there was only so much sleeping one could do during the daytime. My principal memory of that time at K-6 was having the freedom to fly almost at will about what was still a war zone. Reg and I would invent some vitally important errand to be run which required flying up to Seoul or down to Pusan. A trip to Seoul involved a low level flight for about twenty minutes along a railway line; borrowing a jeep to drive into town; a few cold beers and lunch at the Commonwealth Officer's Club which boasted not only a friendly bartender, but wonder of wonders, a swimming pool; a quick dash to do whatever the errand was and then flying back to K-6 for the evening briefing.

One day we were asked if we could provide a plane to fly down to Pusan to pick up the payroll for K-6's Korean workers, the usual armored truck having broken down. I volunteered and was told that I would have to take a ROK (Republic of Korea) officer to guard the money. When we got to Pusan I found a truck waiting with what appeared to be enough paper money to pay the entire ROK army. Inflation had devastated the Won, which was about to be exchanged for new Wan (or vice-versa) on a 1,000 to 1 basis, but my cargo was the old near worthless currency. Looking at the pile of money and the Firefly's rather cramped back seat, I decided that the best thing was to put the ROK officer in first and then pack the money around him. This we did filling the rear cockpit so full that only the little man's eyes could be seen over all the old shabby paper. I started up, climbed to about six thousand feet and headed north. It was a lovely day, not a cloud in the blue sky, and I decided that life would be complete if I did some aerobatics on the way home. I had, I am ashamed to say, forgotten entirely about the precious cargo in the back. Three slow rolls to the left, three to the right, maybe a couple of hesitation rolls: I forget. I was cleared into K-6, landed, taxied up to the ramp where a truck with a guard of ROK MP's was waiting. I noticed that they were all looking rather anxiously at the back of my plane and, when I got out, saw why. The ROK officer had obviously been terribly sick before he finally fainted. Fortunately his English wasn't up to explaining what had happened, and I wasn't about to interpret. We wrote it off to normal airsickness and the MP's were put to work cleaning up the officer, the plane and the currency. It may have been the first time the Koreans were paid in laundered money, but I doubt the last.

Despite constant rumors of truce, the war continued to wind on, each side battling for a few inches of ground that might provide an advantage when hostilities ceased. At night the pyrotechnics over the lines were quite beautiful if you could disregard the damage being done on either side. At five thousand feet we wound our way back and forth over the flares and artillery, kept alert by frequent alarms, but never catching sight of the elusive Bedcheck Charlie. Indeed, with one notable exception, no one saw any of the little biplanes after we arrived, and no further damage was done to the oil tank farms.

The notable exception to the lack of enemy contact was one of the U.S. Navy F4U pilots, who appeared to have almost uncanny luck in finding the little North Korean airplanes. Although each of his engagements took place the enemy side of the lines (meaning that no wreckage was available to permit verification) he was credited with five kills. Each of these was confirmed by the same ground-based Air Force radar operator who would later testify that, yes, he had indeed seen the two contacts merge and that only one survived. The United

States Navy, with no Korean War fighter ace to brag about, was hungry for good publicity and this pilot provided it, scoring his fifth "kill" just before the truce was signed.

Describing the action later he recalled: "The first night we got a call, two of us launched. I got a visual on a Yak-18. I identified it by its exhaust-stack emission. I saw some tracers, pulled up closer and fired like mad."

*Life* Magazine reported with enthusiasm: "This so impressed (Seventh Fleet Commander) Vice Admiral J.J. ("Jocko") Clark that he flew to the pilot's base to give him a Silver Star. While the Admiral's plane was landing, our hero was out bagging two more Charlies. The Admiral awarded him two Silver Stars and promised him a Navy Cross when he got his fifth. On July 17 he did—the first man to become an ace by getting there last with the least."

The man's reputation as the Navy's only Korean War "ace" stood him well for the rest of his time in the service. He later achieved passing fame as the spokesman for the astronauts during some of the early space missions. However, none of the other K-6 pilots, American or British, entirely bought the story. Nor, I suspect, did James Michener who wrote the following in his novel *Space*:

> "There was, for example, the Air Force pilot . . . who returned to base morning after morning claiming that he had overtaken one of the plywood night invaders and had blown him out of the sky. No one could inspect the ground behind enemy lines to identify the shattered plane, but the high command was so eager to create the illusion in Washington that it was dominating the skies that it gave this windbag a medal with two clusters."

Michener, a Navy man loyal to his service, made the fellow an Air Force pilot, but the rest is familiar enough.

The truce that brought a temporary cessation of the fighting was signed on July 27, 1953 but has never gone beyond that. A state of war still exists between North and South Korea, and tension continues to an extent that makes a renewed outbreak of hostilities possible any day. We continued regular patrols along the truce line until, at the end of October, *Ocean* was relieved by the Australian carrier HMAS *Sydney*.

The Royal Navy aircraft carrier HMS *Ocean* (R68) on passage between Korea and Japan. *Ocean* twice deployed to Korea, firstly from May to October 1952 and then from May to November 1953.

I include this very small naval engagement in this book (a) because I was there, and (b) because I think it's still a narrative worth airing.

Written on HMS *Ocean*, on passage, Japan to UK, November, 1953

# 10 SUEZ, 1956
## A Successful Naval Operation Compromised by Inept Political Leadership

*[This article was originally written to note the passage of a half-century since 1956 when the Anglo-French invasion of Egypt, originally headed for rapid success, was halted by a combination of politics and economics. As the article developed it became apparent that much of what happened fifty years ago, and the political and military thinking (or lack thereof) behind it, had significance for today's strategic planners. Indeed, as one contemplates the present situation in Iraq, Santayana's oft-quoted axiom - that those who cannot learn from the past are condemned to repeat it - remains extraordinarily relevant. Suez was a war of choice in a time of peace, largely justified, we now know, by clandestine political arrangements. It was extraordinarily divisive both politically and among the military leadership, the latter going to unusual lengths to try to halt it. Civilian leadership, anxious to sustain their fictional casus belli in the face of rapidly moving events, interfered with tactical operations in a manner well beyond the relationship normal in democracies. Perhaps the most important conclusion to be drawn from Suez is that flawed political decisions are likely to lead to flawed operational strategy. Nevertheless, as one looks at the actual military performance during the invasion, one sees a near copybook operation. Suez goes down in history as a bad event, and*

*carries a bad name, yet those who fought there, however briefly, arguably did a good job. This article thus concentrates on the operational side of the affair as much, or more, as the political, mainly because the author believes that significant actions should be recorded even though the outcome was disappointing. The article was first published in the Naval War College Review (Autumn 2006).]*

\*\*\*\*\*\*\*\*\*\*\*\*\*\*\*

After the end of World War II the Middle East became an area of growing tension. There were many factors responsible, but the most significant was continuing conflict between the new State of Israel and its Arab neighbors. In 1950, Britain, France and the United States issued a Tripartite Declaration in which they agreed to take action to prevent any violation of the 1947 armistice lines separating Israel from its Arab neighbors. Although intended to defuse the situation, the Declaration did little to calm tensions, but it did become a central factor in Washington policy-making. In the fall of 1955 Moscow and Cairo concluded a major arms contract, at which point relations between Egypt and the West started to deteriorate rapidly. Nevertheless, at the end of the year the United States, Britain and the World Bank offered to fund construction of Egypt's prestigious Aswan High Dam. However, both Gamil Abdel-Nasser, Egypt's new head of state and his proposed dam were equally unpopular with Congress, and on July 19, 1956 the financing offer was withdrawn. A week later Nasser announced that the Suez Canal would be nationalized. The French and British, its principal owners and users, deemed this unacceptable, fearing restricted use of this vital international waterway[1].

Although Anglo-French diplomacy throughout the affair appeared at the time to be principally directed at regaining the Canal, events following the nationalization owe much to the fact that British Prime Minister Anthony Eden and French Prime Minister Guy Mollet respectively, believed that Nasser was undermining British prestige in the Middle East, and providing support for the Algerians in their "rebellion" against France. Such feelings resonated with much of popular opinion in the two countries and comparisons with Hitler and Mussolini were rife. Removing Nasser from power could prove a valuable collateral outcome of a successful recovery, but represented a confusing alternative priority for military planners. Although within days the two governments decided to use military force, they never properly defined their political objectives – regime change or Canal access -- and thus could give little clear guidance to their military staffs. As historian Hugh Thomas noted: "The political aims of the campaign remained somewhat obscure to the officers designated to carry it out."[2]

British post-World War II defense policy contemplated two kinds of war: full scale operations against the Soviet Union within the framework of NATO, or suppression of small-scale colonial insurgencies. In the summer of 1956 a major portion of Britain's active duty army was assigned to its Army of the Rhine, where it represented a significant component of NATO's military strength; Royal Marines and paratroopers (Britain's main rapid deployment units) were largely employed on anti-insurgent duties in Cyprus; while other infantry units and Royal Air Force squadrons were occupied in the long-running Malayan Emergency.

French troops, barely recovered from their disaster in Vietnam, were heavily engaged in Algeria. Although Anglo-French planners were fortunate to have significant naval surface and air power available for what would prove to be principally a littoral operation, much preparatory work would be necessary before an eastern Mediterranean offensive could be contemplated. Many units had to be redeployed and retrained, army reservists recalled, and landing craft and troop transports brought out of reserve or requisitioned. London was concerned that Washington remain at least neutral throughout any conflict, but American thinking was dominated by the Presidential election. Eisenhower, who was seeking a second term, urged a diplomatic resolution, but such ran counter to the Anglo-French desire for military action. The transatlantic relationship was further frayed by the extraordinarily bad relations between Eden and American Secretary of State John Foster Dulles, and by Washington's irritation at Britain's apparent inability to accept its reduced status in the world. Evidence of this reduced status was available for the world to see in the form of the United States Sixth Fleet that provided by far the largest collection of naval power in the Mediterranean, a sea the British had always regarded as being part of their Empire[3].

For several weeks following the nationalization, high-level meetings involving Canal users, the British, French and American governments, and the United Nations, struggled to develop compromises acceptable to all. The diplomatic process was slow, but by early October private negotiations with the Egyptians at the United Nations seemed to be coming close to meeting most of the Canal users' concerns, while Egyptian pilots had successfully taken the place of European waterway operators. The Anglo-French *casus belli* appeared to be melting away and with it their excuse for destroying Nasser. However, the Israelis, increasingly concerned with their security in the face of a rising level of Egyptian *feydaheen*[4] attacks, provided the Alliance's political leadership with a convenient solution.[5]

On October 22 representatives of the French, British and Israeli governments meeting in a Paris suburb secretly agreed that the Israelis would launch a major pre-emptive attack on the Canal Zone at the end of the month. The French and British would then demand that the Israeli and Egyptian Governments withdraw all troops to positions ten miles either side of the Canal. If the Egyptian Government did not agree to this ultimatum by the morning of

October 31, Anglo-French forces would begin military operations. Although it had an uneasy relationship with Israel, Britain had an essential role to play: it alone had the air power deemed necessary to destroy the Egyptian Air Force, and the Israelis were understandably reluctant to risk their army in the open desert until that had been done[6].

Future planning was complicated by the fact that almost no one concerned with the Anglo-French operation had any knowledge that the three-way plot existed. A treaty providing that Britain would come to the aid of Jordan in the likely event of hostilities between that country and Israel further confused matters on the British side. Indeed, there was a moment in October when two distinct planning staffs were preparing for war, one against Israel, the other against Egypt, but both assuming the use of largely the same military forces. One Royal Navy squadron commander recalled that he expected to be fighting the Israelis and expressed his surprise when he found the opposite to be true. As Israeli General Moshe Dayan commented later "I must confess to the feeling that, save for the Almighty, only the British are capable of complicating affairs to such a degree[7]."

During October the normal free flow of intelligence information between London and Washington largely dried up. Heavy communications traffic between London and Paris aroused suspicions in Washington, but overwhelmed American de-ciphering capabilities. Reports from Israel indicated a possible large-scale mobilization. Nevertheless, unknown to anyone but a small circle in Washington, there was a new and highly secret presence watching what was going on. On September 27 America's recently introduced U-2 spy planes were instructed to conduct high-level reconnaissance over the eastern Mediterranean. In the ensuing weeks CIA pilots, including the soon to be famous Francis Gary Powers, photographed most of the Middle East. U-2 reports indicated that the number of French jet fighters in Israel significantly exceeded the number the

French were permitted to transfer under the Tripartite Agreement; high-resolution photographs indicated large quantities of weapons being loaded onto French and British ships in Toulon, Malta and Cyprus. However, although British and French military preparations had become widely publicized, their intentions remained unclear. Although, as CIA Director Richard Bissell commented when he saw the photos, all those vessels were not there getting ready for a regatta.[8]

The Anglo-French ("Allied" for this purpose) navies available for the Suez operation would be asked to perform their traditional role in a military expedition: bring the invasion force safely to the enemy shore; soften up enemy defenses prior to the landing; transport the landing force onto the beaches; and provide cover for the troops while they establish a secure beachhead. Royal Marine Commandos, together with army paratroopers, would form the initial assault force. The Royal Navy and its marines were thus following a tradition that went back through Cunningham at Cape Matapan at least to Nelson at the Battle of the Nile: countering a threat to Britain's vital eastward lines of communication, although in 1956 oil from the Middle East rather than trade with India was the prime motivator.

The British at the time had a well-developed network of military bases in the Mediterranean. However those in Libya and Jordan (made available by treaty) were largely unusable for political reasons, while more accessible colonial facilities had their own drawbacks: airfields and harbors in Cyprus had limited capacity; Royal Air Force ground attack aircraft operating from Cyprus did so at their maximum range, thus reducing their effectiveness; and Malta was some 1,000 miles to the west of any likely action. It was thus clear that carrier aviation would prove a vital part of the invasion plan[9].

## NAVAL OCCASIONS - 1939 THROUGH 1956

Three of the five British aircraft carriers involved in the Suez operation: HMS *Eagle* leads HMS *Bulwark* and HMS *Albion*.

The Royal Navy that went into action at Suez had just undergone a major and innovative carrier modernization program. Three years earlier, during the Korean War, it had provided close air support for United Nations land forces using World War II straight deck light fleet carriers and propeller driven attack planes. Now its operational carrier strength consisted of five recently commissioned ships equipped with early model angled decks and the new mirror landing system that together provided improved flight deck safety and a reduced accident rate. Steam catapults not yet having been deployed, the ships remained much at the mercy of the old hydraulic models, and these gave considerable trouble. HMS *Eagle*, a modern fleet carrier already in the Mediterranean, was hastily reinforced by her smaller contemporaries, HMS *Bulwark* and *Albion*. *Eagle*'s operational efficiency was significantly reduced before the outbreak of hostilities by the failure of her port catapult. Obsolete World War II carriers *Theseus* and *Ocean* were rapidly prepared for troop carrying and sailed for Malta in early August. The French Navy promised a battle group consisting of the older carriers *Arromanches* (a sister ship to *Theseus* and *Ocean*) and *Bois Belleau* (formerly USS *Langley*) and the fast 15-inch gun battleship *Jean Bart*. South of Suez the Royal Navy assembled a task force consisting of the cruiser HMS *Newfoundland* with French and British escorts. The initial allied assault force would have eighteen tank and troop landing vessels. Troop ships with larger combat organizations were to follow some hours behind. Altogether, with escorts and auxiliary vessels, the assault force numbered over 100 ships.[10]

The British carrier air groups (other than helicopters and AEW aircraft) were all modern jet or turbo prop, comprising 100 Seahawk and Sea Venom fighter/bombers, nine Wyvern attack planes, and eight AEW aircraft. The twenty-five radar-equipped Sea Venoms embarked in *Eagle* and *Albion* had night and all-weather capability, giving the Royal Navy for the first time the ability to mount round-the-clock operations. The French carriers operated 36 F4U Corsair fighter/bombers and 10 TBM Avenger anti-submarine aircraft, all propeller driven World War II vintage. In his subsequent report the (British) Flag Officer Aircraft Carriers was particularly complimentary regarding the Corsair's operational versatility. In mid-October, belatedly concerned about a possible underwater threat, the Admiralty rapidly equipped *Theseus* with a helicopter anti-submarine squadron that would later prove invaluable in another context. French Avengers also provided anti-submarine capability[11].

There were three other navies operating in the rather crowded southeast corner of the Mediterranean in October 1956. The Egyptian navy in the early 1950's had two former *Hunt* class destroyers, six frigates and a sloop, all World War II vintage and all acquired from Britain. In 1955 Nasser had acquired two more modern Soviet built Skori-class destroyers, as well as four armed minelayers and 20 MTBs. Nasser's possible purchase of Soviet submarines was of some concern to the Allied navies. The Israeli

Navy believed that training of Egyptian navy crews by Poland and Russia had been considerably more effective than that received by her soldiers[12].

Israel's much smaller navy at the outbreak of hostilities consisted of two formerly British Z class destroyers, a frigate and several MTBs and landing craft. As will be seen, it soon received reinforcement from an unexpected quarter.

Finally there was the powerful United States Sixth Fleet, mustering 50 ships, 25,000 personnel and 200 aircraft. Two modernized *Essex* class carriers: USS *Randolph* (CVA 15) and USS *Coral Sea* (CVB 43) made up the fleet's principal striking force. Its air groups included swept wing F9F Cougar fighters that would cause considerable confusion to Anglo-French air crew and, probably unknown to the rest of the world, small detachments of F2H Banshees trained to deliver the nuclear weapons now routinely carried on board. The British and American navies in the theater, normally friendly rivals used to a high degree of informal cooperation, had essentially stopped speaking to each other in mid-October. The Americans claimed that they knew nothing of British plans; apart from having been told to evacuate US civilians from the combat area, Sixth Fleet Commander Admiral Charles R. Brown had no better instructions than a message from Admiral Arleigh Burke (Chief of Naval Operations) saying: "Situation tense, prepare for imminent hostilities." Other participants, despite being unaware of the highly secret U-2 activities, believed that Washington knew exactly what was going on. In fact, Washington did not[13].

The Egyptian Air Force, which represented the principal threat to both the Anglo-French invasion and the Israelis, consisted of 110 MiG 15 supersonic fighters and 48 IL 28 medium bombers, as well as some other older fighters. These were spread among seven different airfields. The MiGs, which outclassed anything possessed by the allies, were of particular concern, particularly if flown by East Bloc "volunteers". However, these new fighter planes had only just been delivered, and Egyptian pilot training was incomplete. The "volunteers" never did appear and throughout the campaign it would be lack of pilots, not aircraft shortage, which would inhibit Nasser's air forces. Egyptian pilots that did resist were more competent than the Israelis had expected[14].

By the end of July the British staff had prepared a preliminary plan and an inter-service command structure; the codeword was Musketeer. The planning process became Anglo-French in early August, under British leadership. Although inevitable differences would occur throughout the planning process, the matter that most distinguished the allies was British insistence on massive and well-prepared force that contrasted with French urging of speed of preparation and execution. It appears that Eden initially favored the French approach until dissuaded by his military advisers whose thinking was predicated on World War II experience, and serious concerns about the new weapons with which the Soviets had generously equipped the Egyptian forces, especially if these were manned by Russian "volunteers." In fact the British military apprehensions were misplaced, while the French political judgment was proved right: the long time that elapsed between inception and action allowed the many voices calling for peace to become mobilized while the reasons for war became less convincing[15].

To the chagrin of the French, who were urging rapid action, and the bored and occasionally mutinous British reservists who badly wanted to go home, the operation was postponed several times while diplomacy ground on. London eventually approved the final plan of attack on September 19. Landings would be at Port Said, but there was still no definite date. Postponements resulted in equipment problems; weapons and vehicles suffered from being at sea without proper maintenance. The Royal Navy's Mediterranean command emphasized to the Chiefs of Staff the weather-related perils of attempting a landing on defended beaches after November 1[16].

By a curious coincidence (that appeared to be too good to be true and probably was) the plans called for a Command and Communications exercise ("Boathook") to be carried out in early November. Thus on October 27 headquarters ship HMS *Tyne* sailed from Malta with Navy and Air Force commanders on board. The following day French naval units sailed from North African ports. On October 29 the Israelis began their Sinai offensive. The British carrier task force left Malta for Exercise "Boathook" with destroyer and cruiser escorts, and more cruisers and destroyers sailed from Aden towards the Gulf of Suez. Unknown to the various combatants, all of this activity was carefully monitored and photographed by the unseen U-2's[17].

The Anglo-French ultimatum was delivered to the Israeli and Egyptian governments on the 30th. Accusations of collusion were already bedeviling the British, despite Foreign Secretary Selwyn Lloyd's flat denial. Israel immediately accepted the *dictat*, which gave them the right to advance more than 100 miles into Egyptian territory. Nasser, for the same reason, rejected it out of hand. The British and French went to war, the latter with much more conviction than the former[18].

Musketeer suffered from three related constraints. The first was Prime Minister Eden's obsession with maintaining the fiction that the allied armada would be landing in Egypt solely in order to separate the Israelis and Egyptians. Second, and because of this, the convoy which would bring the main body of the landing force from Malta could not be loaded, let alone sailed, until the ultimatum had expired and been rejected[19]. The third constraint was the speed of the convoy; the slowest vessels could only make 6½ knots, meaning that a week would elapse before it could arrive off Port Said. Although diplomatic negotiations had provided just enough time to assemble and train the troops, ships and aircraft deemed necessary by the British, the French clearly feared that the preparations were overdone and the ponderous British time schedule was likely to result in the failure of the operation[20].

The campaign began with surface actions. During the night of October 31 the cruiser HMS *Newfoundland* encountered the Egyptian frigate *Domiat* in the Red Sea. The Egyptian captain ignored an order to heave to and *Newfoundland* opened fire at less than a mile. *Domiat* bravely returned fire until incapacitated, after which she was rammed and sunk by *Newfoundland*'s destroyer escort. Only 69 of the of *Domiat*'s crew were rescued. The same evening a series of confused actions took place off the Israeli port of Haifa. As the deadline of the ultimatum approached, the Egyptian frigate *Ibrahim El-Awal* was able to approach within five miles of the Israeli coast and open fire. Israeli security forces had assumed that the vessel was part of an American flotilla that had been cleared into Haifa to evacuate American nationals. Fortuitously, a small French squadron was refueling in Haifa. One of these vessels, the destroyer *Kersaint*, opened fire on the Egyptians, thus leaving no doubt as to whose side the French were on but causing little damage. Soon after, a small force of Israeli ships approaching from seaward also attacked the Egyptian vessel, assisted by a pair of Israeli Air Force jet fighters. Given the assembled firepower it is not surprising that the *Ibrahim El-Awal* surrendered, allowing an Israeli boarding party to bring her into port. After repairs were completed she was given the name *Haifa* and put back to sea under the Israeli flag. On November 1, as the Israelis crossed from Gaza into Egypt, the French cruiser *Georges Leygues* bombarded Egyptian positions around the border town of Rafah, but without notable success[21].

The remaining time before the arrival of the invasion fleet was occupied by a sustained air offensive against Egyptian military targets, designed to soften up Egyptian defenses and reduce the population's will to resist. Phase 1 of the air offensive began at dusk on October 31, and was intended to eliminate any threat from the Egyptian air force. After rather ineffective night attacks by Cyprus- and Malta-based RAF heavy and medium bombers, naval and RAF ground attack aircraft attacked Egyptian airfields, concentrating on runways and parked aircraft. Great effort was made to avoid damage to civilians and it became evident early in the campaign that, under such constraints, medium and high level bombing was ineffective against small military targets. Nearly all the meaningful Phase 1 damage was achieved by low level ground attack aircraft using bombs and rockets. Naval aircraft performed the bulk of this work since RAF fighters operating out of Cyprus carried a reduced weapon load, and even so could only spend some fifteen minutes over their targets. As the attacks began, the EAF (unfamiliar with its new Soviet equipment) began evacuating its bomber force to airfields in the south of Egypt or to friendly Arab countries. Enemy anti-aircraft fire was light and inaccurate, and the few EAF fighters that got off the ground avoided combat. By dusk on November 2 the EAF had been effectively neutralized. Flight to safety proved illusory: on November 4 French F84's destroyed 13 out of 14 IL 28's that had taken refuge on Luxor airfield some 350 miles south of Port Said[22].

Phase II of the air offensive (November 3 through 5) consisted of attacks on non-airfield military targets such as stores, barracks, and military road and rail traffic south of Port Said. Of particular importance was the Gamil Bridge, which carried the only road linking Port Said with its hinterland. Poor intelligence (what was thought to be a swing bridge was actually a causeway for much of its length) meant that twenty-seven bombing sorties were required to render it impassable. The British carriers were close enough to the target, however, to permit returning aircrews to advise changes in bombing technique. Heavy and accurate flak protected the bridge, causing the loss of one Royal Navy Wyvern. Destruction was finally achieved by a low level "skip" bombing attack by eight Seahawks, each carrying two 500 lb. bombs. High priority was also given to preventing the Egyptian block ship *Akka*, which was moored nearby, from obstructing the Canal. Two attacks were unsuccessful, giving the Egyptians time to tow her into place and scuttle her, together with another 47 concrete filled ships, effectively closing the waterway. The Syrian army then destroyed pumping stations on the western owned Iraqi Petroleum Company pipeline. The Anglo-French ultimatum thus precipitated what the two governments had most feared about Nasser's nationalization: an interruption in the flow of oil[23].

The US Sixth Fleet had been ordered to the area in order to protect the evacuation of US nationals, and the Fleet Commander insisted afterwards that was all he did. However, early in the morning of November 4 USS *Coral Sea* passed through the middle of the British task group. The British Admiral asked his American counterpart to move. The latter refused, signaling Washington "Whose side am I on?" Chief of Naval Operations Admiral Arleigh Burke replied "Take no guff from anyone." American submarines and aircraft created problems for Anglo-French air and underwater defenses and risk of an international incident remained high. The Egyptian Air Force MiG 15's, although less of a threat than previously feared, remained a cause of considerable concern to French and British pilots. US Navy swept-winged F9F's, easily confused with the MiGs, were reputed to be making "attacking" passes at Allied formations. The British Flag Officer Aircraft Carriers believed that the 6th Fleet was purposefully obstructing his operations; its adjacent air activities rendered his air warning radar virtually useless. Fortunately both sides showed restraint although, as Allied C-in-C Vice Admiral M. Richmond later reported: "the danger of shooting down an American aircraft with its international repercussions was ever present." What the international repercussions could have been was recalled by Chief of Naval Operations Admiral Arleigh Burke who, when Dulles asked whether the Sixth Fleet could halt the operation, responded: "Mr. Secretary, we can stop them, but we will blast hell out of them." A French attack on an Egyptian PT boat off Alexandria brought a quick rejoinder from the British command, pointing out that American ships were present in the harbor and that no attacks should be made until they were well clear. The problem of the Sixth Fleet became the subject of "polite signals" between the British and American force commanders, and it was a great relief when the evacuation was completed and the latter withdrew, taking with it some 2,000 American civilians[24].

It is fairly clear that Washington wanted to stop, or at least slow down the Allied operation, but was uncertain what course to adopt once diplomacy had failed. But there may have been a further consideration driving the U.S. Navy's actions. Ever since it declared independence in 1776, freedom of the seas had been a basic element of US diplomacy and a constant source of friction with Britain, who had long insisted on its right when at war to stop and search any ship, belligerent or neutral. The War of 1812 was fought largely over this issue, and did little to settle it. It was Germany's resumption of unrestricted U-boat warfare in 1916 that brought the United States into World War I in 1917, and freedom of navigation was an essential component of President Wilson's fourteen points. On this issue Washington recognized no exceptions: "We would as soon fight the British as the Germans," wrote Admiral William Benson, the first Chief of Naval Operations. Each of these actions, and countless more over the years, was taken to demonstrate that Washington would not accept any abridgement of its fundamental maritime rights. Although Admiral Brown's instructions do not appear to reflect this policy directly, it is fair to assume that President Eisenhower was unwilling to allow the Anglo-French action (of which he strongly disapproved) to set a precedent contravening rights fought for over the previous two centuries. As noted earlier, CNO Admiral Burke would have been firmly behind him[25].

Not surprisingly, the Anglo-French-Israeli attacks on Egypt had met with a bitter reaction around the world. The British Commonwealth, other than Australia and New Zealand, was strongly opposed, while British public opinion, fairly supportive of strong action in the summer, was by now bitterly divided. Debate in the House of Commons became so acrimonious that the Speaker had to suspend the session, the first time in 20 years. Eden was paying the price for his unprecedented action in going to war without keeping the Opposition fully informed. There was considerable resentment among the invasion forces towards the parliamentary Opposition which, it was felt, should be supporting those at risk. Britain's armed forces (like America's before Vietnam) were unused to military action opposed by much of the civilian population. Only the French and the Israelis appeared united and untroubled[26].

In Washington, President Eisenhower was furious at what he perceived as an Anglo-French double cross, given the fact that the Tripartite Declaration required both Britain and France to come to Egypt's aid if attacked by Israel. In New York, on October 30, the British and French added fuel to the President's anger by vetoing a United States resolution calling for a cease-fire. Two days later the United States took a similar resolution to the veto-proof General Assembly where it passed by an overwhelming majority, as did a plan for the UN to occupy the Canal in place of the British and French[27].

The Soviet Union added another political complication, attempting to use the crisis to distract attention from its brutal behavior in Hungary, where it had used troops to overturn a short lived rebellion against Russian domination. Soviet Prime Minister Bulganin threatened Britain and France with "rocket weapons," and suggested that the United States and Russian militaries join forces to protect Egypt, an offer that was summarily rejected[28].

Beset by political opposition at home and abroad, Eden was beginning to show signs of the breakdown that would eventually cost him his job. Disapproval also came from the professional head of the Navy, Admiral Lord Louis Mountbatten, a cousin of the Queen, who possessed considerable political influence. Mountbatten felt that the operation was both morally and militarily wrong, and that the adverse political impact of the proposed invasion had been poorly thought through. Most importantly, he felt that the British, if successful, would have to occupy the Canal Zone for a considerable period of time, at significant cost and with a serious impact on their other global responsibilities. He attempted to resign but was overruled by his civilian superior. Mountbatten made a final and extraordinary telephone call to Eden, appealing to him to turn back the assault convoy before it was too late. Eden said no, and hung up the phone[29].

Meanwhile, the assault force steamed on, still due to arrive on November 6. The French, desperate to move before the tide of international opinion overwhelmed their already precarious diplomatic position, urged that the landings be accelerated. The British reluctantly agreed that a parachute drop, originally planned to precede landings on the 6th, would instead take place on the 5th. Awkwardly, however, Israel had by then captured all its objectives and wanted to obey the UN cease-fire resolution, thus removing any rationale for further Anglo-French action. The Allies managed to persuade Tel Aviv to attach sufficient conditions to its cease-fire acceptance that it could not become effective immediately. The landings would go ahead[30].

At dawn on November 5, a small force of only 600 British and 500 French paratroopers descended on Port Said, landing four miles west and a mile south of the town, respectively. The risks they ran were considerable; since there was no way they could be given significant support for the next 24 hours[31]. The drop was successful, largely due to the effective support provided throughout the day by naval aircraft directed by Air Contact Teams dropped with the paratroopers. A "cab rank" of Seahawks and Corsairs were available throughout the day to be called in as needed to the two respective drops; missions were effectively planned on a minute-by-minute basis. The British eastward advance was slowed down by an old coast guard barracks on the beach road that had been turned into an Egyptian strong point. The barracks, which proved impervious to Seahawk rocket attacks, was quickly devastated by 1,000 and 500 lb. bombs placed with great precision by Wyverns of Eagle's 830 Squadron. While this was happening French paratroops, well-trained veterans of colonial wars who lacked their ally's inhibitions about civilian casualties, were blasting their way north. Allied paratroopers emphasized later that their rapid advance and low casualty rate would have been impossible without naval air support[32].

The main assault force arrived on time on November 6, and took up position five miles out to sea. The passage into Port Said had already been swept for contact and magnetic mines by an Anglo-French minesweeping force. Preliminary bombing runs against the landing beaches were followed at dawn by naval support fire. Initially all Naval bombardment had been vetoed by Downing Street, due to concern about civilian casualties. However, the British task force commander determined that what he was about to do was "support fire," not "bombardment", and decided to go ahead. Last minute instructions from Downing Street limited the fire to no greater than 4.5-inch caliber, lasting no longer than an hour. This restriction thus eliminated from the invasion force the French *Jean Bart* and the British cruisers *Jamaica* and *Ceylon*. Warship fire ceased when naval aircraft started strafing the beaches, continuing until a few minutes before the arrival of the first assault craft. In his after-action report, the invasion fleet commander noted how " . . . the development of modern communications, though intrinsically of great value, is inclined to produce a number of last-minute queries and instructions from London which cannot fail to upset the Command on the spot."[33]

Royal Marines of 42 Commando went over the beaches at 6:15 A.M., just to the west of the Canal, followed by tanks of the 6th Royal Tank Regiment. By 9:30 they had reached their first objective south of the town, supported by air strikes. By noon they had linked up with the French paratroops that had been well supported by their Corsairs. 40 Commando, on 42's right, advanced south to link up with British paratroopers moving in from the west. An incident in which Royal Navy aircraft accidentally attacked a British commando unit, inflicting considerable casualties, evidenced the risks inherent in providing close air support in built up areas[34].

45 Commando, held in reserve, came in an hour after 40 Commando in order to clean up the port area. In a battlefield "first" the Commando was brought in by a mixed collection of 22 RAF and Navy helicopters that in an hour and a half brought ashore 415 men and seven tons of stores. None of the aircraft had been designed for

Royal Navy Westland Whirlwind helicopters taking the first men of 45 Royal Marine Commando into action at Port Said from HMS *Theseus*.

the purpose, but the successful operation vindicated Mountbatten's long held belief in the use of helicopters in battle. Having landed the commando brigades, the helicopters turned their attention to evacuating the wounded out to *Ocean* and *Theseus*. On November 7 the weather deteriorated; strong winds and heavy seas over the next few days would have made landings over the beaches impossible. Since the failure of *Eagle*'s second catapult a day earlier had rendered her incapable of flying operations, the Royal Navy could claim to have received its fair share of good fortune[35].

The Allied carrier force made 1,616 sorties during Musketeer, of which 1,164 were offensive, 359 combat air patrols, and the remainder reconnaissance and transport. The proportion of defensive sorties dropped to under 20% in later days as the EAF was seen to represent less of a threat. Seahawk and Sea Venom aircraft, which undertook the bulk of the operations, averaged 2.8 sorties per day, compared with the 1.4 sorties per day by RAF ground attack aircraft. Naval aircraft flew 200 "cab rank" sorties in support of the parachute operations on November 5. Two Seahawks, two Wyverns and one Corsair were lost due to enemy action. The Corsair pilot was killed, as was the pilot of a Seahawk involved in a deck landing accident. These were the only naval losses. Total Allied casualties were 26 killed and 129 wounded.[36]

The Anglo-French forces now on the ground were aware of the possibility of a cease-fire and made every effort to move as far south along the Canal as possible. However, the final outcome of the battle was being decided not by the military, nor by the politicians, but by anonymous central bankers in capitals as far flung as Washington, Delhi and Beijing.[37]

In 1956 the Pound Sterling was the currency most widely used in world trade. It was also an important reserve currency, particularly with respect to the British Commonwealth and those countries that did not wish to trust their financial assets to Washington. Willingness to hold sterling was very much a matter of trust—the loss of which could well precipitate major sales by central banks and speculators. This is what happened in November 1956: maintaining trust required holding the prevailing sterling/dollar parity, and doing so in the face of massive selling pressure required aggressive use of Britain's own reserves, which had begun to hemorrhage. In theory, the reserves could be replenished from Britain's balances with the International Monetary Fund, but this would require American approval and the Eisenhower administration made it clear that such would not be given until all Anglo-French troops were withdrawn from Egypt. Astonishingly, this development took the British by surprise; the French, less trusting of Washington, had prudently arranged a stand-by credit three weeks before the invasion. Eden attempted to bargain for time but with little success; faced with the possibility of national bankruptcy, he had no choice but to agree to a cease-fire. The French reluctantly went along. It was all over[38].

Arguably Suez represents a seminal turning point in European history. Eden resigned and was replaced by Chancellor of the Exchequer Harold Macmillan who took immediate steps to repair the "special relationship" with Washington. Suez marked the final end of Empire. Britain would never again conduct a significant foreign policy initiative without at least token American support, but the British did recall Suez when they refused to assist America in Vietnam. In France, Suez led to further military disenchantment with the 4th Republic, the soldiers' revolt, the recall of de Gaulle, and the creation of the 5th Republic. France turned itself towards Europe and the Treaty of Rome and some might say, would never again trust America[39].

More generally, Arab nationalism remains a potent force in the world. Egypt continues to own the Canal, which still seems to work, although its importance to world trade is vastly diminished. The

Middle East remains a danger to world stability, although Egypt and Israel do have a peace treaty. Wars of choice remain highly controversial.

More than fifty years have gone by, yet it appears that some of the lessons of Suez still require re-learning. Clearly defined political goals, well supported domestically and well communicated to the military, are arguably more important in wars of choice that they are in wars of national survival. Sea borne expeditions take time, and the longer the time the more opportunity for the voices of those demanding peace to drown out the voices of those arguing for force, and the more opportunity for weather to change for the worse, something even the best-organized military can't control. Shore bases continue hostages to political fortune while floating airfields still retain their freedom of action. Task force commanders today must expect political micro-management to an extent unimaginable by Nelson, Jellicoe, or King. An expeditionary force must go in equipped with either an exit strategy or an occupation strategy. Winning is often deceptively easy, what you do after you win is more difficult; Mountbatten was right, no one had thought about what to do with a defeated Egypt, and the associated cost. Debtor nations that value their currency's reserve asset status must be very, very, careful when they choose to go to war.

# NOTES

[End notes are only included when they were part of the original publication]

## CHAPTER ONE

## LOSS OF THE *ROYAL OAK*

1. Padfield, Peter, *Donitz, the Last Fuhrer*, London, 2001,202; *New York Times* October 19, 1939; *Life* Magazine, October 30, 1939;
2. *Time* October 30, 1939; Brown, David, *Warship Losses of World War Two*, London, 1995, 27
3. Roskill, Captain S. W.DSC, RN, The War at Sea 1939-1945, Volume 1: The Defensive, London, 1954, 74
4. Cousins, Geoffrey, *The Story of Scapa Flow*, 1965, 29-31; Frank, Wolfgang, *Enemy Submarine: the Story of Gunther Prien, Captain of U-47*, London, 1954, 43.
5. Cousins, *op.cit.*, 139; Public records Office, Kew, England, ADM 199/158, *Report of the Board of Enquiry into the Circumstances Attending the Loss of HMS "Royal Oak,"* ("ADM 199/158"), 59.
6. Churchill, Winston S. *The Second World War, Volume I, The Gathering Storm*, Boston MA, 1949, 383.
7. ADM 199/158 *op.cit.*, 36 and Appendix 1; Stern, Robert C., *Battle Beneath the Waves: the U-Boat War*, 1999, 86; Roskill, Captain S. W. RN, *The War at Sea 1939-1945: Volume I, The Defensive*, London, 1954, 74.
8. Letter dated from German Naval Historian Bodo Herzog; Cousins *op.cit.*, 83; Doenitz, Grand Admiral Karl, Memoirs: *Ten Years and Twenty Days*, Tr. R. H. Stevens, Annapolis, 1990; Prien, K-L Gunther, *I Sank The Royal Oak*, London, 1954, 176;
9. Stern, *op.cit.*, 84; Macintyre, Captain Donald RN, *Fighting Ships and Seamen*, 1963, 69, 190; Doenitz, op. cit., 69, 175; Frank, *op.cit.* 25.
10. ADM 199/158, 130;McKee, Alexander, *Black Saturday*, New York, 1959, 7-8.
11. Type VIII data from Showell, Jak P. Mallman, *U-boats Under the*

*Swastika*, 1987, 72-76, 96-99.

12. Stern, *op.cit.*, 84; Weaver, H. J. *Nightmare at Scapa Flow: the Truth About the Sinking of HMS Royal Oak*, 1980, 26; Roskill, op. cit, 70-72; Bodo Herzog letter; Frank, *op.cit.*, 45

13. Roskill, *op.cit.*, 70-71; Weaver, *op.cit.*, 31-33,39-40; Bodo Herzog letter.

14. *Fuehrer Conferences on Naval Affairs 1939-1945* ("Fuehrer Conferences"), Annapolis, 1990 (Extract from Log of U-47; copy of this log also obtained from the Royal Navy Historical Branch, London.), 48; Bodo Herzog Letter

15. ADM 199/158, *op.cit.*, 8; Weaver, *op.cit.*, 35(fn.); Roskill, *op.cit.*, 73.

16. Stern, *op.cit.*, 89, Fuehrer Conferences, *op.cit.*, 50; Weaver *op.cit.*, 157

17. ADM 199/158, *op.cit.*, 74-75, 127; Roskill, *op.cit.*, 74.

18. ADM 199/158, *op.cit.*, 76; Smith, Peter *The Naval Wrecks of Scapa Flow* Orkney Press, 1989, 93-94; DNC Department, Admiralty N4/43 "Battleships of the Royal Sovereign Class, 1918-1945.

19. Imperial War Museum Department of Documents, 87/15/1

20. McKee, *op.cit.*, 8, see also Gordon, Andrew *The Rules of the Game*, London, 1996, 477

21. ADM 199/158, *op.cit.*, 77

22. *Ibid.*, 77-81: Weaver, *op.cit.*, 55

23. *Ibid.*, 78

24. *Ibid.*, 246

25. Imperial War Museum, London, Department of Documents, Miscellaneous 2823 (*Royal Oak* Survivors' Memoirs); ADM 199/158,*op.cit.*, 139

# CHAPTER TWO

## *DECIMA FLOTTIGLIA MAS*

1. Sadkovich, James, Ed., Revaluating Naval Combatants of World War II, New York, Greenwood Press 1990, 129
2. Sadkovich, *op. cit.*, 129
3. Sadkovich, *op. cit.* 130
4. Bragadin, 274
5. Bragadin, 274-275
6. Schofield, William and Carisella, P. J., *Frogmen, First Battles*, Boston, 1987, 18-20, and *The Frogmen*, Waldron, T.J., London 1950, 10-12, and Kemp, 25-26
7. Bragadin, 276
8. Bragadin, 277
9. Imperial War Museum, London, Department of Sound Records, Interview with Admiral Birindelli, SR 14236/2. Admiral Birindelli had a successful post war career in the Italian Navy, culminating in his appointment (1970) as naval commander of NATO forces in the Mediterranean.
10. Birindelli interview.
11. Bragadin, 277
12. Borghese, 40-44, Birindelli interview.
13. Birindelli interview
14. Post war accounts of *Decima Mas* operations off Gibraltar are notably silent on the question, but it is hard to believe that the Spanish authorities did not tacitly support them.
15. Bragadin, 277-278; Birindelli interview.
16. Bragadin, 278; Birindelli interview.
17. Borghese 71, Birindelli interview.
18. Borghese, 63-67; Birindelli interview.

19. Bragadin, 278 (fn.); Author's "Hitler's Fleet in Being; *Tirpitz* and the Arctic Convoys" in MHQ; *the Quarterly Journal of Military History*, Winter 2000, 65.
20. Bragadin, 282-284; Borghese 115, 128.
21. Kemp, 28
22. Bragadin, 285
23. ADM 186/801, 224.
24. ADM 186/801, 226-227; Imperial War Museum, document 87/15/1, memoir John Knight.
25. ADM 186/801, 227-228; Borghese, 147-151.
26. ADM 186/801, 228; Holloway, Adrian, *From Dartmouth to War, a Midshipman's Journal*, London, 1993, 201
27. Cunningham, *A Sailor's Odyssey*, 433
28. ADM 186/801, 225
29. ADM 186/801, 225; Kemp, 28-31; Holloway 202
30. Cunningham, 433. John Knight, 77.
31. Holloway, 196;
32. PW3: Police report attached to prisoner interrogation report.
33. ADM 186/801, 225
34. ADM 186/801, 225-226.
35. The Cunningham Papers, Michael Simpson, Ed., 554

# CHAPTER FOUR

# SICILY

1. Morison, Samuel Eliot, *History of United States Naval Operations in World War II, Volume IX, Sicily – Salerno – Anzio*, January 1943-June, 1944, Boston, Little Brown and Company, 1954, 217

2. *Ibid.*, 217

3. Liddell Hart, B. H., *History of the Second World War*, New York, DaCapo Press, 1971, 436

4. Nicolson, Nigel, *Alex: the Life of Field Marshal Earl Alexander of Tunis*, London, Pan Books, 1976, 205, 206.

5. In a private discussion after the war Alexander confided to Samuel Eliot Morison that at Casablanca the Combined Chiefs treated Sicily as the conclusion of the North African campaign and thus looked no further ahead. Only at Trident did they take a broader view (Library of Congress, Papers of Samuel Eliot Morison, Box 8, Notebook #62.)

6. D'Este, Carlo, *Eisenhower, A Soldier's Life*, New York, Henry Holt and Co., 2002, 444

7. Liddell Hart, *op. cit.*, 435.

8. "Our losses are enormous. We are indeed experiencing a sort of second Stalingrad . ." Goebbels Diary quoted in Bryant, Arthur, *The Turn of the Tide, 1939-1943,* London, Collins, 1957, 612, fn. 1

9. Hinsley F.H. et al., *British Intelligence in the Second World War (Volume Three, Part 1)*, London, HMSO, 1984, Chapter 29: Strategic Assessments,3; Clark, General Mark, commanding United States 5th

Army, 1943, Vol 4, The Citadel, Charleston NC., Entry for August 7, 1943

10. Morison, *op. cit.*, 173

11. Sheppperd, G. A., *The Italian Campaign 1943-45*, New York, Frederick A. Praeger , 1968, 57

12. Cunningham, Admiral Andrew B., *Despatch*(sic), Supplement to the London Gazette of Friday, 28 April, 1950: The Invasion of Sicily, Admiral Cunningham, submitted to Supreme Commander Allied Expeditionary Force, January 1, 1944, 2079.

13. Bradley, Omar N. and Blair, Clay, *A General's Life: An Autobiography*, New York, Simon and Schuster, 1983, 198 (fn.);

14. Simpson, Michael, Ed. *The Cunningham Papers: Volume II The Triumph of Allied Sea Power*, London, Ashgate for the Naval Records Society, 2006, 558

15. Liddell Hart, *op. cit.*, 451

16. Bryant, *op. cit.*, 454-455

17. Mitcham. Samuel W. Jr., and von Stauffenberg, Friedrich, *The Battle of Sicily: How the Allies Lost Their Chance of Total Victory*, Stackpole Books, Mechanicsburg, PA, 2007, 63; Reid, Brian Holden, The Italian Campaign, 1943-45: a Reappraisal of Allied Generalship, Journal of Strategic Studies, 135

18. When urged by naval officers to protest against the new plan, Patton said: "No, Godammit, I've been in this army thirty years and when my superior gives me an order I say 'Yes, Sir.' And then do my Godamndest to carry it out." Morison, *Sicily and Salerno*, fn. 15, p. 20.

19. Garland, Lt. Col. Albert N., Smyth, Howard, McGaw, and Blumenson, Martin: *United States Army in World War II, The Mediterranean Theater of Operations, Sicily and the Surrender of Italy*, Center of Military History, United States Army, Washington, D.C.,149

20. Nicholson, *op. cit.*, 245

21. Liddell Hart B. H., *The Other Side of the Hill*, London, Pan Books, 1999, 356.

22. Nicholson, *op. cit.*, 245, Butcher, Harry C., Captain USNR, *My Three Years with Eisenhower*, New York, Simon and Schuster, 1946,

386-387.

23. *Despatch* (sic) by His Excellency Field Marshall The Viscount Alexander of Tunis, The Conquest of Sicily, 10th July 1943 to 17 August 1943, London, England, The National Archives, 24 described the invasion as "an operation ... to seize and hold the Island of Sicily as a base for future operations,(emphasis added)

24. Clausewitz, *On War* (Michael Howard/Peter Paret translation), Princeton University Press, 1976/84, based on the original in German, *Vom Kriege*, Dummlers Verlag, Berlin, 1832. Clausewitz, *On War*, Howard/Paret translation, 1976/4, Chapter XXVII (emphasis added)

25. Blumenson, Martin, *The Patton Papers, 1940-1945*, New York, Da Capo Press, 1996, 257.

26. Churchill, Winston, S., *The Second World War, Vol IV, The Hinge of Fate*, Boston, Houghton Mifflin Company, 1978, 677

27. www.History.Army.mil/brochures/72-16/Map1

28. Dear, I.C.B, Ed. *The Oxford Companion to World War II*, New York, Oxford University Press, 1995,

29. British National Archives, *Battle Summary No. 35 The Invasion of Sicily*, Admiralty Historical Section, 1946, 2.

30. Liddell Hart, B. H., *History of the Second World War, op. cit.* 437. Cunningham's *Despatch* hypothesizes "the weary Italians, who had been alert for many nights, turning thankfully in their beds saying 'tonight at least they can't come!' But they came."

31. Barnett, Correlli, *Engage the Enemy More Closely, The Royal Navy in the Second World War*, New York, Norton and Co., 1991, 632.

32. Six battleships, 7 light cruisers, and several dozen smaller vessels of unknown operational capability.

33. National Archives, London, ADM 1199/*944 Disposition of Italian Fleet*, 1; Morison *op. cit.*, 35

34. Combat Air Patrol

35. *Battle Summary No. 35: the Invasion of Sicily (Operation "Husky).*" Historical Section, Naval Staff, Admiralty S.W.1, February 1946. Also O'Hara, Vincent, *The Struggle for the Middle Sea: The Great Navies at War*

*in the Mediterranean Theater, 1940-1945*, Naval Institute Press, Annapolis, MD, 2009, 214, regarding the role of the Italian Navy: "Would any modern navy, except the Japanese, have sought battle under like conditions?"

36, British Library, Cunningham Correspondence File 52, Pound to Cunningham, July 3, 1943

37. National Archives, London, ADM 199/943, *Operation Husky*, Appendix VII, 1

38. Letter from Pound to ABC, August 24, 1942 Cunningham Correspondence File 52, British Library

39. Report of Commander, Western Task Force, National Archives (UK), WO 204/7607,44

40. *Ibid.*, 87

41. Von Senger und Etterlin, General Frido, *Neither Fear nor Hope*, (tr. George Malcolm), London, Macdonald & Co., 1963, 148.

42. ADM 199/943, *op. cit.*, 4

43. Cunningham, *op. cit.*, London Gazette "This little blow (Force 6-7) had various effects but the most noteworthy was its contribution to our unexpected success in gaining complete surprise." See also Liddell Hart *Second World War*, *op. cit.*, 442

44. Ambrose, Stephen, *The Supreme Commander, the War Years of General Dwight D. Eisenhower*, Jackson MI, University Press, 1999, 218

45. Alexander *Despatch, op.cit.*, 22;

46. Roskill, Captain S. W., D.S.C., R.N., *The War at Sea, 1939 – 1945, Volume III, The Offensive, Part I, 1st June 1943 – 31st May 1944*. Her Majesty's Stationary Office, London, 1960, 142; Pogue, *Supreme Command*, 387-388; Bradley, *A Soldiers Story*, 484-485; Eisenhower, *Crusade in Europe*, 356.

47. Roskill, Captain S. W., D.S.C., R.N., *The War at Sea, 1939 – 1945, Volume III, The Offensive, Part I, 1st June 1943 – 31st May 1944*. Her Majesty's Stationary Office, London, 1960, 142

48. Citation

49. Pogue, *Supreme Command*, 387-388; Bradley, *A Soldiers Story*, 484-485; Eisenhower *Crusade in Europe*, 356.

50. Ambrose, Stephen, *The Supreme Commander, the War Years of General Dwight D. Eisenhower*, Jackson MI, University Press, 1999, 227; Butcher, Harry C., Captain USNR, *My Three Years with Eisenhower*, New York, Simon and Schuster, 1946, 383-4

51. Farago, Ladislas, *Patton, Ordeal and Triumph*, Westholme Publishing, Yardley, PA, 2005, 303

52. The British Official History suggest that these tensions would have been greatly reduced had the senior officers concerned demonstrated a little more administrative efficiency and diplomatic tact (Howard, *op. cit.*, 468-469).

53. Shepperd, G. A., *The Italian Campaign, 1943-45*, New York, Praeger, 1968,

54. Stephen Brooks, Ed., *Montgomery and the Eighth Army*, Bodley Head for the Army Records Society, 1991, 251 (Extract from note to Major General D. N. Wimberly, 21 July, 1943)

55. The 1st Parachute Division, flown in from France, was landed just behind the German front at Catania on July 14

56. Brooks, *op. cit.*, 259, 261

57. National Archives, London, PREM 3/245/4

58. Nicholson, *op.cit.*, 242

59. Howard, *op. cit.*, 469

60. Atkinson, Rick, *The Day of Battle, The War in Sicily and Italy, 1943*, New York, Henry Holt and Company, 2007, 124

61. Reynolds, Michael, *Monty and Patton, Two Paths to Victory*, Staplehurst, Spellmount, date, 136

62. Morison, *op. cit.*, 191

63. Garland, *op. cit.*, 388-403

64. General Hube's biographical material from his *Wikipedia* entry

65. *On War*. Clausewitz, *op. cit.*, 271

66. Howard, *op. cit.*, 474; see also Map Three

67. Ambrose, Stephen, *The Supreme Commander, the War Years of General Dwight D. Eisenhower*, University Press, Jackson MI, 1999, 228.

68. Morison, *op. cit.*, 198-199

69. *Ibid.*, 204

70. *Ibid.*, 205
71. Garland, *op. cit.*, 401
72. This section relies on B.S. 35, *op.cit.* Chapter VII, pp. 80 - 85
73. See page 27 following, fn. 127.
74. Patton to Bradley July 22, 1943: ". . .. even if you've got to spend men to do it. I want you to beat Monty into Messina" (Brighton, Terry, *Patton, Montgomery, Rommel*, New York, Crown Publishing, 2008, 209
75. Nicolson, *op. cit.*, 242
76. D'Este, *Bitter Victory, op. cit.*, 520; Tregaskis, Richard, *Invasion Diary*, University of Nebraska Press, 2004, 89.
77. Alexander, *op. cit.*, 29.
78. Battle Summary 35, *op. cit.*, 8
79. Kent Hewitt Oral History, *op. cit.*, 354, 371, 372.
80. Garland *op. cit.*, 421
81. Pack, *Operation Husky*, NY 1977
82. D'Este, *op. cit., Bitter Victory*, 168-169
83. Atkinson, *op. cit.*, 106, 162
84. Terraine, John, *The Right of the Line: The Royal Air Force in the European War 1939-1945*, Hodder and Staughton Ltd., London 1988, 578 (quoting from narrative of Herrman Goering Division AHB/II/117)
85. Report # 14of the Canadian Army Historical Section, "The Sicilian Campaign, July – August 1943," dated April 15, 1947.
86. The principal source for this section is Hinsley, F. H., *British Intelligence in the Second World War Vol. Three, Part 3*, London, Stationery Office Books, 1988
87. "Ultra" was the British designation for intelligence derived from secret German radio and teleprinter communications, much of it encrypted on the Enigma machine. In discussing intelligence material the terms "Ultra" and "Enigma" are often been used almost interchangeably.
88. Hinsley, *op. cit.* 96
89. Siebel ferries were the workhorse of the evacuation fleet.

Originally designed for the invasion of Britain in 1940, they consisted of a large platform laid over two pontoons, the whole powered by two aircraft engines. Each ferry could carry 450 men or ten vehicles. They were brought from northern France to Italy when evacuation appeared imminent. (Roskill, *op. cit.*, 145.)

90. Bletchley, Bucks, location of British code breaking operations

91. Barnett, Correlli, *Engage the Enemy More Closely: the Royal Navy in the Second World War*, New York, Norton & Co., 1991, 649

92. Hinsley, *op. cit.*, 97

93. Hinsley, *op. cit.*, 97

94. Hamilton, Nigel, *Master of the Battlefield: Monty's War Years, 1942-1944*, McGraw-Hill, 1983, 347, 348

95. Roskill, *op. cit.*,150

96. Alexander *Despatch, op. cit.*, 28, 29.

97. Roskill, *op. cit.*, 213; Admiral of the Fleet Viscount Cunningham of Hyndhope, K.T., G.C.B., O.M., D.S.O., *A Sailor's Odyssey*, Hutchinson & Co., London, 1951, 550

98. Roskill, op. cit., 146

99. Ibid. 149

100. Letter Broadhurst to Coningham, August 3, 1943, reproduced in D'Este, *Bitter Victory, op. cit.*, 528.

101. Roskill, *op. cit.*, 148

102. The Citadel, Charleston SC; The Ruge Collection, A 1974.3 Box 8: Interviews and Articles re British and German Officials, Events in World War II, "*Ruge Report*", 28

103. Barnett Correlli, *Engage the Enemy More Closely*, W.W Norton, New York, 1991, 649.

104. Moorhead, Alan, *Gallipoli*, London, Aurum Press, 2007, 77.

105. See Cunningham's comment (p.9) "It must always be for the General to decide. The Navy can only provide the means, and advise on the practicability . . . of the projected operation. It may be that, had I pressed my views more strongly, more could have been done".

106. Appointed C-in-C Mediterranean Fleet in June, 1939, continued in that position (with a short break in Washington, DC) until he

became First Sea Lord in 1944: salty, vigorous, blunt speaking, "the embodiment of the Royal Navy's best traditions of fighting sailors." Correlli Barnett, *Engage the Enemy More Closely, op.cit.*, 50.

107. D'Este, *Eisenhower*, 454

108. Liddell Hart, *History of the Second World War, op. cit.* 445

109. *Fuehrer Conferences on Naval Affairs, 1939-1945*, Naval Institute Press, Annapolis MD, 1990, 345-349

110. Doenitz, Grand Admiral Karl, *Memoirs: Ten Years and Twenty Days*, Tr. 1959, Annapolis MD, Naval Institute Press, 360-369

111. *Ibid.*, 350-353

112. Ruge Report *op. cit.*, 28

113. *Ibid.*, 29

114. *Ibid.*, 30, 31.

115. *Ibid.*, 32

116. *Ibid.*, 33. 34

117. *Ibid.*, 35

118. *Ibid.*, 38-40

119. *Ibid.*, 41; Von Liebenstein "Final Report.", Enclosure C

120. Final Report, *op. cit.*, 24

121. *Ibid.*, 44

122. In his *Memoirs* Kesselring comments how much the Axis were helped by the "methodical procedure of the Allies."(Kesselring, *op. cit.*, 165)

123. Coles, Michael, *The Channel Dash*, in MHQ, The Quarterly Journal of Military History, Summer 1999, 30.

124. Ruge, *op. cit.*, 33, 34

125. Ruge, *op. cit.*, 32

126. Enclosure to Herman Goering Division Order, August 2, 1943, Also Tregaskis, Richard, *Invasion Diary*, University of Nebraska Press, 2004, 73

127. Ruge, *op. cit.*, 45. Admiral Ruge said later that these were minimum figures: "counting was sometimes inaccurate in the hurry and under bomb attack."

128. Morison, *op. cit.*, 217

129. Max Hastings, in his recent (2011) history of World War II *All Hell Let Loose: The World at War 1939-1945*, provides a cogent summary of CCS directed strategy: "Again and again they failed – as they would again fail in northwest Europe – to translate captures of ground into destruction of enemy forces"(p. 450)

130. Churchill, *op. cit.*, 116-118; Grigg, *op. cit.*, 98.

131. Nicholson, *op. cit.*, 232

132. Coles, Michael, "The Warrior and the Strategist, Cunningham and King, Training for High Command" in *New Interpretations in Naval History*, Annapolis, MD, the Naval Institute Press, 1997

133. D'Este, *Eisenhower*, 531

134. Reid, 136

135. Mitcham and Stauffenberg, 208

136. Speech to the London County Council, July 14, 1941.

137. Grigg, John, *1943, The Victory that Never Was*, London, Penguin Books, 1999

138. Linklater, Eric, *The Campaign in Italy*, London, His Majesty's Stationary Office, 1951, 279

141. Atkinson, 168

# CHAPTER SEVEN

# ERNEST KING AND THE BRITISH PACIFIC FLEET

\* The author would like to thank those who have helped by reading earlier versions of this essay. These include Robert Love, Jon Sumida, H. P. Willmott, and my adviser when I began researching it, Sir Michael Howard.

1. H. P. Willmott, "Just being There: An Examination of the Record, Problems and Achievement of the British Pacific Fleet in the Course of its Operations in the Indian and Pacific Oceans Between November 1944 and September 1945" (Ph.D. diss., University of London, 1986), 2.
2. Edwin Gray, *Operation Pacific: The Royal Navy's War Against Japan, 1941-1945* (London: Leo Cooper, 1990), 163, 176; Richard Humble, *Fraser of North Cape: The Life of Admiral of the Fleet Lord Fraser (1888-1981)* (London: Routledge and Kegan Paul, 1983), 251.
3. John Winton, *The Forgotten Fleet: The Story of the British Pacific Fleet, 1944-45* (London: Michael Joseph, 1969), 36; William L. O'Neill, *A Democracy at War: America's Fight at Home and Abroad in World War II* (New York: Macmillan, 1993), 413.
4. Alex Danchev, *Very Special Relationship: Field-Marshal Sir John Dill and the Anglo-American Alliance, 1941-44* (London: Brassey's, 1986), 65 (Dill headed the British military mission in Washington, D.C., for most of the war); Hastings L. Ismay, *The Memoirs of General Lord Ismay* (New York: Viking, 1960), 253.
5. Richard Hough, *The Longest Battle: The War at Sea, 1939-45* (New York: Morrow, 1986), 337; Samuel Eliot Morison, *The Two-Ocean War: A Short History of the United States Navy in the Second World War*

(Boston: Little, Brown, 1963), 423.

6. Thomas B. Buell, *Master of Sea Power: A Biography of Fleet Admiral Ernest J. King* (Boston: Little, Brown, 1980), 11.

7. Eric Larrabee, *Commander in Chief: Franklin Delano Roosevelt, His Lieutenants, and Their War* (New York: Harper and Row,1987), 153, 188.

8. See, for example, Philip Ziegler, *Mountbatten* (New York: Knopf, 1985), 221, regarding Admiral Louis Mountbatten; Buell, Master of Sea Power, 145, regarding First Sea Lord Dudley Pound; and Ismay, *Memoirs*, 253, regarding General Hastings L. Ismay.

9. Undated note in Thomas B. Buell files, J. R. Tupper questionnaire re Atlantic Conference, 1941, box 2, no. 1, Walter Muir Whitehill Papers, Naval War College, Newport, R.I.

10. Ismay, *Memoirs*, 253.

11. In 1945 the Royal Navy furnished a four-carrier task group, with supporting escort and supply elements, which fought with distinction off Okinawa and the Japanese mainland. The purpose of this analysis, however, is to examine King's position at Octagon in the light of the information available to him at the time.

12. "We have scarcely scratched the surface in breaking down the enemy's power to resist final destruction, although there is no question in the minds of American authorities that the Allies will defeat Japan," *Washington Post*, 28 September 1944, quoting a contemporaneous Office of War Information survey of armed forces and State Department opinion.

13. 4 September 1944, CCS 452/18, *Records of the Joint Chiefs of Staff Meetings--Part I, 1942-1945* (Frederick, Md.: University Publications of America, 1980-1983), microfilm [hereafter cited as *JCS Meetings*).

14. Diary entry for 14 July 1944, Andrew B. Cunningham Papers, ADD 52577, British Library, London, England; for a full account of the British pre-Octagon discussions, see H. P. Willmott, *Grave of a Dozen Schemes: British Naval Planning and the War Against Japan, 1943-1945* (Annapolis, Md.: Naval Institute Press, 1996).

15. President Franklin D. Roosevelt to Prime Minister Winston S.

Churchill, 13 March 1944, in Winston S. Churchill, *The Second World War, vol. 5, Closing the Ring* (Boston: Houghton Mifflin, 1951), 510; Willmott, *Grave of a Dozen Schemes*, 103.

16. Arthur Bryant, *Triumph in the West: A History of the War Years Based on the Diaries of Field-Marshal Lord Alanbrooke, Chief of the Imperial General Staff* (Garden City, N.Y.: Doubleday, 1959), 123.

17. Staff analyses in *JCS Meetings*: "British Participation in the War Against Japan," 4 September 1944, JCS 992/3; Report by the Joint Strategic Survey Committee, 8 September 1944, JCS 992/5; and 13 September 1944, JCS 992/7.

18. 13 September 1944, CCS 452/27, *JCS Meetings*. One account of the meeting implies that its timing was unexpectedly accelerated. General George C. Marshall to Secretary of War Henry L. Stimson, 13 September 1944, in Larry I. Bland and Sharon Ritenour Stevens, eds., *The Papers of George Catlett Marshall, vol. 4, Aggressive and Determined Leadership, June 1, 1943-December 31, 1944* (Baltimore: Johns Hopkins University Press, 1996), 581.

19. United States Department of State, *Foreign Relations of the United States: The Conference at Quebec, 1944* (Washington: GPO, 1972), 315, 317 [hereafter cited as *FRUS*); *New York Times* columnist Hanson W. Baldwin later commented that the Prime Minister showed a confidence "not shared by many in the United States Navy." Baldwin, "Anglo-American Plans for the Pacific," *New York Times*, 4 October 1944.

20. Ismay, *Memoirs*, 374.

21. Papers and Minutes of Meetings, Octagon Conference, Office, U.S. Secretary of the Combined Chiefs of Staff, 1944, 207-13; 14 September 1944, CCS 452/27, *JCS Meetings*.

22. Andrew B. Cunningham, *A Sailor's Odyssey: The Autobiography of Admiral of the Fleet Viscount Cunningham of Hyndhope* (London: Hutchinson, 1951), 612.

23. *FRUS*, 330-35.

24. Gray, *Operation Pacific*, 163.

25. Ismay, *Memoirs*, 375.

26. Samuel Eliot Morison, *History of United States Naval Operations in World War II*, vol. 1, *The Battle of the Atlantic, 1939-1943* (Boston: Little, Brown, 1947), 116.

27. Correlli Barnett, *Engage the Enemy More Closely: The Royal Navy in the Second World War* (New York: Norton, 1991), 877.

28. *FRUS*, 254, 178.

29. Robert E. Sherwood, *Roosevelt and Hopkins: An Intimate History* (New York: Harper, 1948), 773; note from Secretary of State Cordell Hull to Roosevelt, 8 September 1944, *FRUS*, 264.

30. Selden Menefee, "America at War: Public Opinion on the British," *Washington Post*, 28 September 1944; Barnet Nover, "Life's Advice to England," *New York Times*, 15 October 1942.

31. Section 12 of Alanbrooke Papers, quoted in David Fraser, *Alanbrooke* (London: HarperCollins, 1997), 417; John Charmley, *Churchill's Grand Alliance: The Anglo-American Special Relationship, 1940-57* (New York: Harcourt Brace, 1995), 54.

32. *FRUS*, 275.

33. I. C. B. Dear and M. R. D. Foot, eds., *The Oxford Companion to World War II* (New York: Oxford University Press, 1995), 233. While Octagon was in progress, British Empire and Japanese forces were engaged in the epic Imphal/Kohima campaign which resulted in the failure of Japan's last attempt to invade India and, according to one source, "the biggest defeat the Japanese army had known in its entire history"; *ibid.*, 176.

34. E. B. Potter, *Nimitz* (Annapolis, Md.: Naval Institute Press, 1976), 312; Buell, *Master of Sea Power*, 34.

35. Hull memorandum, 8 September 1944, *FRUS*, 262-63.

36. Potter, *Nimitz*, 282; diary entry for 13 April 1944, James F. Somerville Diary, Cunningham Papers, ADD 52564, British Library.

37. Admiral E. J. King to General Douglas MacArthur, 21 July 1944, memorandum, folder 6, box 10, RG 4, Douglas MacArthur Memorial Archives, Norfolk, Virginia.

38. MacArthur to King, 5 August 1944, folder 6, box 10, RG 4, MacArthur Memorial Archives.

39. MacArthur to Marshall, 27 August 1944, folder 2, box 17, RG 4, MacArthur Memorial Archives.

40. King wrote: "I merely pass the information on to you at this time in order that you can be given some forewarning as to proposals that may be made later." King to MacArthur, 21 July 1944, memorandum, folder 6, box 10, RG 4, MacArthur Memorial Archives; Merrill Bartlett and William Robert Love, Jr., "Anglo-American Diplomacy and the British Pacific Fleet, 1942-1945," *American Neptune* 62 (1982): 213.

41. Joel R. Davidson, *The Unsinkable Fleet: The Politics of U.S. Navy Expansion in World War II* (Annapolis, Md.: Naval Institute Press, 1996), 18-19.

42. Ibid., 111, 133, 105, 122.

43. Ibid., 110, 158, 167, 172.

44. 13 September 1944, JCS 99217, *JCS Meetings*.

45. Memorandum by the British Treasury Representative (Brand), 14 August 1944, in *FRUS*, 159.

46. Alan P. Dobson, *US Wartime Aid to Britain, 1940-1946* (New York: St. Martin's Press, 1986), 192.

47. H. P. Willmott, "Reinforcing the Eastern Fleet: 1944," in *Warship* 39 (July 1986) 196.

48. King--Andrew B. Cunningham meeting, 15 September 1944, in *FRUS*, 350-53; Cunningham--James F. Somerville Correspondence, 19 December 1943, Cunningham Papers, ADD 52563; Letter from Charles Lambe, 5 February 1944, General Correspondence: July 1943-1944, Cunningham Papers, ADD 52571; 18 November 1943, SH225, FOLUS War Diaries, ADM 199/268, PRO.

49. Samuel Eliot Morison, *History of United States Naval Operations in World War II, vol. 10, The Atlantic Battle Won, May 1943-May 1945* (Boston: Little, Brown, 1956), 39n; "C-in-C Western Approaches to Admiralty, November 7, 1943: Use of Escort Carriers on Trade Protection," ADM 1/12865, Public Records Office, Kew, England ([hereafter cited as PRO].

50. Signal CinC BPF to CincPac, box 88, RG 38, National Archives

and Records Administration, Washington, D.C.; also Tactical and Staff Duties Division, Historical Section, Admiralty, *Naval Staff History Second World War, Battle Summary No. 47, Naval Operations in the Assault and Capture of Okinawa, March-June 1945, (Operation "Iceberg")* (London: HMSO, 1949), 101; Willmott, "Reinforcing the Eastern Fleet," 35.

51. 9 September 1943, SH201, FOLUS War Diaries, ADM 199/268, PRO.

52. Maurice Matloff, *Strategic Planning for Coalition Warfare, 1943-1944*, a volume in United States Army in World War II series (Washington: Office of the Chief of Military History, Dept. of the Army, 1959), 309; King--Chester W. Nimitz Conference Notes, 1 August and 25 September 1943 Meetings, box 10, series 4, Ernest J. King Papers, U.S. Naval Historical Center, Washington, D.C.

53. Larrabee, *Commander in Chief*, 202; Philip Vian, *Action this Day* (London: F. Muller, 1960), 155.

54. See note 17.

55. Ernest J. King and Walter Muir Whitehill, *Fleet Admiral King: A Naval Record* (New York: Norton, 1952), 581; and Humble, *Fraser of North Cape*, 267; Morison, *The Two-Ocean War*, 423.

56. Historical Section, Admiralty, *Naval Staff History Second World War, War With Japan, vol. 6, The Advance to Japan* (London: HMSO, 1959), 14. Historical Section, Admiralty, *Operation Iceberg*, 101. The U.S. Navy used 5-inch hoses for refueling at sea with a capacity of 140 tons per hour. The British, in contrast, used 4-inch hoses whose capacity was only 70-80 tons per hour. Diary entries for 10 May and 19 May 1944, Somerville Diary, Cunningham Papers, ADD 52564. Barnett, *Engage the Enemy More Closely*, 889.

57. Churchill to Alexander, 4 April 1944, quoted in Peter Nash, "Trains, Trials and Tribulations: the Lessons Learned in Developing a Fleet Train for the British Pacific Fleet Between 1944 and 1946-How Soon Forgotten?" (Ph.D. diss., King's College, London, 1996). See also Gray, *Operation Pacific*, 163. .

58. Gray, *Operation Pacific*, 163; Historical Section, Admiralty, *The*

*Advance to Japan*, 11.

59. Matloff, *Strategic Planning for Coalition Warfare*, 193; King and Whitehill, *Fleet Admiral King*, 581.

60. Historical Section, Admiralty, *Advance to Japan*, 14.

61. Vian, *Action This Day*, 155, 161.

62. Report of Captain L. D. Mackintosh, RN (*Victorious*), 6 June 1943, ADM 205/31, PRO.

63. The *Saratoga*, which had fought with distinction throughout the war, had suffered considerably in the process. In the spring of 1944 Admirals King and Nimitz agreed that, due to her large turning circle and slow elevators, she was no longer suited for fleet duty, suggesting she might be better employed as a training carrier. COMINCWCINCPAC Conference, 5 May 1944, King Papers; Gray, *Operation Pacific*, 161.

64. "Comparison of Royal Navy and United States Navy Take-off and Landing Times," ADM 1/17484, PRO.

65. Baldwin, "Anglo-American Plans for the Pacific."

66. Enclosure to Letter from Admiral Percy Noble, head of British Admiralty Delegation in Washington, D.C., to Cunningham, 30 January 1944, General Correspondence: July 1943-1944, Cunningham Papers, ADD 52571; author's correspondence with Fleet Air Arm Museum, Yeovil, Somerset; and Admiralty, *List of Officers on the Active List of the Royal Navy, April 1945*.

67. Clark Reynolds, "Sara in the East," *U.S. Naval Institute Proceedings*, December 1961, 77.

68. Report from Naval Attaché, London, 12 December 1940, National Archives; Barnett, *Engage the Enemy More Closely*, 40-41; Historical Section, Admiralty, *Operation Iceberg*, 113; Willmott, "Reinforcing the Eastern Fleet," 32, 33.

69. King and Whitehill, *Fleet Admiral King*, 581.

70. Mary Klachko with David Trask, *Admiral William Shepherd Benson, First Chief of Naval Operations* (Annapolis, Md.: Naval Institute Press, 1987), 83, 91; Buell, Master of Sea Power, 165-66.

71. Mary Klachko, "Anglo-American Naval Competition, 1918-1922"

(MA thesis, Columbia University, 1980), 80ff; Stephen Roskill, *Naval Policy between the Wars, vol. 1, The Period of Anglo-American Antagonism, 1919-1929* (New York: Walker, 1968), 63; Captain Ernest J. King, "The Influence of the National Policy on the Strategy of a War" (Newport, R.I.: Naval War College, 1932).

72. Buell, *Master of Sea Power*, 162; Danchev, *Very Special Relationship*, 40.

73. Interview with Admiral Alan G. Kirk, Columbia Oral History Project, 1: 284; Thomas Buell, "The Prewar Career of Ernest J. King," in Robert William Love, Jr., ed., *Changing Interpretations and New Sources in Naval History; Papers from the Third United States Naval Academy History Symposium* (New York: Garland, 1980), 376.

74. King and Whitehill, Fle*et Admiral King*, 461; Danchev, *Very Special Relationship*, 127; Martin Stephen, *The Fighting Admirals: British Admirals of the Second World War* (Annapolis, Md.: Naval Institute Press, 1991), 82, 118.

75. See especially Willmott, "Reinforcing the Eastern Fleet," and Winton, *The Forgotten Fleet*.

76. William T. Y'Blood, *The Little Giants: U.S. Escort Carriers Against Japan* (Annapolis, Md.: Naval Institute Press, 1987), 365.

77. Report by Cdr. Owen, RN, British Pacific Fleet liaison officer on USS *Shangri-La*, 26 August 1945, ADM 1523, PRO; Willmott, "Reinforcing the Eastern Fleet," 50.

78. Dennis Showalter, review of *The First World War: Germany and Austria-Hungary, 1914-1918*, by Holger H. Herwig, *Journal of Military History* 61 (October 1997): 812.

79. Quoted in H. C. Allen, *Great Britain and the United States: A History of Anglo-American Relations* (New York: St. Martin's Press, 1955), 914.

# CHAPTER EIGHT

# FAILED DETERRENCE, KOREA, 1950-1953

1. Acheson, Dean. *Present at the Creation.* 1970. 46.
2. *The New York Times.* September 11, 1950.
3. Wilde, Oscar, *The Importance of Being Earnest.* 1895, Act 1.t
4. Van Evera, Stephen, *Why Cooperation failed in 1914 in World Politics. a Quarterly Journal of International Relations.* Volume 38 (October 1985 - July, 1986), 105.
5. George, Alexander L., *Deterrence in American Foreign Policy: Theory and Practice.* 1974, 185-186.
6. See Paige, Glenn D., *The Korea Decision.* 1968 for an account of these events. Also Department of State, *United States Policy in the Korea Crisis,* 1950.
7. Acheson, Dean, *Present at the Creation.* 1969, 406-413; Truman, Harry, *Memoirs. Volume 2. Years of Trial and Hope. 1946-1952.* 1956, 332-335; and George, *op. cit.* 158.
8. Department of State, *op.cit.* . 7.
9. *The New York Times.* June 29, 1950.
10. Much of the material in this section is taken from the author's Essay *From Containment to Rollback: Changing Political Objectives During the Korean War.* submitted in partial fulfillment of the requirements for a Masters degree in History, Columbia University, December. 1950.
11. See Luard, Evan, *A History of the United Nations: Volume I. The years of western Dominance. 1945-1955.* 1982.
12. See Whiting, Alan, *China Crosses the Yalu: the Decision to Enter the Korean War.* 1960, 1- 19; Gittings, John, *The Role of the Chinese Army,* 1967, 23-26; Pollack, Jonathan D., *The Korean War and Sino-American*

*Relations*. a paper delivered at Conference on Sino American Relations, Beijing, 1986, 6; and *The New York Times*. July 2 and July 16, 1950.

13. See Cumings, Bruce, *The Two Koreas*. Foreign Policy Association, May/June, 1984; Fairbank, John K., *The United States and China*. 1983, 261-262; and *The New York Times*, October 3 and October 8, 1950.

14. Pollack, *op. cit*.. 16, 19.

15. *The New York Times*, August 1 and 29 and September 1 and 2, 1950. Also Nitze, Paul H. with Smith Ann M, and Reardon Steven L., *From Hiroshima to Glasnost: At the Center of Decision - a Memoir*. 1989, 109.

16. New China News Agency, BBC Monitor, November 4, 1950, Public Record Office London, FK1023/92, F0371/84113.

17. PRO., British Charge d'Affaires, Peking, to Foreign Office, October 11, 1950, F0371 84109, FK 1023/8.

18. Whiting, *op. cit.*, 37; Fairbank, *op. cit*. 387.

19. *The New York Times*. July 13, 1950.

20. *Ibid*. August 27, 1950.

21. *Foreign Relations of the United States ("FRUS")*, 1950, Volume 7, 698, 765.

22. *Shiiie Zhishi*. August 26, 1950, as cited in Whiting, *op. cit*. 84-85.

23. *The New York Times*. September 23, 1950.

24. Ibid. September 24, 1950.

25. *Ibid*. August 21, 1950.

26. *Ibid*. August 27, 1950.

27. *Ibid*. July 3, 1950.

28. *The New York Times*. July 13, 1950.

29. MacArthur Memorial, RG-9, Box 39, FEC Survey of Formosa, September 16, 1950.

30. Panikkar, K. M., *In Two Chinas: Memoirs of a Diplomat*. 1955, 108.

31. Panikkar, *op. cit*. 108.

32. *Ibid*. 108-110.

33. *The New York Times*, October 1 and 2, 1950, and FRUS *op. cit*. 852.

34. Whiting, *op. cit.* 108.
35. *The New York Times.* October 3, 1950.
36. *Ibid.* October 8, 1950.
37. Public Records Office, London, ("PRO") PREM 8, 1405, UKHICOM India to FO, October 3, 1950.
38. FRUS, *op. cit.*, 850.
39. Whiting, *op. cit.*, 108.
40. *The New York Times.* October 12, 1950.
41. Schelling, Thomas C., *Arms and Influence*, 1966, 36-38.
42. See Coles, *op. cit.*
43. Collins. J. Lawton. *War in Peacetime: the History and Lessons of Korea.* 1969, 172, 173. See also *MacArthur Memorial Archives memorandum of February 23, 1951 Regarding Washington Intelligence Estimates re Communist Chinese intervention in Korea.* October 4, page 4.
44. FRUS, *op. cit.* 849-850.
45. *The New York Times.* October 5, 1950.
46. *Ibid.* September 21, 1950.
47. The CIA too agreed that from a military standpoint the time for intervention had passed. FRUS, *op. cit.* 934, 953.
48. Pollack, *op. cit. The New York Times.* September 24, 1950.
49. Truman, *op. cit..* 362.
50. Panikkar, *op. cit.* and PRO, F0371/83558 FC1909/13 *Biographical Note and personality sketch of Sardar K. M Panikkar, Indian Ambassador to China.* November, 1950.
50. Acheson, *op. cit.* 420
51. Author interview with former Secretary of State Dean Rusk, March 9, 1990.
53. *Newsweek.* November 6, 1950.
54. Truman. *op. cit.* 340.
55. *The New York Times*, August 14-17, 1950
56. Whitney, Courtney, *MacArthur: His Rendezvous with History.* 1956, 36-37.

57. Manchester, William, *Doulas MacArthur: American Caesar 1880-1964* 1978, 547.
58. *The New York Times,* October 1, 1950.
59. FRUS, *op. cit.* . 449-454, 624. Also Nitze, Paul H. with Smith, Ann M. and Reardon, Steven L., *op. cit.* 107
60. *Ibid.* 600.
61. *Ibid.* 514.
62. NSC 73/4 and NSC 76.
63. FRUS, *op. cit.* 781.
64. *Ibid.* 458-461.
65. Schnabel, James F., and Watson, Robert J., *The History of the Joint Chiefs of Staff, the Joint Chiefs of Staff and National Policy, Volume 3. The Korean War.* 1978, 242.
66. See for example Pogue. Forrest C., *George C. Marshall: Statesman, 1945-1959.* 1987, 457.
67. FRUS, *op.cit* . 953.
68. MacArthur, Douglas, *Reminiscences.* 1964, 362. See also Schnabel and Watson, *op. cit.* 262.
69. PRO, Tokyo to FO, October 3, 1950, FK 1022/373/G, FO 371/84099.
70. Bradley, Omar and Blair, Clay, *A General's Life.* 1983, 178.
71. *The New York Times.* September 11, 1950.
72. Hastings, Max, *The Korean War.* 1987, 127.
73. See for example, Hastings, *op. cit.* 138.
74. Manchester, *op. cit.* 604.
75. Ridgeway, Matthew B., *The Korean War.* 1967, 150.
76. See Schalling, Thomas C., *Arms and Influence.* 118.
77. See Trachtenberg, Marc, A *"Wasting Asset:" American Strategy and the Shifting Nuclear Balance.* 1949-1954. in *International Security,* Winter 1988-9, Volume 13:3, 12.
78. See for example, Whelan, *op. cit..* 235-236.

# CHAPTER TEN

# SUEZ, 1956

1. Foreign Relations of the United States: *The Suez Crisis, 1956* ("FRUS"), 723, (fn.); *The Times*, London, November 26, 1956; Diane B. Kunz, *The Economic Diplomacy of the Suez Crisis*, (Chapel Hill, NC, University of North Carolina Press, 1991), 71-72. Hugh Thomas, *Suez*, (New York, Harper and Row Publishers, 1967), 39, 45-46

2. Hugh Thomas *op.cit.*, 111; Nutting, Anthony, *No End of a Lesson, the Story of Suez, 1967,* 34; London Times, Leader, August 1, 1956; Lucas, Scott, *Britain and Suez: The Lion's Last Roar*, (Manchester, Manchester University Press, 1996), 53.

3. *Ibid.*, 49, 55, 64; Robert Murphy, *Diplomat Among Warriors*, (New York, Doubleday & Company, 1964), 378; Kyle, Keith, *Suez*, (New York, St. Martins Press 1991),168-169; Grove, Eric, *Vanguard to Trident: British Naval Policy Since World War II*, (London, Bodley Head, 1987), 186; Cooper, Chester, L., *The Lion's Last Roar: Suez, 1956*, (London, Bodley Head, 1987), 63, 80; Philip Alphonse Dur, *The Sixth Fleet: a Case Study of Institutionalized Naval Presence, 1946-1958*, (unpublished Ph.D. Thesis, Cambridge MA, Harvard University, 1975)

4. Holy warriors sworn to defend the prophet and serve the cause of freedom.

5. Anthony Nutting, *op.cit.*, 78; Hugh Thomas, *op.cit.*, 83, 86-87; Eric Grove, *op.cit.*, 187

6. There are several accounts of this meeting, including a summary in *Foreign Relations of the United States, 1955-1957, the Suez Crisis, ("FRUS")*, (Washington, DC, State Dept., Bureau of Public Affairs, Office of the Historian United States Government Printing Office, 1990), 776, but the account in Kyle, *op.cit.*, 315-331 and Appendix A, is the most recent and thus probably the most complete; Kennett

Love, *Suez, The Twice Fought War*, (New York, McGraw-Hill Book Company, 1969),449.

7. Air Marshall D.H.F Barnett, *Report of the Air Task Force Commander on Operation Musketeer, November 27, 1956* ("Air Task Force Report"), 2; Lt. Cdr. Roy Everleigh, RN quoted in Brian Cull, David Nicolle and Shlomo Aloni, *Wings Over Suez, Air Operations During the Sinai and Suez Wars of 1956*, (London, Grub Street, 1996), 169; Kennett Love, *op.cit.*, 449; Dyan comment in Hugh Thomas, *op.cit.*, 107.

8. Michael R Beschloss, *Mayday: Eisenhower, Khrushchev and the U-2 Affair*, (New York, Harper & Row, 1986), 137-138; Leonard Mosely, *Dulles*, (New York, Dell Publishing, 1978), 446.

9. Hugh Thomas, *op.cit.*, 43; Keith Kyle, *op.cit.*, 168-169; ADM116/6209, Naval Report on Operation Musketeer. ("Naval Report"), (National Archives), 69

10. Hugh Thomas, *op.cit.*, 72. Norman Friedman, *British Carrier Aviation: The Evolution of the Ships and Their Aircraft*, (Naval Institute Press, Annapolis, MD, 1989); Donald Neff, *Warriors at Suez*, (New York, Linden Press/Simon and Schuster, 1981), 289; Naval Report, *op cit.*, 7 and 216-218

11. National Archives, Kew, England, ADM 1/27051, *Carrier Operations in Support of Operation Musketeer, 1959*, ("Carrier Operations"), 18; Naval Report, *op.cit.*, 70, 72.

12. Robert Henriques, *A Hundred Hours to Suez: the Epic Story of Israel's Smashing Victory in the First Sinai Campaign*, (New York, Pyramid Books, 1957 180-181); Carrier Operations, *op.cit.*, 19, 43.

13. Sarandis Papadopoulos, *"The Steel Grey Stabilizer," The Sixth Fleet in Three Crises, 1946-1958*, (unpublished), (Washington, DC, Naval Historical Center), 23, 37, 39; FRUS *op.cit.*, 790, 815.

14. Carrier Operations, *op.cit.*, 19, 43; Brian Cull, et.al., *op.cit.*, 123, 169; FRUS, 939.

15. Hugh Thomas, *op.cit.*, 72; Terrence Robertson, *Crisis: the Inside Story of the Suez Conspiracy*, (New York, Athenaeum Press), 1965, 76-77; Anthony Nutting, *op.cit.*, 35. Jackson, General Sir William and Bramall, Field Marshal Lord, *The Chiefs: the Story of the United Kingdom*

*Jackson Chiefs of Staff*, (London, Brassey's), 1992, 298.

16. Naval Report, *op.cit.*, 29-30, 68, 168-171; General Andre Beaufre, *The Suez Expedition 1956*, London, Faber and Faber, 1969, 64; Eric Grove, *op.cit.*, 188-189; ; Keith Kyle. *op.cit.*, 340

17. Naval Report, *op.cit.*, 171-172; Michael Beschloss, *op.cit.* 137.

18. London *Times*. November 1, 1956; Hugh Thomas, *op.cit.*, 130; Andre Beaufre, *op.cit.*, 82

19. Naval Report, *op.cit.*, 173; Kennett Love *op.cit.*, 512-3.

20. Willmott, "The Suez Fiasco" in *War in Peace, Conventional and Guerilla Warfare Since 1945*, Thompson, Robert, Ed., 1981, 93; Kyle, *op.cit.*, 341

21. Keith Kyle, *op.cit.*, 409, 410, 413; Robert Henriques, , *op.cit.*, 184-188; Brian Cull et.al, *op.cit.*, 125-127; Naval Report *op.cit.*, 73.

22. Eric Grove *op.cit.*, 192; Carrier Operations, op cit. 50; Naval Report, *op.cit.*, 78, 173.

23. Ibid., 77-78; Hugh Thomas, *op.cit.* 134; Donald Neff, *op.cit.*, 398; Brian Cull *op.cit.*, 271.

24. Naval Report, *op.cit.*, 73; Appendix A to Report of the Air Task Force Commander (ATF/TS.287/56), 3; Vice Admiral Charles R. Brown, 6th. Fleet Commander, interview in *US News and World Report* November 14, 1956; Burke quotation from Keith Kyle, *op.cit.*, 412; Eric Grove, *op.cit.*, 194; Sarandis Papadopoulos, *op.cit.*, 38. Brian Cull, *op.cit.*, 229, 240.

25. Stephen Howarth, *To Shining Sea: A History of the United States Navy 1775-1991*, (New York Random House, 1991) 299, 323 – 324; Captain Ernest J. King, USN *The Influence of the National Policy on the Strategy of a War*, (Newport, Naval War College, 1932)

26. *Chicago Tribune*, October 31, 1956; *Pittsburgh Post-Gazette*, October 31, 1956; London *Times*. November 1, 1956; Neff, *op.cit.*, 388; Thomas, *op.cit.*, 75, 143; Nutting, *op.cit.*, 128-129; Lt. Cdr. John Hackett RN *in Fly Navy, the View from the Cockpit, 1945-2000*, 75.

27. FRUS, *op.cit.*, 867; Ibid., 873; Donald Neff, 397; Anthony Gorst and Lewis Johnman, *The Suez Crisis*, (New York, Routledge, 1997), 106, 115.

28. *New York Times*, October 23, 25, 27, November 2, 4; Anthony Gorst and Lewis Johnman *op.cit.*, 123.

29. Anthony Nutting, *op.cit.*, 165; Jackson, General Sir William and Bramall, Field Marshal Lord, *The Chiefs: the Story of the United Kingdom Chiefs of Staff*, London, Brassey's, 1992, 298; Eric Grove, *op.cit.*, 193; Mountbatten Papers, University of Southampton Archives; MBI/N106, Paper 3: "File on the Suez Affair of 1956," notes written in1966; Donald Neff, *op.cit.*, 400.

30. Hugh Thomas, *op.cit.*, 141; General Andre Beaufre, *op.cit.*, 89, 90

31. H. P. Willmott, *op.cit.*, 95.

32. Naval Report, *op.cit.*, 75-76; Carrier Report, op, cit., 60; Rathbun, Major R.W. USMC, *Operation Musketeer: A Military Success Ends in Political Failure*, paper delivered at "War Since 1945 Seminar", Quantico VA, 1984; Carrier Report, *op.cit.*, 60; Naval Report, *op.cit.*, 178; Donald Neff, *op.cit.*, 407; Eric Grove, *op.cit.*, 191.

33. Hugh Thomas, *op.cit.*, 36; Naval Report *op.cit.*, 1, 98,99

34. Keith Kyle, *op.cit.*, 462; H. P. Willmott, *op.cit.*, 96; Carrier Report, *op.cit.*, 62; Naval Report, *op.cit.*, 78.

35. Carrier Report, *op.cit.*,61; John Hackett, *op.cit.*,75; Air Task Force Report, *op.cit.*, 8; Keightley Report, *op.cit.* 5334; Naval Report, 178.

36. ADM 1/27051, *op.cit.*, Report dated July 10, 1958 by Admiralty Department of Operational Research, 2-4; Carrier Report, *op.cit.*, 36, 129; Kennett Love, *op.cit.*, 635

37. H. P., Willmott, *op.cit.*, 97.

38. For an excellent description of the Suez related sterling crisis see Kunz, *op.cit.*, particularly 131-145. I am indebted to Yale Professor Paul Kennedy for drawing my attention to this work. See also Chester Cooper *op.cit.*, 192 and Hugh Thomas, *op.cit.*, 156

39. General Andre Beaufre, *op.cit.*, 14; Harold Macmillan, *Riding the Storm, 1956-1958*, (New York, Harper and Row, 1971), 259; Chester Cooper, *op.cit.*, 269, 275; New York Times, May 13, 1958.

# ABOUT THE AUTHOR

Michael Coles, born in England in 1932, was educated privately there until 1951, when, following the start of the Korean War, he joined the Royal Navy. He served as a carrier pilot on the HMS *Ocean*, a light fleet carrier that provided close air support to British Commonwealth forces fighting in Korea under the command of the United Nations.

On return from Korea he spent a further two years in carrier borne flight operations, followed by two years as a flight instructor. He concluded his naval career on the staff of the Royal Navy Admiral responsible for the Middle East, based in Cyprus.

On leaving the Royal Navy in 1959 he married the former Joan Collins of Boston MA, and obtained a Master's Degree in Business Administration from Harvard. Following Harvard he joined Goldman, Sachs & Co in New York, and eventually became Chairman of its International Corporation.

After retiring from Goldman, Sachs in 1987 he earned a Master's Degree in History from Columbia University.

During his retirement years he has devoted considerable time to not-for-profit activities, as well as studying and writing naval, military and political history.

His first wife died in 1999, and he has since remarried Dr. Edith Langner. They live in Shelter Island, NY.

Made in the USA
Lexington, KY
17 May 2019